Understanding Others

Understanding Others

Cultural and Cross-Cultural Studies and the Teaching of Literature

Edited by

Joseph Trimmer
Ball State University

Tilly Warnock
University of Arizona

National Council of Teachers of English
1111 Kenyon Road, Urbana, Illinois 61801

NCTE College Editorial Board: Rafael Castillo, Gail E. Hawisher, Joyce Kinkead, Charles Moran, Louise Wetherbee Phelps, Charles Suhor, chair, *ex officio*, Michael Spooner, *ex officio*

Manuscript Editor: Amita Kachru

Interior Design: Tom Kovacs for TGK Design

Cover Photograph: Carl Pope

Cover Design: Doug Burnett

NCTE Stock Number 55626-3050

Library of Congress Cataloging-in-Publication Data

Understanding others : cultural and cross-cultural studies and the teaching of
    literature / edited by Joseph Trimmer, Tilly Warnock.
        p. cm.
    Includes bibliographical references and index.
    ISBN 0-8141-5562-6 : $21.95
    1. American literature—Minority authors—Study and teaching. 2. Plu-
ralism (Social sciences) in literature—Study and teaching. 3. Literature
and society—United States—Study and teaching. 4. Ethnic groups in
literature—Study and teaching. 5. Minorities in literature—Study and
teaching. 6. Ethnicity in literature—Study and teaching. 7. Culture in
literature—Study and teaching.
    I. Trimmer, Joseph F. II. Warnock, Tilly.
    PS153.M56U53   1992   92-31580
    810.9'920693—dc20   CIP

Contents

Introduction

Most of us who have spent our careers teaching literature probably agree with Clifford Geertz that "something is happening to the way we think about the way we think" (1983, 20). Although we would revise that statement to read "something is happening to the way we think about literature," we would see the irony in citing a cultural anthropologist to announce a change in the direction of literary study. Indeed, given the themes of recent scholarship, public debate, and professional chatter, we might even suggest that literary study is being revised into cultural studies.

To some, this change may seem no more than an extension of conventional practice. We have always believed that studying culture was virtually synonymous with studying literature, because *culture*, in Matthew Arnold's sense of the word, referred to those great works of literature that contained "the best that has been known and thought" (42). We have also believed that our literature students needed cultural "background." We have introduced them to historical periods (the Middle Ages), artistic monuments (the Elizabethan stage), and intellectual movements (Romanticism) so that they could understand the forces that influenced the literature we have asked them to interpret.

For others, however, this shift toward cultural studies has prompted a revolution in theory and practice. The problem begins with the word *culture*. Although Arnold used it to define an exclusive and coherent literary tradition, Raymond Williams sees it as "one of the two or three most complicated words in the English language" (1983, 87). Its historical origins twist through the worlds of art and work, and its current usage evokes both *"material* production" and *"signifying* and *symbolic* systems" (91).

Borrowing insights from disciplines as diverse as anthropology, linguistics, and philosophy, contemporary theorists have explored the multiple meanings of culture to determine how those meanings enrich and complicate our study of literature. Their speculation has uncovered questions that encourage teachers of literature to rethink the fundamental assumptions of their practice: How do words and worlds interact? How does this interaction create cultural contexts? How do texts reproduce traces of those contexts? What is a literary text? How does a literary text relate to other texts? What do we do when we study texts, and which ones should we study?

The "cultural studies" set in motion by this line of inquiry is complicated further when it is conducted in a comparative setting. "Cross-cultural studies" is an inevitable result of our life in the "global village." But theorists who speculate on different cultural formations within and across the borders of Western culture discover questions that alert teachers of literature to the territorial constraints of their practice: How do cultures represent themselves to outsiders? What roles do class, gender, race, and ethnicity play in that representation? How are these terms in conflict, and how are they subject to change over time and in different places? How do texts written in one culture address multicultural audiences? How do outsiders interpret and evaluate texts written in other cultural contexts? How do texts from other cultures contest and reconfigure the kind of literary works canonized by Arnold's sense of culture?

The poetics, politics, and pedagogy involved in answering these questions were the subjects of the 1989 (Cultural Studies) and 1990 (Cross-Cultural Studies) Summer Institutes for Teachers of Literature sponsored by the College Section Steering Committee of NCTE. The conversations begun at those institutes have continued in various forums, prompting teachers throughout the country to begin reporting on the way cultural and cross-cultural studies have changed their thinking about literature.

This book attempts to represent the energy, diversity, and complexity of those conversations. The ideas and images that surfaced at the two Summer Institutes certainly provided ample evidence for Williams's assertion that *culture* is a difficult word to define. Other theorists, such as Gloria Anzaldúa, Kenneth Burke, Terry Eagleton, Clifford Geertz, Trinh T. Minh-ha, Mary Louise Pratt, Robert Scholes, and Catharine Stimpson have helped us see how the complicated and contrary definitions of culture connect to literary study. And the two hundred manuscripts we read in making this book have convinced us that cultural and cross-cultural studies have started to revise and reanimate the teaching of literature.

We have organized the seventeen essays in this collection under three subtitles, "Theories," "Contexts," and "Texts." The authors did not write their essays to fit this arrangement, but our selecting and sorting suggested that these terms provide a focus for certain groups of essays. The terms are interconnected, however, in many subtle and significant ways, so that a case could be made for rearranging essays in any one section under the subtitle of another section.

In our introduction to each of these sections, we suggest several ways to interpret the organizing subtitle and provide commentary on the contributions of each essay. But like Williams, we find our terms difficult, conflicted, and problematic. So rather than use them to create a false sense of coherence, we encourage readers to use them as points of departure, as prompts for interrogating individual essays and for discovering connections among and barriers between the essays in this collection.

Theories

The section opens with two essays that theorize about cultural studies: Mary Poovey traces the history of the movement from Raymond Williams through feminism and poststructuralism; James Slevin explores genre as a cultural formation that shapes our views of literature and literacy. The second pair of essays speculates on the problems of cross-cultural studies: Reed Way Dasenbrock suggests a theory for interpreting texts from other cultures; Anuradha Dingwaney and Carol Maier explain how various mediations complicate such acts of interpretation.

Contexts

The essays in this section exhibit various approaches to cultural and cross-cultural contexts. The first three essays consider context in social and school settings: Judith Scot-Smith Girgus and Cecelia Tichi examine the contexts that television has created for their students; Mary C. Savage reveals how the ethnic backgrounds of four teachers from the Bronx interact with the multicultural patterns in their neighborhoods and schools; and Norma Alarcón probes the political and personal contexts that mark the historical conflicts in her culture. The last three essays define context in university settings: Reginald Martin recounts how literary theorists have evoked either the "integrationist" or the "separatist" context for interpreting literature; Robert S. Burton questions the kind of academic multiculturalism that turns complex contexts into simple categories; and H. W. Matalene reports on his attempt to provide contexts for a text to students in another culture.

Texts

The essays in this section focus on individual texts. The first three essays employ different strategies of interpretation: Sandra Jamieson uses rhetorical theory to disclose the contexts embedded in three African American texts; Chauncey A. Ridley uses African mythology and folklore to explain the contextual assumptions in Toni Morrison's *Beloved*; and Pancho Savery uses the history and politics of bebop to enrich his reading of James Baldwin's "Sonny's Blues." The next three essays present new texts from different cultures: David Leiwei Li surveys the variety of literature written by contemporary Chinese Americans; Renny Christopher argues for the study of texts by Vietnamese American authors; and Suzanne Evertsen Lundquist introduces us to the narrative strategies of Egyptian novelist Naguib Mahfouz. The last essay focuses on the work of Leslie Marmon Silko as Patricia Riley reveals the "mixed blood" traditions that mark *Ceremony*.

The essays in this collection are distinguished by their mixture of theory and practice, their discovery of the hidden in the known, and their struggle to make the unfamiliar accessible. We thank the speakers and participants at the Summer Institutes for providing the rich conversation that enabled us to find and arrange these engaging essays. We also thank College Section members, manuscript reviewers, and three special readers—John Trimbur (Worcester Polytechnic Institute), John Warnock (University of Arizona), and Patti White (Ball State University)—for their comments and criticism on the preparation of this manuscript.

Works Cited

Arnold, Matthew. 1966–1977. *Collected Prose*. Vol. 3. Ann Arbor: University of Michigan Press.

Geertz, Clifford. 1983. *Local Knowledge: Further Essays in Interpretative Anthropology*. New York: Basic Books.

Williams, Raymond. 1983. *Keywords: A Vocabulary of Culture and Society*. Rev. ed. New York: Oxford University Press.

I Theories

A theory is a scheme of ideas which attempts to explain practice. As Terry Eagleton suggests, "Without some kind of theory, however unreflective and implicit, we would not know what a 'literary work' was in the first place or how we were to read it" (1983, viii). But theory is not an absolute scheme. Indeed, as Trinh T. Minh-ha points out, "Theory no longer is theoretical when it loses sight of its own conditional nature, takes no risk in speculation, and circulates as a form of administrative inquisition" (1989, 42). Literary theory is best understood as provisional and plural, as projecting different ways of representing the practice of interpreting texts and their relationship to their cultural contexts.

The four essays in this section "speculate" on the intricate system of cultural forces that inform and impede our teaching of literature. Mary Poovey uses her experience at a Bruce Springsteen concert to introduce the major issues that mark the movement toward cultural criticism. She outlines the humanist and structuralist versions of this movement before moving on to consider the contributions of feminism and poststructuralism. By combining these theories, Poovey proposes a three-tiered enterprise that calls for "the study of culture as an interdependent set of institutional and informal practices and discourses; the study of the traces this larger social formation produces in individual texts; [and] the study of the role of our own practice . . . plays in reproducing or subverting the dominant cultural formation."

James Slevin also uses an extended example, his analysis of *Don Quixote*, to illustrate how genre functions as a cultural formation. His literary analysis prompts him to consider how the socializing genres of academic discourse define and control what we learn. He examines three earlier theories on this subject to demonstrate that the university is not a unified discourse community; that students need to critique,

1

not merely mimic, the genres in this community; and that teachers and students need to rethink the power relationship in the university culture. This examination leads Slevin to theorize and practice new ways to use literary and literacy texts in the classroom.

Reed Way Dasenbrock redefines the "practical difficulties" of reading texts written in another culture as a "theoretical issue." Contemporary theorists, he reminds us, have revalued the role of the reader by arguing that meaning is not what "an author 'put[s]' in' a work, but ... what we can make of the work here and now." But such theories assume an undifferentiated concept of reading, and thus fail to represent the cross-cultural situation. For that reason, Dasenbrock uses the ideas of analytic philosopher Donald Davidson to construct a new theory that enables readers to come to terms with the cultural anomalies they encounter in alien texts.

Finally, Anuradha Dingwaney and Carol Maier demonstrate how an understanding of multiple mediation is crucial to any theory of reading Third World texts. For their example, they analyze *I . . . Rigoberta Menchú: An Indian Woman in Guatemala*, a text that was dictated by Menchú (in her recently acquired Spanish) to Elisabeth Burgos-Debray (a Colombian anthropologist living in Paris) and then translated into English by Ann Wright. As they sort out these mediations, including their own interaction with the text and their students, Dingwaney and Maier reveal how acknowledging the interplay of appropriation and inaccessibility leads to a more informed cross-cultural teaching of literature.

Works Cited

Eagleton, Terry. 1983. *Literary Theory: An Introduction.* Minneapolis: University of Minnesota Press.

Minh-ha, Trinh T. 1989. *Woman, Native, Other: Writing Postcoloniality and Feminism.* Bloomington: Indiana University Press.

1 Cultural Criticism: Past and Present

Mary Poovey
Johns Hopkins University

In September 1988, I joined 75,000 other people in Philadelphia's J.F.K. Stadium for one of three U.S. performances of the Amnesty International rock and roll tour. After six hours of driving music, hard bleacher seats, and all of the distractions of a restless crowd, Bruce Springsteen, "the Boss," took the stage. Just above the roar of thousands I could make out a few bars of music—a solo piano, then a plaintive harmonica, straining coarsely, longingly. A hush fell over the crowd; then, perfectly in unison, seventy-five thousand voices lifted the words into the night:

> The screen door slams
> Mary's dress waves
> Like a vision she dances across the porch
> As the radio plays. . . .

From "Thunder Road" to "Cover Me," from "Jungleland" to "Cadillac Ranch," the crowd never missed a word. It was a moving, eerie experience. Although I could hear Springsteen's guttural voice amplified a hundred times beneath the burden of the devoted, the music I heard him sing was no more authentically "Springsteen" than was the image, also amplified a hundred times and projected onto a giant screen just to one side of the stage. From where I sat, the "real" Springsteen was a figure the size of a matchstick; the image that made this match figure larger than life was curiously, infuriatingly, out of synch with the words that the crowd carried so reverently. So there it was: the miracle of rock and roll in a technological age—that phenomenon in which the familiarity of the art object so completely anticipates the experience that the "event" as such only exists as a repetition, and there is never

This essay appeared in a somewhat different form in *College English* 52(6) (October 1990): 615–25. Used with permission.

an "original," not even in the moment of supreme presence, the moment of performance itself.

The next day, seeking to capture what I felt I had just missed at the concert, I went out and replaced the Springsteen records I had lost in my divorce. Even with state-of-the-art stereo equipment, however, the recordings no more captured the authentic Springsteen than the concert had. In fact, ironically, the recordings brought back to me primarily the memory of the concert, with those seventy-five thousand devotees singing the memorized words, singing over Bruce but somehow making him more real even than himself.

The decentering of Bruce Springsteen that I experienced then is only one example of the postmodern art phenomenon. The tiny figure displaced by the giant image has already been displaced by records, CDs, and now by videos, all of which are readily available for purchase at your neighborhood store. But such simulacra do not so much repeat the live performance as they substitute, and even prepare, for it. Even if you have never experienced Bruce Springsteen "live" (and even if you have, you've probably not *seen* him), you know what it's like because you've seen (and even bought) the video, even though you know that most of the video's "concert" footage was choreographed and edited for the tape. Then, too, there's MTV and the snippets of rock and roll used to sell all kinds of products on TV and radio, from Levi's 501 jeans to Oldsmobile cars. And here it might interest you to know that Springsteen was *the* most valuable rock and roll figure in 1985–86 (worth 12 million to Lee Iaccoca's Chrysler Corporation) precisely because Springsteen *refused* all endorsement deals. As a consequence, ad agencies recruited an army of Springsteen look-alikes—all the while exploiting the irony that if Springsteen *did* endorse a product, his value would plummet (Frith 1988, 90). Even Springsteen, whose "authenticity" and "sincerity" are carefully produced and marketed to sell his unique status in rock and roll, doesn't exist as such. "Springsteen" is only an effect of multiple representations, which allude to and quote each other, while the original recedes into a haze of nostalgia, a fantasy of what rock "used" to be.

The purpose of this essay is not just—or even primarily—to argue that college teachers of English ought to teach rock and roll (or even, to give it its more respectable title, "popular culture"). Instead, my argument, which will be partly defensive and partly—mostly—celebratory, will be about what we can learn from the rock and roll art object. The defensive part is this: for most of our undergraduates, the experience of MTV, television, and rock and roll constitutes an important part of the training they have received in how to read before they enter our classrooms. To ignore this and teach only close readings of texts that we present as static and centered is to risk making institutionalized education seem even more irrelevant to many of our students' past experiences and extra-curricular lives than I suspect it already feels. The celebratory part will take me longer to develop. It goes something like this: the reconceptualization of the art object urged upon us by the postmodern phenomenon of rock and roll can be seen as part of a turn in contemporary "literary" criticism. I'm not going to argue that rock and roll single-handedly caused literary criticism to take a new direction; rather, this turn is as much the product of the cultural and material forces that have produced this stage of rock and roll as is the postmodern rock and roll phenomenon itself. For the purposes of this essay, I want to look at this turn as the conditions that have made possible the practice that has been called "cultural criticism."

I want to sketch out one history of cultural criticism now, as a strategy for moving toward a definition of its practice and so we can see what's at stake in this critical turn. In an essay on "Cultural Studies," Stuart Hall describes the emergence of this kind of criticism in the 1950s as a "significant break" in the history of criticism. In such a break, Hall writes, "old lines of thought are disturbed, older constellations displaced, and elements old and new, are regrouped around a different set of premises and themes" (1980, 57). Cultural criticism, in short, changes the basic paradigm of our interpretive practice; as a consequence, the nature of the questions we ask changes, as do the forms in which they are posed and the kinds of answers that will be considered adequate or even relevant.

Significantly, of the three texts with which Hall associates this break, only one—Raymond Williams's *Culture and Society*—deals extensively with literary texts. What Richard Hoggart's *The Uses of Literacy* and E. P. Thompson's *The Making of the English Working Class* and *Culture and Society* have in common is not a preoccupation with texts that are considered to be "the best that has been thought and said" but the constitution of "culture" as an object of analysis. Each of these writers argues that without some concept of culture, we cannot understand historical transformations or the place of those texts considered to incarnate "the best that has been thought and said." The self-consciousness of the three texts Hall cites, moreover—their attention to the fact that such critical work invariably participates in (rather than simply reflecting upon) what counts *as* culture—dovetailed with the agenda of the New Left so as to place the politics of intellectual work squarely at the center of cultural studies. In practice, this means that cultural criticism necessarily takes itself as one of the objects of its own scrutiny, since critical practice—whether in the form of teaching, lecturing, or writing—is viewed as a constitutive part of culture and therefore as always already political—as a participant, or even an intervention, in the exercise of power.

Hall's essay focuses on two of the dominant paradigms by which culture has been conceptualized within the practice of cultural studies. The first paradigm emphasizes the coherence of culture and its availability to rational investigation and human action. One facet of this paradigm comes from Williams's work; it defines culture as "a general social process: the giving and taking of meanings . . . the process of community" (quoted in Hall 1980, 59). Not only do meanings form part of social process, but so too do the social practices that we normally think of as separate. Culture is therefore conceptualized as the patterns of organization that underwrite and link all parts of the social formation, making of it a "common" culture, a social totality. Even when conflict is written into this model, as it is in its second formative facet—that offered by E. P. Thompson—culture is still a whole, encompassing both the meanings and values that social groups create and the lived practices through which individuals experience those meanings. For literary critics and teachers of writing, the point of this is that it militates against separating literacy and literary texts from other kinds of social activity; to do so, the argument goes, is artificially to rupture (or repress) the totality of which literacy and the literary text are integral parts.

If this first paradigm is "humanist," in the sense that it emphasizes the experience and agency of individuals within the social totality, then the second paradigm Hall describes is "structuralist," in the sense that it emphasizes the systems of relations that underwrite and determine *what counts as* individual experience. Derived from the linguistics of Ferdinand de Saussure, the anthropology of Levi-Strauss, and the structural Marxism of Louis Althusser, this paradigm describes culture as the ensemble of categories and signifying systems that provide the terms through which humans understand our world, from which we derive our identity, and in which we formulate and express desire (including what seems to be, but is not, "free" choice). For the most part, these categories and systems are not visible; we participate in them unconsciously, and one of the effects of ideology is to obscure the operation of these determinate deep structures. Here is Althusser, writing on the relation between "structures" and consciousness:

> Ideology is indeed a system of "representations," but in the majority of cases these representations have nothing to do with

"consciousness." ... It is above all as structures that they impose on the vast majority of men, not via their "consciousness." ... It is within this ideological unconsciousness that men succeed in altering the "lived" relation between them and the world and acquiring that new form of specific unconsciousness called "consciousness." (quoted in Hall, 1980, 66)

This structuralist paradigm therefore pushes experience, intention, and rationality away from the center of culture and analysis; it recasts experience, intention, and (what seems like) rationality as the *effects* of representations and signifying systems, not their unproblematic origins. For teachers of literature and writing, this means that any analysis that focuses on the reader's report of her experience of reading, the author's intention, or the referential meaning of a text (what is it about?) is seen as participating in the ideological masking of the system of relations in which reading and textual production take place.

These paradigms clearly have limitations which need to be carefully worked through. Williams's notion of "community," for example, simply assumes the existence of a nation-state at the same time that it leaves unclear how the various dialects that problematize the nation-state's ideal of a "common language" fit into this "community." Althusser's emphasis on ideology as an unconscious determinate, meanwhile, makes it difficult to imagine how human beings can know or challenge the "structures" that give them their places and identities. Instead of developing these points now, however, I want to highlight the productive implications of Hall's second paradigm in particular; I also want to supplement Hall's genealogy with two more contributors to what I take to be cultural criticism. I want to make it clear from the beginning that I do not intend to offer an alternative definition of culture in this essay. Indeed, one of the outcomes of my line of argument may well be to show why no stable definition of culture is as useful as a definition that remains strategic—that is, always contestatory and that is always defined in relation to a particular context and set of political needs. Most of us who define ourselves as cultural critics try to start from practice—the practice of reading, of writing, of teaching. What is called cultural criticism, then, is not the criticism of a static object (culture) but a method of critique—a set of questions and some suggestions of the criteria we might use to determine the adequacy of answers.

To my mind, one of the most provocative implications of the revision that the structuralist paradigm works upon the humanist paradigm is that it restores to the model of culture the fact of *difference*. That is, whereas Raymond Williams's emphasis on community (and even, in a different way, Thompson's celebration of class "experience") stresses the homogeneity of culture, the structuralist position directs us to examine the *specificity*—the *difference*—of practices, institutions, and discourses. Beyond this, moreover, this paradigm implicitly directs us to uncover the exclusions by which any entity (such as culture) achieves the illusion of coherence and autonomy. In other words, in the humanist paradigm (and here I'm going to extend Hall's analysis beyond the humanist paradigm of early cultural studies to *any* humanist paradigm—indeed, to humanism itself) difference is repressed in order to produce the illusion of a unified, totalizing, universal truth. This repression is not always conscious, nor is it always attributable to identifiable individuals. Instead, this process of repression, which produces and proceeds by exclusions, is a function of any process of definition in an epistemological system that depends upon non-contradictory logic and unitary identity. This process of repression, in other words, is the process by which any concept is stabilized as a self-contained and coherent entity. Once we see this repression of difference as constitutive of the (illusion of) autonomy, coherence, and universal truth, then differences become available as a terrain for contestation. To explain more fully what I have in mind here, let me turn to two of the contributors that Hall's account excludes: feminism and poststructuralism.

This is not the place to rehearse the history of the feminist movement in the United States, inside or outside the academy (but I ask you all to have that in mind as the subtext for my comments). For my purposes, it is sufficient to note one of the unexpected effects of the political movement that developed in the 1960s alongside (and in a complex relation to) the Civil Rights Movement. One part of the feminist argument was that what was taught in schools—the canon—did not represent "human nature" or "universal truth" because the canon excluded a significant part of the human population. This argument inadvertently called attention to the fact that any claim to totality, representativeness, or universality depends upon excluding some groups from that totality—precisely because the differences among those groups cannot be assimilated into an internally coherent whole. In practice, this meant that attempts to rectify the inadequacies of the canon—to add women (or peoples of color) so as to make the totality more "representative"—paradoxically exposed the fact that what had counted as representativeness did—and always would—involve exclusions, which were constitutive of (the illusion of) coverage or representativeness in the first place.

Within the women's movement, this principle became painfully clear in the 1970s, as some women of color and lesbians argued that feminism itself involved significant exclusions—that feminism systematically repressed the differences among women in order to reify a single, homogenized entity—Woman—which could be opposed to (the also falsely homogenized entity) Man. Within the practice of literary studies, meanwhile, this principle was also being driven home—uncomfortably—by various poststructuralists, who argued, among other difficult things, that the very assumptions of humanism (including the humanist version of feminism) systematically repressed the differences within the individual, that humanism translated the differences within the individual into a difference between individuals so as to manage the threat to autonomy that difference posed.

For the purposes of this discussion, I want to emphasize only two tenets of poststructuralism, and I will plead guilty in advance to the crime of oversimplification. The first relevant tenet of poststructuralism is the critique of stable identity. As developed most provocatively by Jacques Derrida and Michel Foucault, this argument suggests that the identity of any entity is stabilized only by repressing the play of differences within and between what look to be (but are not) separate things. This means, for example, that "life" derives its essential identity not through some fixed difference from (or opposition to) another stable entity, "death," but by simultaneously invoking and repressing the degrees of difference that actually link life to death. In some ways, the most telling demonstration of this principle is offered by the "border cases," those points along the chain of differences that problematize the very ideas of an oppositional definition and stable identity. Typically, these border cases will be sites of the most aggressive social contestations, for they threaten to undermine the certainty upon which humanism bases its claim to authority. So, for example, abortion and euthanasia are fiercely contested, for the one points to the uncertainty of life, the other to the indeterminacy of death.

The second relevant poststructuralist principle is the critique of referentiality. Derived from Saussure's linguistic theories, this principle holds that words do not generate meanings by referring to their originals—things—but rather through the orderly (but artificial) operations of the self-contained system of language, or the signifying chain. The implication of this thesis is that a metaphysics, like humanism, that is based on presence—that says that the original is more authentic than the representation, the idea is more important than the sign, and the intention is more significant than the additional effects words generate—excludes any recognition of the operations of language, which always produce meanings other than and in excess of the original idea or intention. Taken together, these two critiques—of the unified subject and of reference—virtually reverse the practices of humanism. Whereas humanists want to investigate origins, stability, truth, identity, mimesis, and the rational subject, poststructuralists focus on representation: language as a system of relations, the instability of meaning, the artificiality of truth, the contradictory nature of identity, the generative capacity of language, and the de-centered subject.

When the critiques of identity and reference derived from poststructuralism and (more complexly) from feminism are added to the preoccupation Stuart Hall describes with culture as the ground of human activity, the result is something like the three-tiered enterprise that I am calling cultural criticism: the study of culture as an interdependent set of institutional and informal practices and discourses; the study of the traces this larger social formation produces in individual texts; the study of the role our own practice—in this case, teaching— plays in reproducing or subverting the dominant cultural formation. What are the implications for teachers of literature and writing of conceptualizing literature as somehow a part of the social formation called culture? This is, of course, a complex issue, which has already been addressed by writers such as Richard Johnson (1986–1987) and John Trimbur (1988). I want now just to offer my contribution to the subject.

The basic premise, as I see it, of a cultural criticism informed by poststructuralism is that concepts we treat as if they were things are seen as the effects of representations and institutional practices, not their origins. A recent essay by Paula Treichler (1987) about AIDS provides a good example of how this fundamental change in the problematic mandates new questions and new answers. Whereas the humanist approach would assume that the disease entity AIDS has been scientifically proven to exist and would examine either the accuracy of various representations as measured against the original or the interrelation of various representations to see what they reveal about the original, the new problematic argues that what counts as AIDS at any given moment is partly a function of representations. This doesn't mean that what we now call AIDS would no longer be transmitted by sexual contact if we changed the way we talk about it, but it does mean that the way individuals experience the disease and the social resources devoted to treatment, prevention, and cure *do* depend on the various signifying systems in which the representation of AIDS is lodged. As long as AIDS is conceptualized primarily by one mode of transmission, for example—as a *sexual* disease—it will belong to the signifying chains that include, on the one hand, syphilis, gonorrhea, and hepatitis and, on the other, transgression, sin, dirtiness, contagion, death. Sexual intercourse is only one means by which AIDS is transmitted, of course, and its mode of transmission is only one feature of the retrovirus, but because this mode of transmission has dominated discussions of the disease, AIDS now seems to be bound to the moralistic equation of the 1980s: sex = sin = death; those who practice illicit sex deserve to get sick and die. That this equation is not necessarily the only interpretation of AIDS available, however, is clear from the work of gay activists and members of groups like ACT UP, who have promoted other sets of associations by insisting on alternative representations of the disease.

If we accept the notion that what we think of as autonomous entities are actually the effects of representation, then we are faced with the dissolution of the entity that has grounded our institutional authority and expertise—literature. The kind of cultural criticism I am describing argues that what has come to count as a literary text since the nineteenth century has depended on a set of institutional practices which includes a system of schooling, the disciplinary division of knowledge, and the departmental division of labor. These practices allow some kinds of human productions to be received as textual embodiments of values that are held to be important and representative (if not universal). Defining some kinds of human productions as "literature," moreover, depends upon privileging and stabilizing the individual work—a process that depends, in turn, upon ignoring the differences among various editions of the work, not to mention the difference between, for example, the textual version of a play and its various performances. Defining some productions as literature also depends upon repressing the connections between texts and the cultural processes of which they can be said to be a part, whether these processes are understood as the mode of production of the text (its composition, publication, marketing, and place within the system of advertising and reviewing) or its participation in the production of social meanings and effects. Defining some productions as literature also depends upon defining some other kinds of productions as "not-literature": journalism, for example, is clearly not literature. But then there are those problematic border cases. If *Moby Dick* is literature, what about *Uncle Tom's Cabin?* If *Uncle Tom's Cabin* comes to be counted as literature, what about Harlequin romances? political tracts? journalism?

In part, such exclusions and the systems of repressed relations to which I have just alluded are what cultural criticism restores to visibility.

To do this, one version of the practice takes as its object of study not just the individual text, but something extrapolated from a wide variety of texts and reconstructed as the ideological and material conditions of possibility *for* these texts. This new object of analysis—not culture as some reified entity, but an abstraction that constitutes the field from which what counts as culture comes into visibility—is in the first instance formal: it is a principle of organization, or, better still, a system of relations that stabilizes identity by provisionally inscribing differences. Inevitably, of course, this formal principle also has content, for it exists only in and through representations. In the mid-Victorian period, for example, the conditions of possibility for all kinds of texts and practices consisted of a binary conceptualization of reality, which was articulated most "naturally," hence persuasively, upon the sexual difference. That is, the most characteristic formal feature of mid-Victorian culture was the articulation of identity as a series of binary oppositions, the most fundamental of which—and here is the content— was the opposition male/female (Poovey 1988, 4–15).

To describe this object of analysis as a "system" of institutions and practices or even a characteristic "relation" conveys the impression that it is internally organized, coherent, and (relatively) static. But there is another, equally important dimension to this object of analysis: it is uneven. In the most fundamental sense, this unevenness is a function of that process I have already described—the process by which our non-contradictory system of logic artificially reifies entities by (momentarily) repressing the play of differences. This unevenness is also a function, however, of the relative autonomy of various parts of the social formation. That is, various institutional practices change according to pressures specific to those institutions as well as in relation to deep structural changes within the entire social formation. Unevenness means, on the one hand, that there is no strict parallelism among the different parts of the social formation. It also means, on the other hand, that, occasionally and to some groups of people under conditions that need to be discussed, the underlying contradictions and instabilities become visible and available for analysis and resistance (Poovey, 1–4).

Depicting culture as an uneven system of relations dissolves the conventional opposition between texts and institutional practices or events because it casts all of these supposed entities as effects of— but also participants in—the play between a culture's deep structure and its various representations. It suggests that one important subject for analysis will be the specificity of a culture's deep structure—its particular combination of coherence and incoherence, which under- writes the society's identity and its susceptibility to change. The privileged sites for such analysis will be, on the one hand, the mechanisms that efface the constitutive instability of institutions and texts and, on the other hand, the contexts in which differences that have been repressed threaten to emerge into visibility. This model also suggests that cultural critics should abandon the goal of devising "complete" interpretations of individual texts in favor of analyses that reconstruct the debates and practices in which texts initially participated. The privileged sites of this analysis will be textual details that (also) belong to (other) contemporary vocabularies and discussions and the textual contradictions or symbolic solutions that make what we now think of as the text's "context" part of the fabric of textuality itself. (For examples of this kind of work, see Brown 1987, 41–61; Poovey 1988, 89–125.)

This kind of analysis, then, will most typically have a historical component (although the kind of comparative work anthropologists do is also relevant). The historical component is important because one is initially trying to describe how and under what determinant conditions entities and concepts acquired coherence: how did "literature" as a set of texts, reading procedures, attitudes, and institutional practices come into being? As part of this analysis, critics will look at the historical process of reification: the specific exclusions by which concepts have come to be stabilized, the processes of institutionalization, credentialization, and professionalization that occur alongside and in relation to the emergence of discrete categories. Because of the importance of the dynamic of exclusion as part of this process, and because of the particular exclusions that have characterized Western civilization, race, gender, class, and ethnicity will assume particular importance in such analyses. While these categories have particular importance now, however, I do not want to exempt race, gender, class, and ethnicity from the kinds of historical and critical scrutiny I am calling for. Each of these categories has also been artificially homogenized and reified by historical processes that have been characterized by strategic exclusions. I suggest that we ask how race, gender, class, and ethnicity work—how they produce and disrupt meanings—but I also suggest that we ask, for example, who is included under the designation "black" at any given moment? Who is excluded? How does this term relate to other culturally laden signifiers—not just "white," but also "evil," "unemployed," "unwed," and "beautiful"?

Changing the object of analysis as I have suggested here constitutes an intervention in the current definition and practice of literary criticism and the teaching of writing. Implicitly, it calls into question many of the institutional structures in which most of us teach—the disciplinary division of knowledge, the reification and reproduction of a literary canon, the departmental segregation of teachers within the academy, a tenure process that rewards primarily specialized scholarship. It also calls for some new organizations of our time and resources: more team-teaching, more interdisciplinary teaching (or "de-disciplinary" teaching, as Cornel West phrases it [1987, 200]), a more systematic willingness to examine the conditions of possibility for our own classroom practice, the commitment to problematize the syllabus and examine its strategic exclusions, a willingness to look at the social construction of such apparently unassailable entities as "literacy," "aesthetic value," and "literature." I also realize that the practice I've sketched out here doesn't solve—or even raise—all of the problems this kind of inquiry introduces. More theoretical work needs to be done on the nature of the relationships among different parts of the social formation, the role pleasure plays in the production of meaning, and the question of how power can be seized and wielded once we have problematized agency and the individual subject. We also need some ways to tackle the practical problems that emerge from the conflict between such a radical transformation and the institutions in which most of us work. What role, for example, could canon-revision play in such a transition? Can one teacher change her practice without demanding department-wide changes (or incurring the wrath of her colleagues)? How can those of us who have a traditional training in literary history and composition as a process learn to ask the kinds of questions this practice implies?

In even suggesting that we change the object of critical analysis, I may sound like a visionary, but I don't suffer from the delusion that these changes are on the horizon. For one thing, we work in an institutional structure that resists such radical transformation—and here I'm not talking just about the school system but also about a publishing industry that makes millions of dollars every year from the textbooks, anthologies, and editions that keep most of us teaching (more or less) the same thing year after year. For another thing, most of us—I, anyway—have considerable investment in literature—and here I don't mean just that we've spent years learning how to read and teach but also that we *care* about certain texts and authors and even canons. "Think of the *loss*," I sometimes tell myself, even though I also think, "Just imagine the *gain!* Just think what's at stake!"

If I'm not a visionary, imagining that this change will transform our teaching overnight, then neither am I a pessimist. For, no matter how rigid the institutional or curricular constraints we work under, one of the conditions that almost always obtains in the work of teaching is the relative autonomy of our power over what actually occurs in the classroom. Even if one must teach from a textbook, even if one must prepare students to succeed in a standardized examination, the way one teaches is, in almost all cases, left up to the individual teacher. The kinds of changes I have been describing here can begin in the individual classroom—even if one does not teach Bruce Springsteen. I don't think that changes at the individual level are enough, in the final analysis. Changes in one's own practice need to be accompanied by attempts to reconsider the curriculum, the organization of the major, who is hired and at what age. Nonetheless, we don't need to wait for sweeping institutional changes to begin rethinking what we do. Our students, after all, are already living the changes I have only sketched out here.

Works Cited

Brown, Laura. 1987. "The Romance of Empire: *Oroonoko* and the Trade in Slaves." In *The New Eighteenth Century: Theory, Politics, English Literature,* edited by Felicity Nussbaum and Laura Brown, 41–61. New York: Methuen.

Frith, Simon. 1988. "Picking up the Pieces." In *Facing the Music,* 88–130. New York: Pantheon.

Hall, Stuart. 1980. "Cultural Studies: Two Paradigms." *Media, Culture and Society* 2: 57–72. London: The Open University.

Johnson, Richard. 1986–1987. "What Is Cultural Studies Anyway?" *Social Text* 16: 38–80.

Poovey, Mary. 1988. *Uneven Developments: The Ideological Work of Gender in Mid-Victorian England.* Chicago: University of Chicago Press.

Treichler, Paula. 1987. "AIDS, Homophobia, and Biomedical Discourse: An Epidemic of Signification." *Cultural Studies* 1(3): 263–305.

Trimbur, John. 1988. "Cultural Studies and Teaching Writing." *Focuses* 1(2): 5–18.

West, Cornel. 1987. "Minority Discourse and the Pitfalls of Canon Formation." *Yale Journal of Criticism* 1(1): 193–201.

2 Genre as a Social Institution

James F. Slevin
Georgetown University

Part One

> He knows his genre from the inside out; his genre is his fix on
> the world.
>> —Rosalie Colie, *The Resources of Kind*

In Cervantes' *Don Quixote,* home is the site of boredom, disillusionment, anxiety, and even betrayal. And journeying, which is actually only wandering, only "getting away" without necessarily having anywhere to go, originates in the need to escape the unsettled and unsettling problems of home. Ennui is the most conspicuous of these problems. Going mad helps.

Alonso Quixana, who, as we first meet him, is about to rename himself Don Quixote, is a lonely, childless, aging man, with not much to do and no one to do it for. In this condition, we are told, he turns into an avaricious reader, disregarding his duties to the estate, abandoning his other pleasures, and even selling his lands in order to devote himself to the reading of chivalric romances.

> In short, he so immersed himself in those romances that he spent
> whole days and nights over his books; and thus with little sleeping
> and much reading, his brains dried up to such a degree that he
> lost the use of his reason. . . . So true did all this phantasmagoria
> from books appear to him that in his mind he accounted no
> history in the world more authentic. (Cervantes 1957, 58)

And, to act rather than just continue to be, he decides to restore to his own time the world of these books.

Instead of his home, he elects to inhabit a discursive institution, a genre, and through him that genre inhabits the world. He wants, in our more modern terms, to be more fully and grandly the author of his own life. He wills to invent in his acts, however intertextually, the narrative that another will transcribe. He wants both to choose the character he will be and to choose the genre he will be written in, so that every action of his life may become, unashamedly, both originating and intertextual. His life thus becomes a genre, and Don Quixote, as he leaves his home for the first time, imagines how his departure will be narrated by some future, adoring chronicler. Home, for him, becomes this anticipated narration of the life he is setting out to author. His anticipation takes this form:

> Scarcely had the rubicund Apollo spread over the face of the vast and spacious earth the golden tresses of his beautiful hair, and scarcely had the little painted birds with their tuneful tongues saluted in sweet and melodious harmony the coming of rosy Aurora, . . . when the famous knight Don Quixote of La Mancha, quitting his downy bed of ease, mounted his renowned steed, Rozinante, and began to ride over the ancient and memorable plain of Montiel. . . . O happy era, O happy age, wherein my famous deeds shall be revealed to the world, deeds worthy to be engraved in bronze, sculptured in marble, and painted in pictures for future record. (62–63)

For Don Quixote, the romance genre becomes a form within which experience is not only understood but made possible. But it is embedded, here and throughout the book, within another genre—one we now call a novel. So we as readers are provided another, quite different lens—a counter-genre, as it were—to inhabit as a context. For *we* have previously encountered an alternative rendering of Don Quixote's departure, a clear, realistic, straightforward account of his abandoning home—the same event we have just seen through Don Quixote's chivalric eyes.

> And so, without acquainting a living soul with his intentions, *and wholly unobserved*, one morning before daybreak (it was one of the hottest in the month of July), he armed himself cap-a-pie, mounted Rozinante, placed his ill-constructed helmet on his head, braced on his buckler, grasped his lance, and through the door of his back yard sallied forth into the open country, mightily pleased to note the ease with which he had begun his worthy enterprise. . . . And . . . he rode slowly on while the sun rose with such intense heat that it would have been enough to dissolve his brains, if he had had any left. (62)

In my epigraph, Rosalie Colie argues that Don Quixote "knows his genre from the inside out; his genre is his fix on the world" (31). But she adds that this does not necessarily distinguish him from the rest of us. *We* are instructed, we come to learn from this novel, that what we see and how we see it are intimately related to the discursive genres we inhabit at any given moment. Our world seems to be a construction of available forms; we see, think, feel, in what the Renaissance called "kinds" (31).

And so our way of grasping and living in the world depends on the genres to which we give precedence, on our personal generic hierarchy. And this, in turn, depends on what and how we have learned.

Part Two

> Genres may have several mutual relations, such as inclusion, mixture [and] contrast. Another is hierarchical: relation with respect to "height." So classical critics regarded epic as higher than pastoral.... [H]eight was more than a rhetorical dimension: its normative force is unmistakable.
>
> —Alistair Fowler, *Kinds of Literature*

What are the "kinds" that we ask our students to learn and inhabit? What are we doing to introduce them to these forms? And what are the ideological dimensions of this process?

Most critics and theorists identify a limited number of aspects of discourse that form the basis for generic identification. I will draw here on the fifteen categories suggested by Alistair Fowler in his book, *Kinds of Literature: An Introduction to the Theory of Genres and Modes* (1982). His catalogue of generic features is consistent with most of the work in this field, but more exhaustive and helpful. Unlike Fowler, I am concerned not just with literary genres but with the whole range of discursive forms, literary and nonliterary, polite and popular. I have grouped Fowler's catalogue of features into five more general categories.

1. Aspects of the subject matter (topics, character types, conventional plot devices, etc.)
2. Aspects of meaning (thematic properties, thesis)
3. Aspects of organization (relation of parts among themselves)
4. Pragmatic aspects (the relation between speaker and implied or actual audience)
5. Aspects of style (diction, syntax, figures)

A genre is characterized in part by the manner in which these properties can be chosen, emphasized, and integrated according to established and publicly available codes. Tzvetan Todorov emphasizes the social nature of this process:

> In a society, the recurrence of certain discursive properties is institutionalized, and individual texts are produced and perceived

in relation to the norm constituted by this codification. A genre, literary or otherwise, is nothing but this codification of discursive properties. (1976, 162)

That is, a genre is an inherited social form, a "discursive institution," within which a writer fuses meaning, structure, linguistic features, and pragmatic purposes and effects.

Generic institutions can be embedded in other institutions, and serve these interests, as Richard Ohmann has shown us in the Pentagon Papers and as all of us know from teaching students forms of discourse in the academy. So, when we discuss student writing, and especially when we try to identify the qualities that deserve our attention and reward, we often practice disguised forms of genre theorizing. We are arguing about the features that mark a particular genre, and we often propose (either directly or indirectly) that genre and those features as the normative code for discursive practice generally. In seeing our work this way, I hope to encourage a more satisfying analysis of our own efforts to identify, promote, and question certain norms in writing. We might even come to understand how we can help students think critically about these norms as well. This is crucial, because every course we teach, I believe, proposes at its core a system of generic norms into which students are expected to grow. Such growth will depend on their capacity to question as well as to understand our norms.

Part Three

Don Quixote is certainly not alone in living a literary text. Indeed, the roads and mountains that he travels seem overpopulated by men and women who have left their urban dwellings or country manor houses to take up residency among rocks and sheep. As in Shakespeare's comedies, there seems to be a pastoral compulsion, as characters assume idyllic disguises, frequently reversing sexual roles, usually to pursue personal desire or to escape the unwelcome desires of another. Not pastoral alone, however; there is also what Claudio Guillen (1971) calls pastoral's "counter-genre": picaresque. Generic disguise, it seems, is how you protect your inner life, or find an inner life you lack or have lost, when you can no longer protect or find yourself at home. In the case of the picaresque hero, it's also a way to elude the cops.

Many of the characters enter the narrative as self-consciously living literary kinds. They are used to it and find in Don Quixote an epitome of generic style, around whom they gather by choice. By the end of

Part I, no fewer than thirty characters are staying at an inn with him, and most are engaged in an elaborate drama, extending to fifteen chapters, to fool him into returning home. Let me see if I can say this succinctly: these are characters, dissatisfied with their social roles, who assume literary roles, and then go on to play an additional role in an elaborate "chivalric romance" plot that is really in the genre of the "hoax."

How different, really, is Don Quixote from all the other, "normal," characters in this novel? All seem to suffer from an epidemic of literary madness.

Part Four

In the past ten years, there have been numerous investigations of the generic hierarchies that form the aims of the introductory English course; these investigations have focused specific attention on the question of "academic discourse." I want to look particularly at three of the earliest of these inquiries, articles which can be said to have originated this critical process and which have served as points of reference for later discussions.

Elaine Maimon was among the first to undertake such study, and in her article "Maps and Genres: Exploring Connections in the Arts and Sciences," she seeks to expand the range of genres to which we should introduce our students. "A required composition course," Maimon believes, "should be an introduction to composing academic discourse in the arts and sciences" (1983, 117). To that end, she has devoted much of her work to finding out from her colleagues in other fields the generic conventions that govern the discourse they require from students. In this essay, she describes the genre of the "lab report," noting such basic elements as voice and form, both of which "reflect the scientist's disengaged stance on experience" (114); and she sets forth a neoclassical "decorum" of required, permissible, and inappropriate features (e.g., precise reporting and clear subdivisions are required, but humor or cleverness is not permissible).

She compares this process to an apprenticeship whereby one not only develops a skill but enters a new community. Maimon sees "liberal education [as] a process of learning how scholars behave, in the general academic community and in the small social groupings of their disciplines," and our purpose in a writing course is to "help students become socialized into the academic community" (122). "Our real goal is to initiate beginners into the community of educated people" (120–

21), to lead them "from the community of the less educated to the community of the culturally literate" (122).

I welcome the generic orientation of her work and her expansion of generic considerations beyond the literary. But I wish to raise some questions about the approach she takes, and to suggest some difficulties I have found in trying to work with it in my university's writing-across-the-curriculum program.

First, it is not clear to what extent the analogy with apprenticeship precisely corresponds to the aims, methods, and realistic possibilities of a broad first-year writing course. Genuine apprenticeship (which still exists in some crafts) is a long process, sometimes extending for as many as ten years. Because it involves intensive guidance and rigorous review by an expert, it in some ways trivializes this practice to compare it to what can be done in one fourteen-week course.

Moreover, the analogy carries with it an association of indenture, of the young and powerless to the established and powerful, which explains, I believe, why it is attractive to some faculty but also why I encounter from others serious objections to the whole notion of apprenticeship. I have many colleagues, some of them accomplished teachers and scholars, who think that *apprenticing* students to the discipline, or to academic discourse, is not what they are about at all. They resist any effort to define our educational goals as "socializing students into the academic community," because they object to the act of socializing, period. Perhaps they are naive. My point is simply that we should realize that, following Maimon's model, we might be preparing students for a view of disciplinary study not universally shared, one that might do them a disservice in comprehending the goals of many of their courses later on.

Second, the variety of discourses marking different academic disciplines makes clear and indisputable that the academy is not a unified discourse community. Moreover, from my twelve years of experience working with colleagues from other disciplines, I am not sure that I believe that even individual disciplines are in fact discourse communities, or even communities. In advancing her notion that "genre conventions are constructed by a community that has practiced writing particular kinds of texts," Maimon cites Stanley Fish and *his* notion of the authority of "interpretive communities" (Maimon 1983, 112–13). But such a view confronts the same problems that Fish encounters: How does one account for differences within the community? Although the sciences may be an exception (I really am not sure), humanities and social science disciplines are profoundly heterogeneous. At my institution, there are widely varying and often competing forms of discourse and methods of investigation not only between but within the individual disciplines of philosophy, economics, political science, English, sociology, and theology. Now I realize that community members don't have to agree; but these folks are at each other's throats, often claiming (occasionally with pride) that they cannot comprehend what the others are doing. (Perhaps they are more aptly compared to families?) So, when we imagine the composition course as introducing students to the discourse of each community, I am not sure I know what referent the term "discourse"—not to mention what referent the term "community"—might have.

In his influential article, "Inventing the University," David Bartholomae addresses many of the same questions raised by Maimon, though his approach differs in several important ways. While Maimon studies specific disciplinary genres and conventions, Bartholomae is concerned "with university discourse in its most generalized form—as it is represented by introductory courses—and not with the special conventions required by advanced work in the various disciplines" (1985, 147). And, while Maimon derives her generalizations from faculty in the different fields (the "masters," as it were), Bartholomae looks at papers written by basic writers, examining how these apprentices try to approximate "university discourse" and where and why they succeed or fall short. Just as Maimon demonstrates a talent for analyzing and synthesizing what she learns from her colleagues, Bartholomae is an intelligent and sensitive reader of student texts and draws from that examination astute generalizations about the features of student writing in academic situations. Like Maimon's, his essay is important because it addresses a number of very good questions in a sophisticated way.

He orients his discussion by drawing a contrast between his own work and that of the cognitivists, objecting to their psychologizing of writing, their setting the writer's "thinking" apart from its textuality. In summarizing his position, he notes that "it should be clear by now that when I think of 'knowledge' I think of it as situated in the discourse that constitutes 'knowledge' in a particular discourse community, rather than as situated in mental 'knowledge sites' " (145). He is arguing, really, for the primary importance of generic repertoires in our appreciation of a student's rhetorical situation. He locates the student within "a language with its own requirements and agendas, a language that limits what we might say and that makes us write and sound, finally, also like someone else" (142).

Sounding like someone else seems to be the nature of academic discourse for the beginning writer. Bartholomae examines hundreds of placement exams to understand the features of the most successful papers, and I think we can abstract from his observations a Bartholomaean description of the universal "academic" genre. Aspects of subject and theme focus on the transcendence or complication of naive positions, so that the writer establishes his or her own view in relation to another view which seems inadequate to the question being addressed. The form of the essay reflects this self-conscious dialectical strategy—from the organization of the whole piece to paragraphs to sentences—so the style will be marked by just such a contrastive syntax and a specialized vocabulary that, in its reliance on Latinate terms, approximates academic diction. The audience for the genre of academic discourse is always someone more knowledgeable than the writer, creating rhetorical difficulties in the creation of the writer's persona, which must, somehow, earn the right to be heard.

Bartholomae sees the development of students as writers as a means of "writing their way into a position of privilege" (157), and he seems specifically to want to define a form, which in the hands of others risks becoming a formula, for achieving this position of privilege. While Bartholomae, in this article and elsewhere, has problematized this notion of privilege and sought ways of reconceiving power relations within the academy, that nuance has not always been noticed by those who have derived their own analyses, curricula, and pedagogies from him. Indeed, their narrow focus on the students' need to earn the privilege to speak is, for one thing, inconsistent with the way many faculty envision students in their classes. The word "privilege," in all its current and even obsolete meanings, implies a special advantage over others, an advantage usually awarded (without necessarily being earned) by a superior authority. Not just sentimental egalitarians, but even many of the most traditional curmudgeons, grant students the right, even in bad grammar, and even in an egocentric style, to have their say and have it taken seriously. Thus, a narrow focus on the students' development of a position of privilege ignores the practice of even the most traditional teacher who takes students' idiosyncratic positions as rightfully theirs.

But the more basic problem, as I see it, is that if students are to understand their positions as writers within the complex generic system (not the single genre) we call "academic discourse," they need to avoid imitating its surface form and receiving instruction in its conventions; rather, they must engage in the kind of analysis in which Bartholomae himself is engaged. That is the point Bartholomae himself makes, his most important point, really, and unfortunately the one that has often been lost. Students need, consciously and rigorously, to examine their discursive predicament as he does, and with the same unsentimental eye. They need to think about the *form*, think about the *situation* in which they find themselves, and think about the various *alternatives* open to them. This critical examination is more important than the production of the form and is, at any rate, crucial to its mastery. Students might conclude that apprenticing themselves to this form is the best or only alternative, but it would help if they were fully aware, through their own investigation and analysis, of the situation that makes it so. And then again, they might conclude, to invoke Bartholomae's own title, that it is time to "reinvent the university" and to rethink for themselves their position in this institution. This "reinvention of the university" need not be a matter of developing counter forms, or resorting exclusively to personal forms that may only perpetuate the predicament students are already in. What it can be, however, is an active, politically, and socially conscious examination of academic forms that proceeds from a critical appropriation, and not from an imitation, of those very forms.

Part Five

Sancho Panza is not entirely unlike Don Quixote. To begin with, they are much alike in their need to find or make something different of their lives. Sancho wants to be a governor, or a count, maybe even a king, and he is willing to take an apparently absurd risk to achieve what he wants. And he believes (truly believes) what he must (for example, that this old, lean man is somehow really a knight) to keep alive his hope and greed.

But mostly they differ. Where the knight sees giants and chivalric armies, Sancho sees windmills and sheep. When Don Quixote seeks to fast and fight, Sancho Panza eats and retreats. But primarily they differ because one can read and write, and the other cannot. Indeed, the main contrast between the two characters, especially at the beginning of the novel, resides in the contrast between literacy and orality that concerns Cervantes throughout. Don Quixote, the literate man gone mad in his literacy, a generic lunatic, lives in a fictional history, guided by his predecessors in kind. In contrast, Sancho Panza, the man who keeps reminding us that he cannot read or write, lives in the discursive resources of oral culture: folk wisdom embodied in the genres of proverbs, maxims, and folktales. There is a generic hierarchy here, though, and it is not just Sancho's constant "babbling" that bothers Don Quixote—it is Sancho's utterly alien, proverbial, ahistorical way of thinking about the world. The knight tries everything he can think of to silence this illiteracy, insisting that the proper squire must earn the privilege of speaking by speaking well. In other words, Sancho must ascend in the generic hierarchy.

The book suggests that illiterates are not the most cooperative pupils, but they learn well. Sancho will not, in fact, shut up, even though he isn't listened to. As the narrative proceeds, however, he begins to enter the world—the linguistic world—of the chivalric romance, serving what might be called an "apprenticeship" to his master, and he becomes more and more a proper squire in *this* great tradition. He learns—from direct instruction but mostly from immersion in the living text he follows—how to win the right to be heard. So the first half of the novel closes on the squire's lament, an elevated genre, over the body of his apparently dead knight. The bathos here depends on his almost complete mastery of the *form*.

> O flower of chivalry, one single blow of a cudgel has finished the course of your well-spent years! O glory to your race, honor and credit to all La Mancha, and even to the whole world, which, now that you are gone, will be overrun with evildoers, who will no longer fear punishment for their iniquities! O liberal above all the Alexanders. . . . In a word, knight-errant, which is the highest thing anyone could say! (511–12)

What is happening here is not just a command of a style; it is the absorption of an attitude, a way of looking at the world, which constitutes for the character a second language and a second culture. The process of Sancho's initiation into this language and culture, this fix on the world, is explored throughout, and his maturing eloquence is perhaps most evident during his encounter, in the novel's second part, with a duke and a duchess who mysteriously cross their path. Sent by his master, Sancho greets the duchess with the following complex, rather elegant, and characteristically prolix introduction. Let me remind you that this is the (still) illiterate peasant speaking.

> This same Knight of the Lions, who was called a short while ago the Knight of the Rueful Figure, sends by me to say that your greatness be pleased to give him leave that, with your good pleasure and consent, he may come and carry out his wishes, which are, as he says and I do believe, nothing else than to serve your lofty nobility and beauty, and if you give it, your ladyship will do something that will redound to your honor, and he will receive a most marked favor and contentment. (740)

In its diction, careful subordination, and elevated tone, it constitutes a striking contrast to the powers of language with which Sancho began his discursive "apprenticeship." By this point, his initiation is complete, and he has been confirmed, literally "so to speak," in the dominant discursive institution.

For his master, too, this is a moment of confirmation. Accustomed to a less than gracious treatment, he is taken aback at the reception provided by these two nobles, who actually extend to him all the conventional courtesies of the genre, receiving him entirely in the forms of romance. At this critical juncture in the plot, we read that

> All this astonished Don Quixote, and for the *first* time he felt *thoroughly* convinced that he was a knight-errant *in fact* and not in imagination, for he saw himself treated in the same way as he had read that such knights were treated in past ages. (745; emphases added)

This moment of reception constitutes a completed initiation for one, a complete confirmation for the other. As we might understand it in the academy, it is the moment a first-year student receives his or her first "A," the moment a graduate student receives his or her first "this may be publishable." It is surely a moment too precious to spoil. So let us leave them for the time being in their contentment, this special moment in which genre and social context form one harmonious whole, and turn to matters of genre less comfortable.

Part Six

In several fine essays, Patricia Bizzell has contextualized the situation of students in ways that few other scholars have even attempted, especially with respect to academic discourse. Her ground-breaking 1982 review article on writing-across-the-curriculum textbooks, "College Composition: Initiation into the Academic Discourse Community," uses the work of Bordieu and Passerson, Bernstein, Shaughnessy, and others to show how inequalities of social class affect students' abilities to master academic forms. She asserts that

> We have not examined the relationship between the academic discourse community and the communities from which our students come: communities with forms of language use shaped by their own social circumstances. We have not demystified academic discourse. (193)

In examining current textbooks, she asks whether they "initiate students into academic discourse in such a way as to foster a productive critical distance on the social processes whereby knowledge is generated and controlled" (197). The ultimate goal is, in her terms, to "demystify disciplinary activity" (203), and she praises those texts that explain that academic genres derive from the specific discursive and methodological conventions of individual disciplines. The best textbooks teach students that disciplinary conventions are not "part of nature," but socially constructed conceptual models that are shared by members of any academic discipline.

This admirable review clarifies important issues, though it remains ambiguous about two key terms that have marked subsequent work in this area: "initiation" and "demystification." Initiation, in the passive modality usually invoked, has the connotations of a ritualistic introduction into some secret, mysterious, or even occult knowledge; it is an action performed by someone in authority, on and for another. In this case, the student is the receiver of an action, an "initiate." Haunting this ceremonial or ritualistic sense of the term is its original meaning in Latin and in English, "to begin, commence, set going, originate" (*OED*), a meaning preserved in our sense of the term "initiative." But it is precisely this meaning that is usually suppressed in the metaphor of initiation. Instead, we have a sense of someone led and let into an understanding of the mystery but not into an active, initiating relationship with that mystery, and not even into a critical examination of it. In this process of being ritually initiated, one takes for granted, and more unfortunately, one is often asked to *serve* the mysterious practices that accompany this otherwise secret knowledge.

This service is related to the ambiguity of the term "demystification." It can mean, in a way consistent with the metaphor of initiation, that one simply comes to understand practices that were not understood before. *That* meaning and aim should be clearly distinguished from another sense of the term—the sense evident in Bizzell's most recent work—in which demystification is part of a genuinely critical examination that not only clarifies an otherwise mysterious knowledge, but questions and even challenges it. Of course, it is hard to know how beginners could do that, could be the agents, the active initiators, of this kind of scrutiny. But that's a pedagogical problem (to which I will soon turn), not a problem of the aims of education. If we think they should, then we will figure out how to help them do it. If we simply provide descriptions and explanations of academic conventions, the students are not, for all that, active subjects engaged in the critical process of analyzing, questioning, and genuinely demystifying. They remain instead passive initiates.

Significantly, this critical process is the very project that Bizzell herself has undertaken and invited her readers to join:

> Thus, *our* examination of new college textbooks takes *us* beyond
> the question of what is happening in composition studies. Because
> of the centrality of writing to the academic enterprise, *we* find
> *ourselves examining the worth* of academic intellectual work itself
> when *we question* the conventions of academic discourse. . . . (205–
> 6; emphases added)

It is "we" (herself and us, her readers) who have entered into this
analysis, and it has led us to examine the worth of academic intellectual
work itself through the "question[ing]" of academic discourse.

It is not clear why *students* couldn't do that, as a part of learning
the forms. One can agree that it is desirable to join this community
and one can value what is made possible when students control the
genres of academic discourse without wishing to see students as
initiates. I think the problem we face rests in the tension between the
metaphor of initiation in which we have become ensnared, and our
desire, finally, to provide for students a critical distance that makes
the process of joining the academic discourse community something
quite different from an "initiation."

As I have noted elsewhere (Slevin 1988), providing such a critical
distance has more than a pedagogical rationale. It seems to me a
necessary aim if we are, in fact, to prepare our students for the highly
complex and often unpredictable world of academic disciplines as they
now exist. In his discussion of what he terms "the refiguration of
social thought," Clifford Geertz notes:

> This genre blurring [among and within the disciplines] is
> philosophical inquiries looking like literary criticism . . . scientific
> discussions looking like belles lettres morceaus . . . histories that
> consist of equations and tables or law court testimony . . . theo-
> retical treatises set out as travelogues . . . methodological polemics
> got up as personal memoirs. . . .
>
> [T]he present jumbling of varieties of discourse has grown to
> the point where it is becoming difficult either to label authors . . . or
> to classify works. . . . Something is happening to the way we think
> about the way we think. (1983, 19–20)

What's happening is precisely what students need and have a right
to know. Academic genres and conventions are not stable, ahistorical
entities; they change and merge. The whole issue of what the academic
genres are, and what writers do with them and within them, cannot
be grasped apart from a critical perception of their institutional and
historical contexts.

This critical dimension of the students' encounter with academic
genres cannot be deferred; it cannot be seen simply as some later stage
of a process that begins as uncritical acquiescence. At the very least

we should be wary of any desire to be exempt, in our own classes, from a critical impulse we will require everywhere else. And anyway, it seems to me impossible ever to attain a critical distance on anything unless you can, from the beginning, seek to question its assumptions, examine what it does and does not do *for* you, and consider what it is doing *to* you—that is, explain it socially and historically. Even *literacy*, and especially academic literacy, must be examined in this way, from the beginning of the process of attaining it; it must be examined in terms of what one gives up as well as what one gains, in terms of what it makes possible and what it takes away. The process of critical education must examine education itself as a social and institutional practice among others. Nothing should be exempt from such critical inquiry, *least of all* the immediate objects and aims of the introductory writing course.

Part Seven

Suspended, contented, for this long interruption, are our heroes from La Mancha, enjoying their moment of harmony and confirmation on the esplanade of a lovely country manor in the second part of their adventure. All is well with them.

Actually, no. For, you see, the duke and the duchess are themselves avid readers of romances and, what's more, they have read with great delight Part I of *Don Quixote*, which now appears as a material text, a real book, in the second part. Many of the privileged characters in Part II have read it, but not Don Quixote and Sancho Panza. Life is like that: You live your text, but you can't seem to get a copy of the damn thing.

Discursive forms are social properties, and they are related to the uses and abuses of social power. The duke and the duchess have only perverse literary interests in the two main characters, whose arrival is simply an opportunity for these nobles to play out and control *in life* what they love in their reading. Playful and detached, they treat the central characters as puppets; they appropriate control of the genre, reducing it from romance to farce. They are, in this respect, a function of a traditionally scripted social institution and are, in this functioning, emblems of all institutional figures, perhaps even those employed by universities.

So we witness the transformation of Quixote's and Sancho's lives into another's drama, well scripted and often quite spectacular. From this point on, in scene after scene, what happens to them is the result not of their own folly, but of the machinations of the "nobles" who are toying with them for their own pleasure and self-esteem. There is thus a sense in which Don Quixote is no longer at the center of the narrative, no longer the "subject" of his own imagined history, because *he* is no longer the one imagining it.

For now, in immediate ways, Don Quixote and Sancho are being written by their noble hosts, who spend their time—for lack of anything else to do—creating dramas of all kinds in which the two central characters are deceived into participating. In these twenty-five chapters, the longest section of the novel, we find contrived love stories, chivalric contests, political adventures, and even blasphemous resurrection rituals. The duke and the duchess supplant Don Quixote as the agent of his actions, and hence as the author of his life.

Cervantes is concerned here with "authorship" in the specific sense of who gets to create the life of whom. The power to author one's life becomes a test of critical consciousness and a function of "class," and Don Quixote has neither. Cervantes explores this theme of the authorship of the *social text* throughout his novel, suggesting that a society not capable of a critical examination of its own conventions is engaged in nothing more than a game played by those in power in order to manipulate others.

Of course, this only makes apparent by grotesque exaggeration what has been happening to the novel's protagonists all along. The manipulation by the duke and the duchess can be read as a metaphor not just for the abuses of genre, but for the nature of genre as a social institution, not unlike other institutions that control what individuals do and think and become. So it is fair to say that, all along, it is the genre that has been writing its "inhabitant," Don Quixote, and through him, his initiate, Sancho, not the other way around. They have never really been in charge—discursive institutions have. The apparently simple truth is the novel's most resonant point: Don Quixote doesn't know how to read.

Cervantes uses his novel to provide and invite a critical examination of this social-aesthetic practice. The novel, a generic innovation that transforms as it joins the literary system, thus establishes a critical perspective not just on the genre of chivalric romances, an easy target, but also on the social processes of inhabiting genres and of being initiated into them. And to that extent, Cervantes, by reshaping the generic hierarchy through this particular narrative, provides a model for the interpretation and critical study of discursive forms, of genres as social and *socializing* institutions.

In a period of generic transformation, very much like our own, he provides a comprehensive exploration not just of romance, but of picaresque and pastoral, dialogue and treatise, literary criticism and surveys of rhetoric, theological meditation and political tract, song, farce, sonnet, lampoon, elegy, lament, and many other forms. Cervantes' book includes and examines them all, demonstrating that, through a study of genres—a book about books and specifically about kinds of books—we can explore our ways of seeing and our ways with words, genuinely demystifying what they are and what they do.

And this is what, I believe, education means. This is how I have tried to teach in my first-year courses.

My allusions are to two books I ask my students to read. *Ways with Words* (1983) is Shirley Brice Heath's important study of language learning and life somewhere in rural Carolina, and it is quite simply one of the best studies of genre as a social institution to appear in the last twenty years. It traces, in gripping detail that supports and in some cases carries her analysis, the relationship between the social position of children, their forms of discourse as embedded in social structures, and their capacity to master, or be mastered by, the dominant modes of school reading and writing. My students and I begin there, learning together from her how to undertake such study, how to investigate these matters as she does. We also consider what is perhaps a more important point: Heath writes in a genre, ethnography, the status of which is at best problematic among humanities scholars. If not exactly an outcast, it is a suspect form, low in the generic hierarchy of academic discourse. So Heath's book both talks about and enacts the problem of genre as a social institution.

We move then to John Berger's *Ways of Seeing* (1972), a study of painting and the discourse about it. This book's genre, too, a television documentary transformed into print, is of problematic status. Berger examines the relationship between several genres of painting (the portrait, the nude) from a Marxist-feminist perspective that relates visual conventions to the social structures and economic exchanges that enable them.

We read Richard Ohmann's analysis (1980) of the genre he terms "discourse of plural authorship," a genre that embraces Terkel's *Working* and Rosengarten's *All God's Dangers*, among other "disestablished" books. We read studies of the essay form as it has been historically available, or rather unavailable, to women. We read texts that explore the nature and processes of literacy and literate action (Douglass's *Narrative of the Life of An American Slave*; Shaw's *Pygmalion*; Silko's *Storyteller*). Of course, woven through the course from beginning to end is *Don Quixote,* to see what we can make of it and what such making can itself make of what we are trying to do.

While the focus of the course is student writing—examined in the institutional context of the academy's expectations for them and its own uses of writing—the reading list makes clear that we are at least partly concerned with finding a new use for literature and, perhaps, a new way of envisioning its academic study, at least in the introductory course. Cervantes' multi- and metageneric narrative offers a way of reading and seeing that resituates students' relationships to literature in terms of their own work as writers. By not restricting the generic focus of the course to the genres of academic writing, we open up more traditional literary genres to the same critical scrutiny, engaging them as cultural practices with political and social implications. In a "general" way, the course thereby bridges gaps between literary and non-literary texts and forms. But it tries to do something more as well.

Specifically, it helps literature speak more immediately to our students about the situations in which educators and students find themselves. Among the debates that now mark the discipline is this one: Does "literature" belong in the literacy class—or does it distract the students and teacher from the students' writing, in favor of endless, tiresome interpretations of canonical books? Since I find this question itself somewhat endless and tiresome, I would simply turn it around. Rather than "the place of literature in the classroom," the question becomes "the place of the classroom in literature." That has been, to some degree, the tendency of my reading of *Don Quixote,* but that text is not exceptional in this regard, as contemporary readings of Silko, Douglass, and Shaw make immediately clear.

So, let me conclude with one more example, which just happens to be the last text in the course I have been sketching. When teaching *The Tempest,* we look for sites of teaching and learning as they are explored in a play about the relationship between learning (study, "Prospero's Books") and life (political action and responsibility); we consider this learned magician, for whom "the liberal arts . . . being all [his] study, . . . [he] to [his] state grew stranger, being transported / And Rapt in secret studies" (1.2.73–77). And, noting Prospero's claim to be Miranda's unparalleled "schoolmaster" (1.2.172) and Caliban's master, we can examine the educative forces for and against "literacy" that are at work in the formation of these characters as objects of Prospero's tuition. I would suggest that ideas about personal responsibility, freedom, dialogue, and "education," very broadly conceived, have an important place in this way of reading Shakespeare's great play of writing, politics, and the powers of the imagination. For that reason alone, this work has a critical place in the class that introduces students to the work of the academy.

We use all of these texts to write about and to write *from*, trying their conventions ourselves and examining those conventions. And, as we think and write about these texts, we do the same with specific academic genres, inviting teachers from other departments to bring in their writing for our consideration. But we do this work in conjunction with a reading of Maimon, Bartholomae, and Bizzell not just to learn what they know, but to learn how to do the kind of analysis and probing of generic conventions that they have done, perhaps adding some questions they do not entertain. And, finally, if I think my students can bear the tedium, I ask them to read this article. If I've done anything like a reasonable job, they'll be able to take it apart almost as well as my gentle reader has already begun to do.

Works Cited

Bartholomae, David. 1985. "Inventing the University." In *When a Writer Can't Write: Studies in Writer's Block and Other Composing Process Problems*, edited by Mike Rose, 134–65. New York: Guilford Press.

Berger, John. 1972. *Ways of Seeing*. London: Penguin.

Bizzell, Patricia. 1982. "College Composition: Initiation into the Academic Discourse Community." *Curriculum Inquiry* 12: 191–207.

Cervantes. *Don Quixote*. 1957. Translated by Walter Starkie. New York: New American Library.

Colie, Rosalie. 1973. *The Resources of Kind*. Edited by Barbara Lewalski. Berkeley: University of California Press.

Douglass, Frederick. 1960. *Narrative of the Life of Frederick Douglass, An American Slave*, edited by Benjamin Quarles. Cambridge, MA: Harvard University Press.

Fowler, Alistair. 1982. *Kinds of Literature: An Introduction to the Theory of Genres and Modes*. Cambridge, MA: Harvard University Press.

Geertz, Clifford. 1983. "Blurred Genres: The Refiguration of Social Thought." In *Local Knowledge: Further Essays in Interpretive Anthropology*, 19–35. New York: Basic.

Guillen, Claudio. 1971. *Literature as System: Essays Toward the Theory of Literary History*. Princeton: Princeton University Press.

Heath, Shirley Brice. 1983. *Ways with Words: Language, Life, and Works in Communities and Classrooms*. Cambridge, MA: Cambridge University Press.

Maimon, Elaine. 1983. "Maps and Genres: Exploring Connections in the Arts and Sciences." In *Composition and Literature: Bridging the Gap*, edited by Winifred Bryan Horner, 110–25. Chicago: University of Chicago Press.

Ohmann, Richard. 1976. *English in America: A Radical View of the Profession*. New York: Oxford University Press.

————. 1980. "Politics and Genre in Nonfiction Prose." *New Literary History* 2: 230–41.

Rosengarten, Theodore, comp. 1974. *All God's Dangers: The Life of Nate Shaw.* New York: Knopf.

Shakespeare, William. 1987. *The Tempest,* edited by Stephen Orgel. Oxford: Oxford University Press.

Shaw, George Bernard. 1916. *Pygmalion: A Romance in Five Acts.* London: Penguin.

Silko, Leslie Marmon. 1981. *Storyteller.* New York: Arcade Publishing.

Slevin, James. 1988. "Genre Theory, Academic Discourse, and Writing Within Disciplines." In *Audits of Meaning,* edited by Louise Smith, 3–16. Portsmouth, NH: Heinemann and Boynton/Cook.

Terkel, Studs. 1974. *Working: People Talk About What They Do All Day and How They Feel About What They Do.* New York: Pantheon.

Todorov, Tzvetan. 1976. "The Origin of Genres." *New Literary History* 8: 159–70.

3 Teaching Multicultural Literature

Reed Way Dasenbrock
New Mexico State University

For the purposes of this article, I am going to assume that I do not have to argue for the inclusion of works from non-Western cultures, and from marginalized groups and peoples in our own country, in the curriculum of our schools and colleges. Demographics and economics make virtually moot any argument about this. As our schools are increasingly comprised of minority students, and as we realize how badly those schools are failing those students, it should be obvious to almost everyone that we cannot go on acting as if American literature has been written primarily by white males, most of whom are from New England. And as trends in our own and in the world economy create an increasingly interdependent world economy, non-Western nations are playing an increasingly powerful international role. It should, again, be obvious to virtually everyone that we cannot go on talking about just the Western tradition, as if the West Asia that developed mathematics and monotheism and the East Asia that invented printing and gunpowder and that increasingly finances our debt-ridden economy can or should be ignored. We need to incorporate the heritage of a variety of peoples and cultures into our curriculum. I hope I can safely assume agreement on this point, and I will not devote space here to arguing for this proposition.[1] The question to take up now is: how?

I think it only sensible to be cognizant of every difficulty that stands in the way. Many teachers who are prepared to grant the abstract case that this is something we ought to be doing still have a substantial reservation about actually doing it. This is usually expressed to me in fundamentally the same way: "I'd like to teach something non-Western

In the original draft, this chapter was titled "Understanding Others: Teaching Multicultural Literature." The editors wish to thank Reed Way Dasenbrock for allowing them to use the first part of his title in the title of the book.

but it's not really my field." Or, "I don't really feel that I have control
over the text." Or, most directly, "I don't think I know enough about
it to teach it." Now, this may seem like a practical difficulty, to be
solved by such practical means as teachers' aids and curricular materials.
But I think it is really a theoretical difficulty, for such statements imply
a consistent set of theoretical beliefs. I think that those beliefs are
wrong, and seeing how they are wrong may help us in the present
instance.

To say "I don't know enough to teach this literature" is to reaffirm
a model of interpretation in which the "proper" interpreter is the
already informed interpreter. This is the model behind most forms of
literary scholarship, but it takes on a particular form when dealing
with cross-cultural communication. When dealing with texts situated
in another culture, we feel that what is needed is someone knowledgeable about the cultural and historical contexts of the work. The
proper interpreter of an African novel is therefore an expert about
Africa, and in practice this usually leads to the conclusion that the
proper interpreter of African literature is an African. In fact there have
been fierce—if inconclusive—debates in the criticism of African literature about whether non-Africans should be writing about African
literature at all. European critics have been attacked as "colonialist
critics," and the choice of the political metaphor here is telling.[2]
Europeans once illegitimately "owned" Africa and were ousted only
after a struggle for decolonization and independence. Comparably,
those African critics and writers calling for the "decolonization" of
the study of African literature are calling for the cultural independence
of Africa. And though I use African criticism as an example because
the dispute has been fiercer here than elsewhere, comparable tensions
exist in other "new literatures" in English.[3]

If the choice of the proper critical standpoint is described in this
way, as a choice between colonialist and decolonized mentalities, then
clearly the decolonizers have the stronger argument. If readers from
the outside who read texts from non-Western countries can be described
as taking possession of these texts, just as the Europeans once took
possession of these countries, then indeed this should justly be criticized. And certainly some of the attempts to study the new literatures
in English emerging around the world have fallen into such a pattern.
But that way of dividing the terrain—in proclaiming the local perspective the right one—discourages more than just a colonialist appropriation of the literature. It discourages outside reading of any kind.
In this way, a movement insisting on the importance of the study of
non-Western literature ends up arguing that the only culture one can

study is one's own. Such a view logically leads away from—not toward—the incorporation of non-Western literature in an American curriculum, as in this view the only literature most of us could know well enough to teach would be American literature. And in this view, the American literature the predominately white professoriate could teach would be precisely and exclusively the old canon, since by the same logic no white professor can know the African American or Chicano experience well enough to teach these literatures.

However, it seems more than a little ironic that these metaphors of possession and exclusivity would take hold in this field when they have been coming under such attack elsewhere. For certainly the dominant trend in literary theory over the past generation has been in a direction diametrically opposed to this way of thinking. The logic of arguing that only Africans are in a position to read African literature well is an intentionalist or author-oriented one. The position of authority is the author, and the aim of the interpreter (and the teacher) is to try to approximate as much as possible the position of the author, to know what the author knows. But a number of currents in literary theory have sharply challenged this by arguing that it is either impossible or illogical to approximate to the author's position, and have tried in a number of ways to revalue the position of the reader as opposed to the author. This is explicitly the agenda of reader-response criticism, as seen in the work of Stanley Fish, Wolfgang Iser, and others. It can also be seen in the hermeneutics of Hans-Georg Gadamer. Meaning, for Gadamer, is not what an author "puts in[to]" a work; rather, it is what we can make of the work here and now. For Gadamer as well as for Fish, the meaning of a work of art is not fixed, but can be seen as a kind of trajectory through time and across history. Fish argues that meanings are authorized not by the author or by the text, but by shifting and plural interpretive communities. Gadamer assigns the text a greater role in the creation of meaning than does Fish, but for Gadamer as well as for Fish, the standpoint of the reader is much more decisive than that of the author.

A more radical position is that advanced by deconstruction. According to Jacques Derrida, the traditional mode of interpretation, which consists of attempting to capture an author's intended meaning, what the author wished to say, is an impossibility, a notion radically at odds with the drift inherent in all written texts. The error made in such an approach is that we impose the condition of speaking on writing: because a written text is capable of being meaningful in the absence of the author and even in the absence of the intended receiver, writing breaks with any writer's controlling intentions. Writers have no control over what use will be made of their texts, over the contexts in which they will be placed, which means ultimately that they have no control over the meaning of their writing.

So all of these analyses of reading leave room for a reader different from an author; the problem, particularly for the study of cross-cultural texts, is that they leave too much room. The reader is everywhere, the author is nowhere. Hermeneutics, reader-response criticism, and deconstruction all insist that we understand only on our own terms. We understand what is like us, or, to put it another way, the way we understand is precisely by making the artwork like us. This general point would be stated differently by these three schools: Gadamer would say that we can understand only what we are connected to historically; Fish would say that to assert understanding is to assert connectedness; and Derrida and Paul de Man would say that this assertion is always necessary for reading but is always a bit hollow. For all these critics, to read is to take possession, to take control: for Fish, this move always succeeds; for Derrida and de Man, it always fails; for Gadamer, it succeeds where we share a cultural horizon with the work.

There are, of course, important differences among these schools that it would take a long and detailed exposition to convey with any adequacy, but none of these approaches is adequate to the cross-cultural situation, the situation where we encounter a work of art from an entirely different society. Reader-response criticism, hermeneutics, and deconstruction all fail us here because of their undifferentiated concept of reading: in every act of reading, we seem to do the same thing. Yet we are not always in the same position vis-à-vis what we read, and it seems to me that every teacher is reminded of this in every class. We read differently from our students, and for any teacher to have any success in the classroom, he or she needs to know and respect, to use the revealing current phrase, "where our students are coming from." But that can coexist with a desire to have them end up someplace else, to teach them to read differently (which means to be different) by the end of the course. Where they are coming from is not necessarily where they will, or want to, end up. And I think we should be able to see that current theories of interpretation fail to describe the classroom for just the same reasons that they fail to describe the cross-cultural situation. These different schools presuppose that what is necessary for interpretation is a confident possession of the text, something we may have for works of Western culture but not for non-Western works, something our students may not have for any of the classics of our own cultural heritage. Teachers aware of this, and aware that the canon is contested anyway, often move, sometimes in desperation, to finding works students can "relate to," works they already possess with some confidence. Cultural studies provides support for this when it argues that we need to move from studying a few "classics" at the top of the cultural pyramid to looking at the various systems of cultural signification that constitute our culture; in practice, this can mean discussing Bruce Springsteen rather than Dante's *Commedia*, as Mary Poovey does, which is undoubtedly far more likely to allow our students the successful possession of what they study from their own culture.

But what I am interested in instead is questioning the logic of interpretive possession. I don't think our students need to be encouraged to study their own culture or our own culture, however we define it; they will probably do so anyway, whether with our tools or their own. What I would encourage instead of cultural studies is cross-cultural studies, the development of curiosity about—if not any "expert" knowledge of—other cultures, other peoples. If we are to do this, we must break with our assumption that the only proper place from which to apprehend a work of art is the position of possession, the position of the expert. What we need is a model of reading, of interpretation, which redescribes the scene of reading not as a scene of possession, of the demonstration of knowledge already in place, or as a failure of possession, but as a scene of learning.

Learning, particularly the position of needing to learn, is something literary theory has always, unfortunately, disvalued in relation to the position of being an expert. When I took my son at the age of four to see Mozart's *The Magic Flute*, I was surely the more "expert" spectator, more informed about what we were seeing and what lay behind it, but my concentration and excitement could not equal the rapt attention of someone utterly engrossed in his first opera. The informed position is not always the position of the richest or most powerful experience of a work of art. And this becomes even more true when crossing cultural barriers: the unknown can be powerful precisely because it is unknown. But this is not to defend ignorance, to defend remaining unknowledgeable. For one can see something for the first time only once; after that, the choice is to become more knowledgeable, more expert, more informed, or to stay uninformed without the intense pleasure of initial acquaintance.

Thus there is no real choice to be made between the initial uninformed response and the later expert one; the experience of art ideally leads one from the first to the second. Knowledge does not come first and control the experience of the work of art; the experience of the work comes first and leads the experiencer towards knowledge. Therefore it is not the expert reader who counts, but the reader willing to become expert, for only by becoming expert do we gain as well as lose in the process of gaining familiarity with art. Here, I am restating—with a crucial reemphasis—the old dictum descending from Longinus that the test of a work of art is the test of time, the test of how long it continues to be of interest to a reader or a community of readers. The reemphasis is that remoteness can be a function of cultural difference among contemporaries as well as a difference in time. The test of time is also a test of space.

But how can we overcome such remoteness in space or time? The contemporary analytic philosopher Donald Davidson, in his work on communication and interpretation, has given us a useful set of terms for describing this process.[4] Davidson says that when we encounter someone else for the first time, we encounter that person with a "prior theory," a set of expectations about the meanings of the words that person will employ. If we have no information about that person, we will employ, to use another of Davidson's terms, "interpretative charity," which is to say that we will assume that the person speaks the same language, has the same beliefs, means the same things by the same words that we do. To begin to interpret, we begin by assuming similarity, a backdrop of similarity. But this "prior theory" is never adequate to the task of interpretation, for the only person who speaks exactly the way I do, means exactly what I mean by my words, is myself. Oscar Wilde once said that England and America were two countries divided by a common language, but this is only a striking formulation of what is always the case. Even within shared languages there can be remarkable differences, which is why interpretation is necessary. And if this is true for speakers of the same language, it is much more obviously true for speakers of other languages. So if we interpret according to a prior theory and the prior theory never works, what do we do? According to Davidson, we develop a "passing theory," which is to say that as we gather information and inferences about the person being interpreted, we make subtle adjustments to our prior or general theory to fit the particular person being interpreted. If I say, "It's a cold day out," and the person to whom I am speaking says, "No, it's quite hot," I am faced with an interpretive anomaly. Two interpretations are possible. The speaker could mean the same thing by hot that I mean by cold, in which case the difference between us is a matter of words; or, what is rather more likely, the difference between us is a matter of beliefs, that what strikes me as cold strikes the other person as hot.

This is a simple example, but it is not a trivial one, for Davidson's point is that it is meanings and beliefs that keep us apart as much as words. We can share a language but not share a set of beliefs, and the beliefs will dictate our particular use of the language. This is particularly true of a language like English, the official language of more than forty countries, countries that share a language but not much else. Anyone who has ever been asked in England what time one would like to be knocked up in the morning knows what I am talking about. Meanings—not words—keep us apart here.

Davidson's papers on interpretation theory, mostly collected in *Inquiries into Truth and Interpretation* (1986), do not discuss the interpretation of literary works,[5] nor do they give us everything we need for a theory of cross-cultural interpretation, but they give us the crucial starting point. Three aspects of his work are crucial. First, the central movement in interpretation is from an assumption of similitude to a location of and an understanding of difference. Second, this understanding of difference leads not to an inability to interpret but to an ability to communicate across that difference. It is not essential for us to use the same words or mean the same things by those words—what is essential is that we understand what others mean by their words and what they understand ours to mean. We can understand someone, even if we do not share a set of beliefs or a language, as long as we know what the other's beliefs are. What enables us to do this is our ability to construct passing or short-term theories to interpret anomalous utterances. Faced with an anomaly, with something that doesn't fit our prior theory, we adjust that prior theory, incorporating what we learn from encountering that anomaly into a new passing theory. This leads into the final crucial point about Davidsonian interpretation, its stress on how the interpreter changes, adapts, and learns in the encounter with the anomalous. In short, we assume similarity but inevitably encounter difference. The encounter with difference, however, is productive, not frustrating, because it causes change in the interpretive system of the interpreter.

Davidson's stress on the evitability of change in the interpreter differentiates his work sharply both from traditional intentionalist, author-centered accounts of meaning, and from the newer reader-oriented schools of interpretation. The rock on which intentionalist, authorial accounts of interpretation have foundered is the irreducible plurality of our responses to a work of art, and it is this plurality that has given rise to reader-oriented schools of interpretation. How can the author's meaning be relevant or discernible if so many readers have read the text so differently? Davidson is not concerned with the meta-interpretive question of whether our interpretations can ever really be said to be true. His more descriptive account of interpretation simply notes that we continue to adjust our interpretations until we think they are true, until we stop having to adjust them because of the anomalies we perceive. For Davidson, interpretation is not an arena of certainty, an arena in which one interpretation is proven correct, as much as it is an arena of change. And this again seems right when applied to art. In the encounter with a great work of art, we do not remain unchanged, and our experience of art is not just analytical and cognitive, concerned solely with the truth of the statements we and others make about it.

If Davidson's account of an interpreter creating a passing theory in response to the anomalous seems generally right for all artistic interpretation, it seems particularly accurate for the encounter with the works of another culture. The uninformed reader is often the reader whom writers of the new literatures in English have primarily in mind, for a variety of complex reasons, many demographic and economic. A Chicano writer writing in English has many more non-Chicano than Chicano readers, and a Kenyan writing in English many more non-Kenyan than Kenyan readers. The power of such works is precisely their effect on the uninformed reader, their ability to provoke such a reader to construct a passing theory. A literary work created in such a situation is not simply a work to be read by those who know its world already; it is truly a site of learning and is often designed to be. This learning can take place on many different levels, often simultaneously: the lexical, the syntactic, the formal or generic, the cultural, the religious.

I would like to give one, extremely brief example of this to help make my discussion more concrete. Let me quote a paragraph from an Ethiopian novel written in English, Sahle Sellassie's *Warrior King:*

> "It is a long story, Aberash. I am afraid you will be bored by it. Besides, my throat will crack open with dryness if I try to tell you all about him now."
> "Don't worry about my being bored, father of Gebreye. And I will bring you tella to drink so that your throat will not crack up with dryness," she said, understanding what he wanted. She trotted away to the guada, to return instantly with a jar of the home-made beer and a wancha. She filled the utensil and handed it to her husband after tasting the drink herself as was the custom. (1974, 4)

A reading of this passage provides a perfect example of Davidsonian radical interpretation at work for anyone unfamiliar with the Ethiopian context of the novel. The paragraph is in English, and except for three words, all of the semantic elements of the paragraph are in recognizable English. We begin, therefore, in the spirit of interpretive charity, assuming equivalence between the meaning of the words here and the meaning we would assign to those words. Only three words do not seem to be in English, "tella," "guada," and "wancha," and we instantly infer two things about them. First, they are words in another language, presumably the Ethiopian language these characters are speaking, Amharic. (This is an historical novel, so we know they are not speaking English.) Second, these are in Amharic because they have to be. Sellassie has used our language as much as he could—his use of words that our prior theory is not going to work for must have a reason. So we infer that the reason for the usage of words that are not translated is that they cannot be.

But these three words are handled differently, and the difference is instructive. Tella gets translated, in a way, in the next sentence after its initial use: "She trotted away to the guada, to return instantly with a jar of the home-made beer and a wancha." The normal principles of English cohesion are functioning here, so we understand "home-made beer" as substituting for and translating tella. But what is a wancha? We are given a rough equivalent for that in the next phrase: "She filled the utensil." But we are never told what the guada she "trotted away to" is. Presumably the place where the tella and the wancha are kept. A kitchen? A pantry? A storage shed? We are not told. Does that mean we are at a loss? In a sense, yes; in a sense, no. Sellassie gives us three words in Amharic and handles each of them differently, giving us a precise translation of one, a ballpark translation of another, and no translation at all of the third. The passing theory we develop in this situation therefore works something like this: every time Sellassie frustrates the prior theory, he does so only so far as he must. Tella is close enough to beer that a translation is offered; wancha is named only by its function, which indicates that there is no precise English equivalent. It is not a cup or a mug or a glass, though these are all utensils. So we know less about it than tella, but we know that we know less. We know even less about guada, as not even a function is named, though some of that function can be gleaned from the context. So by the end of the paragraph, our prior theory has been modified to include these new lexical items and some sense of how close and how far away they are from English-language equivalents. But Sellassie builds this bridge between his world and ours only to kick it away once we are across. The terms homemade beer and utensil never appear again. On the very next page, we read:

> Ato Mulato paused here to have his wancha refilled. He loved
> tella very much, so much so that he could empty a whole jar by
> himself at one sitting and still remain sober.
>   "Go on. Go on." Aberash urged him, refilling his wancha. (5)

What has happened here is, I think, quite significant, though on a
small scale. Any reader attentive to the way English works has now
enlarged his or her vocabulary and begun to learn something about
the form of life instantiated in the new vocabulary. You cannot read
Warrior King without your prior theory undergoing modification and
expanding by the end of the book. Drinking tella in a wancha seems
a familiar thing to do, even if you do not quite know what tella tastes
like or what a wancha looks like. The reader has changed, has adapted,
has learned, and this example of how individual words work could
be replicated on a number of more complex levels.

Now, do you need to know what a guada is to teach or write about
this novel? No, I have just done it, and I still do not know what a
guada is. The novel is written not for those who know about guadas,
but for those with some desire to figure it out. When the book resists
easy interpretation, it does so precisely so as to provoke change in the
reader, to force a modification in his or her interpretive schema or
prior theory. And this means that where a reader does not know what
is going on, where a student may ask the teacher that embarrassing
question "What is a guada," the answer "I don't know" is a perfectly
acceptable one. The full answer has to be "I don't know, what do you
think? Why aren't we told?" In other words, the teacher leads the
class through the experience of constructing a passing theory; to do
otherwise, to annotate the unannotated text would be to prevent the
students from experiencing the meaning of the work.[6] To reverse T. S.
Eliot, they would have had the meaning but missed the experience.

As literature in English becomes an increasingly international phenomenon, and as we slowly realize that the best writers in English
today come from all over the world—from Samoa and New Zealand,
from India and Pakistan, from Somalia, Kenya, and Nigeria, from
Guyana and Trinidad, and in this country from Native Americans,
Asian Americans, and Chicanos—if we feel we need to control the
text, to be an authority, we are all going to throw up our hands and
refuse to face this inordinately rich and complex world. That would
be a disservice to our students, ourselves, and these writers. As any
tourist on a first trip abroad can testify, the cross-cultural communicative
situation is a rich experience even—or perhaps especially—when it is
most confusing. The only way to swim in this situation is to jump in
or get pushed. The life buoy I would offer has two sides to it, a

practical and a theoretical side. The practical side is that these writers are themselves intimately familiar with the perils and confusions of cross-cultural communication, so you can trust them—the best of them anyway—to give you the assistance you need. The theoretical side is that, if Davidson is right, this is simply a more extreme version of what we do anyway. All interpersonal communication involves translation and interpretation. We are never in complete command of the language produced by others, yet to live is to come to an understanding of others. Theories suggesting that we never manage to do so are both inaccurate and are likely to confirm us in the prison of our own narrow cultural horizons.

Notes

1. I have, in any case, argued for this elsewhere (see my "English Department Geography" [1987] and "What to Teach When the Canon Closes Down" [1990]). In the present intellectual climate, I perhaps need to make it clear that in my view, admitting the claims of other cultures into the curriculum does not involve any critique of the Western heritage; see my "The Multicultural West" (1991).

2. The term was coined by the Nigerian writer Chinua Achebe, in his essay "Colonialist Criticism" (1976, 3–24).

3. Chinweizu's *Toward the Decolonization of African Literature* (1983) remains the fullest statement of this perspective in the study of African literature; Saakana's *The Colonial Legacy in Caribbean Literature* (1987) is an example of how Chinweizu's approach has influenced the study of other non-Western literatures in English.

4. The terms "prior theory" and "passing theory" were advanced by Davidson in his recent "A Nice Derangement of Epitaphs" (1986). The term "interpretive charity" comes from *Inquiries into Truth and Interpretation*, which has an entire section on "Radical Interpretation" (1984, 123–79).

5. For the first thorough look at what is involved in applying Davidson's work to literary texts, see my *Literary Theory after Davidson* (forthcoming).

6. As I have argued in "Meaningfulness and Intelligibility in Multicultural Literature in English" (1987), this can be true even when the text is partially unintelligible.

Works Cited

Achebe, Chinua. 1976. *Morning Yet on Creation Day: Essays.* New York: Anchor.

Chinweizu, Onwuchekwa Jemie, and Madubuike Ihechukwu. 1983. *Toward the Decolonization of African Literature.* Washington, DC: Howard University Press.

Dasenbrock, Reed Way. 1987. "English Department Geography." *ADE Bulletin* 86(Spring): 16–23.

————. 1987. "Meaningfulness and Intelligibility in Multicultural Literature in English." *PMLA* 101: 1–12.

————. 1991. "The Multicultural West." *Dissent* 38(Fall): 550–55.

————. 1990. "What to Teach When the Canon Closes Down: Toward a New Essentialism." In *Reorientations: Critical Theories and Pedagogies,* edited by Bruce Henricksen and Thaïs E. Morgan, 63–76. Urbana: University of Illinois Press.

————., ed. (Forthcoming). *Literary Theory after Davidson.* University Park: Pennsylvania State University Press.

Davidson, Donald. 1986. "A Nice Derangement of Epitaphs." In *Truth and Interpretation: Perspectives on the Philosophy of Donald Davidson,* edited by Ernest LePore, 433–46. Oxford: Basil Blackwell.

————. 1984. *Inquiries into Truth and Interpretation.* Oxford: Clarendon Pess.

Saakana, Amon Saba. 1987. *The Colonial Legacy in Caribbean Literature.* Trenton: Africa World Press.

Sellassie, Sahle. 1974. *Warrior King.* African Writers Series. London: Heinemann.

4 Translation as a Method for Cross-Cultural Teaching

Anuradha Dingwaney
Oberlin College
Carol Maier
Kent State University

Third World cultures, peoples, and texts are "in." They have been declared "fashionable and grantable" by major cultural institutions, to adapt Guillermo Gómez-Peña's remarks about the sudden attention being showered on Latinos (1989, 24). This includes academe, where more and more courses about Third World cultures are being tacked on to already existing curricula. Although we welcome this challenge to the canon, our experiences in teaching such courses have often proved disconcerting. In particular, the repeated appropriation of these cultures under the categories of the familiar (same) or the unfamiliar (different)—which inevitably seems to characterize student/reader responses—has made us aware of the need for a pedagogy that would guide the teaching of cross-cultural texts and has led us to question our own work as mediators.

The possibility that translation itself might offer a method for making students aware of the organizing principles at work in their readings of Third World texts, thereby enabling them to read the "other," resulted unexpectedly from a short story in English translation. After a presentation about Rosario Ferré's "Pico Rico Mandorico" that Carol Maier made to one of Anu Dingwaney's classes, a student asked if a basket of Puerto Rican fruit would really contain cherries. In fact, in her translation, Diana Vélez had replaced several tropical fruits, whose names would most likely be unfamiliar to North American readers, with cherries, bananas, and passion fruit (1988, 68). The student's question led to a discussion about the difficulties of translating culture-bound terms. It also led to the first of many conversations between the two of us about the possibility of merging Carol's theory and practice in translation with Anu's work on postcolonial theory and Third World writers. What gradually evolved was a conceptualization of translation as a cross-cultural activity in which the goal of immediacy or readability is tempered by a simultaneous willingness— even determination—to work in difference. Practicing within this definition, a translator does not strive to make possible a rush of identification with an "other" unencumbered by foreignness. Rather, the goal is a more complex verbal "transculturation" in which two languages are held within a single expression.[1]

Translation has long been considered a rather questionable tool for language acquisition. When one grants to the practice of translation, however, the broader task of mediation discussed by contemporary theorists, translation involves far more than looking for the closest lexical equivalent.[2] Rather, it involves the creation of a complex tension.[3] That is, ideally, translation makes familiar, and thereby accessible, what is confronted as alien, maintaining the familiar in the face of otherness without either sacrificing or appropriating difference. This means that the translator must have a foot in each of two worlds and be able to mediate self-consciously between them. It is our belief that cross-cultural reading based on this model of translation can give rise to a potentially disquieting but highly interactive situation by ensuring that the mediations in cross-cultural literary texts, including the mediation of reading itself, will be recognized and scrutinized.

In order to illustrate our model and its development, we have chosen as our primary text *I . . . Rigoberta Menchú: An Indian Woman in Guatemala*. This is an exemplary text for two principal reasons: (1) it is multiply mediated; (2) it is rapidly acquiring canonical status among scholars and students of minority experience, who do not necessarily attend to these multiple mediations. In the account that follows, we describe the process we underwent as we read and reread *Rigoberta Menchú*, critically examining our initial assumptions and expectations to expose their fault lines. In class, we try to provoke our students to undertake a similar (if not identical) process.

When we decided to write about *Rigoberta Menchú*, our discussions revolved around the many textual layers of discourse that distance Menchú's testimony from her readers. We were, after all, reading Ann Wright's English translation of *Me Llamo Rigoberta Menchú: y así me nació la concienca*, based on Elisabeth Burgos-Debray's transcription and reworking of Menchú's testimony. The testimony had been spoken in recently acquired Spanish and tape-recorded in a metropolitan setting, Paris, where Burgos-Debray lives. There were other mediations as well. Our own, for instance, were informed by years of interpreting literary texts—in Carol's case, by acts of interpretation she brings to bear on her translations—and by our more recent reading of critical commentaries on transcription and reworking of life histories by ethnographers who seek to understand and render the experiences of non-Western cultures and peoples. Contemporary critical analyses of life histories insist that these histories are not transparencies through which we glimpse the "reality" of the cultures being described. Nor do these histories simply speak for themselves. Rather, "oral history depends for its existence on the intervention of an ethnographer who collects and presents a version of the stories gathered" (Patai 1988, 1–2). The ethnographer's acknowledged and unacknowledged assumptions—social, cultural, political—about the speaker and her culture are implicated in the rendering of the life history. Mediations, therefore, are very much at issue, in that readers, with their expectations and assumptions, interpret a life history, which is itself an ethnographer's interpretation of a speaker's oral testimony. And the speaker's testimony is an account constructed by an individual who has her own agendas and motives for telling the story, and therefore has a stake in what gets represented and how.[4]

As we focused on the role of Burgos-Debray, shuttling back and forth between her "Introduction" and her textual rendition of Menchú's oral testimony, we were struck by both what she says and by what she either leaves unsaid or actively suppresses. In her "Introduction" Burgos-Debray explains how she became involved in the project, explicitly identifying her potential handicaps as an ethnographer. Because she had never studied Maya-Quiché culture, and never done fieldwork in Guatemala (1983, xix), she was worried at first about the quality of her relationship with Menchú—the anxieties and stresses that her lack of background might generate (xiv). As soon as they met, however, Burgos-Debray says, she "knew that [they] were going to get along together" (xiv). We felt, however, that Burgos-Debray glossed over her handicaps, not overcoming them so much as displacing them by appropriating Menchú's identity, her world, her cause, even her voice itself—an impression confirmed by the Spanish version, where Burgos-Debray is named as the author of *Me Llamo Rigoberta Menchú*. Furthermore, a quick, not fully monitored reading of *Rigoberta Menchú* allows the "I" of the "Introduction" to slide seamlessly into the "I" of Menchú's testimony, conflating, indeed conjoining, Burgos-Debray's identity with Menchú's. (Here we might also recall Burgos-Debray's problematic assertion that "for the whole of that week, I lived in Rigoberta's world" [xv], when, in fact, it is Menchú who lives for a week in Burgos-Debray's home in Paris. Who inhabits whose world, then, becomes an appropriate question to ask.)

Our discomfort with Burgos-Debray's claims about her complete identification with Menchú ("I lived in Rigoberta's world"; "I became her instrument, her double" [xv, xx]) undoubtedly arose from our experiences teaching and analyzing literary texts from the Third World, or non-European cultures, in universities in the United States, which is viewed as part of the First World. The sheer inequities in the material and discursive power that the First World wields over the Third necessarily affects First World readings of such texts. For this reason, it is important to disclose and scrutinize the prior understandings and ideological stances vis-à-vis the Third World that U.S. readers bring to bear upon their reading. Such disclosure and scrutiny will, of course, not guarantee an informed understanding, but they could clear the ground for it. More important, a revelation of the interpreter's ideological investments, her "location"—political, intellectual, etc.—will make those investments explicit to other (subsequent) readers. We should add that contemporary criticism of life histories emphasizes that self-reflexivity is required of an ethnographer who edits and interprets these histories from (an)other culture. In such instances, as in teaching and writing about Third World texts, a great deal is at stake in terms of representations of and evaluations about (an)other culture.

Burgos-Debray, as John Beverley notes, is a "Venezuelan social scientist, [who was] living in Paris at the time she met Menchú, with all that [that] implies about contradictions between metropolis [read "First World"] and periphery [read "Third World"], dominant and emergent social formations, and dominant and subaltern languages" (1989, 19–20). She actively fosters the impression of a single first person, however, by erasing all marks of her "intrusions" in and "refashioning" of Menchú's story: "I soon reached the decision to give the manuscript the form of a monologue: that was how it came back to me as I re-read it. I therefore decided to delete all my questions" (xx). Although Burgos-Debray explains the erasure of her "intrusions" as a gesture that allowed her to become Menchú's "instrument"—her "double"—we questioned whether, in fact, anyone (Burgos-Debray included) can simply abandon her identity and take on that of another. Or, less charitably, we questioned whether this gesture did not violate Menchú's identity: in the chapter headings, for example, Menchú is referred to in the third person, and the epigraphs are attributed to her, as if she herself were not already speaking.

None of these contradictions is given "voice" in Burgos-Debray's "Introduction" or in the "refashioned" testimony that follows. The reader's awareness of them is nevertheless crucial to an understanding of Burgos-Debray's project. As readers, teachers, and "translators," we felt it incumbent upon us to attend to Burgos-Debray's suppressions and evasions and to reconstitute the text according to its silences and invisibilities.

Ironically, at first, our attempt to reconstitute Menchú's text by looking insistently for signs of mediation that Burgos-Debray might have suppressed had the peculiar (and undesired) effect of displacing Menchú's testimony: Burgos-Debray increasingly came to occupy the foreground of our interpretive concerns while Menchú's story receded into the background.[5] At the same time, however, it was this realization that directed us toward the following question: What if Burgos-Debray had deliberately erased most signs of her mediation to let Menchú's testimony speak to its readers in all its immediacy and urgency? Menchú's testimony, as we began to recognize, is, after all, the testimony of a political activist. Indeed, that testimony itself is a form of activism ("a manifesto on behalf of an ethnic group" is how Burgos-Debray characterizes it [xiii]) insofar as it seeks to engage the reader's sense of morality, justice, and compassion through its graphic account of the atrocities and dehumanization the Maya-Quiché suffer at the hands of a minority *ladino* population. "Words are her only weapons" (Burgos-Debray, xi) in making a distant, alien culture and a community's struggle for survival *real* to an audience that has not, in all likelihood, ever experienced the kind of repressions Menchú describes. Words matter. To call their referentiality into question, as our emphasis on Burgos-Debray's mediating presence tended to do, defuses their intense political charge and could even be considered the "irresponsible luxury" (Sommer 1988, 120) we should have been trying to avoid.

This discomfiture with our initial interpretive move and its displacement of Menchú's testimony also provoked a complementary question: What if Menchú had collaborated with Burgos-Debray in producing this textual simulation of an unmediated narrative?[6] By concentrating on Burgos-Debray's (lack of) mediation, our initial discussion had evaded, perhaps ignored, Menchú's active agency in crafting her own narrative. Such a view failed to account for "the authority and creativity of the speaker weaving her own text" (Patai 1988, 8). Our assumption that Menchú had no agency also risked reproducing the classic colonizing gesture, identified by Edward W. Said, whereby representatives of a hegemonic (colonizing) culture invest themselves with *the* authority to speak about, describe, and represent the colonized/subaltern subject (1979, 1985).

How, we asked ourselves, do we go about accounting for Menchú's active role in the construction of her story? Where to begin? As an

activist for her community and as a representative in Europe and the
United States of the Guatemalan activist group, 31 January Popular
Front, it was only reasonable to suppose that Menchú had—and
continues to have—a stake in telling her story. For example, the fall
1990 issue of *Report on Guatemala* notes Menchú's appearance at a
recent conference where "she requested solidarity from North American
friends in supporting the demands of popular organizations and of
Guatemala's indigenous majority" (Gorin 1990, 14). Telling her story
was, and is, a political task for her. To influence a diverse, international
audience, that story had to be readily accessible, which meant that
Menchú may well have had a far more active role in the construction
of her story than Burgos-Debray's retelling of it first suggests.

Once we had granted Menchú this accessibility as a strategy, the
extended descriptions of her culture—its presiding deities, its rituals,
family, and community life—could be read as marks of a deliberate
effort to render an unfamiliar culture less alien to her readers in the
West in order to enlist their support. Certainly a great deal of her
extended descriptions about her culture are a part of her political
program: "I'm an Indianist, not just an Indian," Menchú declares. "I
defend everything to do with my ancestors." But this is not her sole
motivation. As Burgos-Debray notes, "She talked to me not only
because she wanted to tell us about her sufferings but also—or perhaps
mainly—because she wanted us to hear about a culture of which she
is extremely proud and which she wants to have recognized" (166;
xx). Nevertheless, some of these descriptions also seem designed to
accommodate Western notions about "primitive" peoples.

Self-consciousness about her political task and about the self-
representations she mobilizes are signaled at various moments in
Menchú's testimony. We will mention only two examples. First, she
reflects on her community's subversive uses of the Bible to underscore
her people's more "moral" grasp of its precepts and teachings:

> We began studying [the Bible] more deeply and, well, we came
> to a conclusion. That being a Christian means thinking of our
> brothers around us, that everyone of our Indian race has the right
> to eat. (132)

> [F]or us the Bible is our main weapon. It has shown us the way.
> Perhaps those who call themselves Christians but who are really
> only Christians in theory, won't understand why we give the
> Bible the meaning we do. But that's because they haven't lived
> as we have. And also perhaps because they can't analyze it. (134)

Second, Menchú accounts for her transgressive move to learn Spanish,
despite her father's forbidding it because he felt it would take her

away from the community, by spelling out its political implications: "They've always said, poor Indians, they can't speak, so many speak for them. That's why I decided to learn Spanish" (156).

Those instances of reflection and the explicit reference to the use of language as a political strategy made clear to us the fundamental paradox that Menchú's testimony turns on, and of which she was certainly "conscious." On the one hand, to affect its readers with its full and urgent political force, the testimony must be, or seem to be, unmediated—a transparency that makes *visible* the brutalities and repressions it witnesses. On the other hand, such *immediacy* can so overwhelm readers that they identify with, indeed feel they become, Menchú. This "identification," of course, is problematic at best, dishonest at worst. Menchú's reader is not Menchú. Protected and distanced from Menchú's "battlefield"—her severe material conditions and struggle for survival—the First World reader can only masquerade as a Third World oppressed, subaltern subject.[7] As Menchú insists: "It's not so much that the hungrier you've been, the purer your ideas must be, but you can only have a real consciousness if you've really lived this life" (223). Her challenge, then, is to enable a reader to *identify* with her cause, her political agenda, without assuming her identity, even though to identify with her cause may entail imagining oneself in her place.

Menchú's testimony ensures this im-mediated response by deploying another paradox. Her testimony is replete with details about her culture, community, family, even the events that lead to her politicization and development into a leader for her people. At the same time, however, she insists that there are secrets she will not disclose, and she concludes her testimony by reminding us: "Nevertheless, I'm still keeping my Indian identity a secret. I'm still keeping secret what I think no-one should know. Not even anthropologists or intellectuals, no matter how many books they have, can find out all our secrets" (247). This maneuver compels readers to inhabit that space of uncertainty where they know that they do not know everything. Moreover, it compels readers to respect[8] the "prior" text—Menchú's testimony— knowing all the time that, from their first encounter with it, the text has been interpreted (and transformed) in their consciousness—an act for which they bear responsibility.

When we thought of Ann Wright's mediation in *Rigoberta Menchú*, our initial response was quite negative, much as it had been with Burgos-Debray. Wright had done a creditable job of rendering Menchú's Spanish into English, but she had just as clearly taken pains to repeat some of the gestures in the Spanish edition that we felt might lead to

a reader's unexamined compassion. Like Burgos-Debray, Wright wants
her own words to be as much as possible like Menchú's. As she
explains in her "Translator's Note," she hopes that her own presence
as mediator will go virtually unnoticed, and this goal of transparency
has determined her practice (Menchú 1984, viii–ix). She has followed
Menchú's "spontaneous narrative" and "original phrasing," even at
times when Menchú's expression might seem awkward, and she has
transcribed rather than translated many words from Quiché. Indeed,
in large part, her "Translator's Note" reads like a translation of the
Spanish "Introducción" that it replaces. In that "Introducción" (Burgos-
Debray 1983, 7), which is omitted in the English (where the "Introduction" is in fact a translation of Burgos-Debray's "Prológo"), Burgos-
Debray reiterates her determination not to "betray" Menchú by altering
the content of her narrative.

What's more, as if to follow Burgos-Debray's example and insert
herself unobtrusively into the same space Burgos-Debray occupies vis-
à-vis Menchú—and therefore ensure for her reader "the impact"
Menchú's words had on her—Wright draws no attention to specific
strategies she might have used to prepare the English version. Nor
does she speculate about the changes in Menchú's narrative that
Burgos-Debray may have made when *she* translated Menchú's spoken
words to written prose. This allows Wright to state, for example, and
without qualification, that "I have tried, as far as possible, to stay with
Rigoberta's original phrasing" (Menchú 1984, viii).[9] In addition, ironically, Burgos-Debray, not Wright, is pictured with Menchú on the
back cover of the English edition of the book; Wright is not even
mentioned. A translator, of course, can hardly be blamed for a
publisher's failure to acknowledge her and her work. Wright's determination to make herself as invisible as possible, however, in effect
contributes to a second layer of mediation or, to use Richard Seiburth's
term (1989, 239), "covering" of Menchú's text which, with respect to
the reader in English, acts as a second distancing or even a second
erasure.

What is curious about this second erasure, however, as we discovered
when we began to study Wright's version with a view to Burgos-
Debray's Spanish, is that Wright does, in fact, give evidence that she
translates not only Burgos-Debray's invisibility, but also Burgos-Debray's editing of Menchú's tapes. This is to say that, contrary to what
her "Translator's Note" might lead one to believe, Wright has apparently been guided as much by Burgos-Debray's mediating principle as
by a "fidelity" to the words in her text: "I only hope that I have been
able to do justice to the power of their message . . . and convey the

impact they had on me when I first read [Menchú's words]" (ix). As we studied Wright's own English words we found in them definite indications of will or agency.

The substitution of Burgos-Debray's "Introducción," for instance, is just one of several alterations that suggest Wright believed she could do more "justice" to the "power" of Menchú's testimony by making it accessible to the English-language reader. Other alterations include the "I" at the beginning of the English title, the absence of *conciencia*, and the use throughout of the word "Indian" rather than "Quiché." What's more, Wright has not reprinted either Burgos-Debray's acknowledgments or her dedication to Alaide Foppa. She has changed the epigraphs of several chapters, shortened many chapter titles, and omitted an appendix of documents about the Comité de Unidad Campesina (CUC). Finally, her use of ellipses is not consistent with the Spanish, and on several occasions she has Menchú speak to a second person, something that does not occur in the Spanish version. These last two alterations are especially important because they lead one to speculate about whether Wright believed her changes could restore some of the orality sacrificed in Burgos-Debray's initial transcription: "Something I want to tell you" (165), Menchú says in Wright's English, or "It's not so much the hungrier you've been" (233), or "I'd need a lot of time to tell you all about my people" (247). (The changes involved in the transcription of oral narratives are discussed in Patai 1988; Tedlock 1983; and Watson and Watson-Franke 1985.)

As our discussion of *Rigoberta Menchú* demonstrates, our grasp of the "demands" Menchú's testimony makes on its readers was achieved through a circuitous route. We constantly interrogated our premises— repeatedly doubling back on our initial assumptions and expectations— at the same time that we tried to be alert to the various positions (Menchú's, Burgos-Debray's, Wright's) implicated in the crafting of Menchú's testimony. In this way, our work revolved around diverse mediations, including those involved in erasing the marks of mediation itself, the readings and retellings that intervene between the reader and the "realities" Menchú describes.

Our assessment that an unmediated narrative is simulated in order to engage Menchú's reader is almost as important as insisting that the very fact of mediation can be extended, we believe, so as to formulate a theory of reading other cross-cultural Third World texts as well. In these texts, as we have come to understand them, the sense of unmediatedness or immediacy is the means by which some form of identification is produced. Simultaneously, however, mediation assumes distance and difference between readers and the subjects-objects of their reading. Reading, then, can be based on a similar, subtly dialectical interplay of identity (identification) and difference. The dangers of mobilizing solely one or the other category are many. An uncritical assumption of identity is, as we have shown through *Rigoberta Menchú,* a mode of appropriation. Similarly, identification is a function of recuperating the unfamiliar "other" in terms of the familiar; reading this way relies on the stereotypes one culture utilizes to understand, and domesticate, (an)other. An uncritical assumption of difference, which presumes that (an)other is never accessible, allows readers to abandon, indeed exonerates them from, the task of ever reading cross-cultural texts.[10] Deployed solely, each category produces an impasse.

Invoking the idea and activity of translation and attending to the specific strategies translators employ offer one way out of this impasse. As an activity, translation starts from the assumption that something of one language *can be* "borne across" or recovered in another. Although translation is often construed as an activity that simply copies or repeats a "prior" text, it is also, and more importantly, construed as one that interprets (and transforms) a "prior" text. It is, after all, an activity that presumes a translator, a subject who intervenes, mediates, between one language and another. Thus, recent theorists emphasize not the "accuracy," or even the product, of translation, but rather the appropriateness of a translator's choices, the strategies used to render one language in terms of another, the inclusions and exclusions.

When a cross-cultural work is seen as an author's translation of a culture, it becomes possible to read that text itself as a reading—a construction of social, political, cultural "realities"—by an individual who inserts herself and her work (and is embedded) in that culture in particular ways, for particular purposes. Such a view warns against easy judgments about how an individual or a work represents (or is representative of) a culture.[11] When readers see their reading as an activity involving translation, it becomes possible for them to scrutinize their own "locations"—the interpretive choices and strategies—which are implicated in their readings. At the same time, however, this emphasis on individual and individualized interpretation involved in translation should not lead to a domain of pure relativity, where every reader can only read in terms of personal experience. The text being translated resists and constrains the reader from this absolute appropriation. While translation requires, according to James Boyd White, "an act of creation, a making of something new . . . the original text cannot be forgotten, for fidelity is always due to it. Indeed, it is upon the prior text that our right to speak at all depends. One has no authority to disregard it and substitute for it texts of one's own composition" (1990, 246).

In light of what we have said above, a desirable goal in teaching and reading cross-cultural texts as an exercise involving translation is to nudge students/readers to occupy that space or tension where they are "faithful" to the text at the same time as they acknowledge that their "fidelity" is itself refracted through their ideological formations as "subjects" in the First World. As Catherine Belsey notes in a different context, "It is here that we see the full force of Althusser's use of the term 'subject,' originally borrowed, as he says, from law. The subject is not only a grammatical subject, 'a center of initiatives, author of and responsible for its actions,' but also a *subjected* being who submits to the authority of the social formation represented in ideology as the Absolute Subject (God, the king, the boss, Man, conscience)" (1985, 49). Being "faithful," then, entails constructing, in as informed a way as possible, the author's "purposes"—examining, that is, "the process of production—not the private experience of the individual author, but the mode of production, the materials and their arrangement in the work" (Belsey 1985, 54).

How might this function in class? More specifically, to return to our first thoughts about using informed translation as an antidote to translation practiced unawares, how might it function with respect to *Rigoberta Menchú*?

Even students who have no knowledge of Spanish might be asked to look carefully at the book's front cover and consider it with respect to the statements in Menchú's opening paragraph. They could be asked about the "I" at the beginning of the title, in the context of Menchú's assertion that "it's not only *my* life, it's also the testimony of my people" (Menchú 1984, 1); about the use of the word "Indian," or the advertisement of a film "featuring" Menchú. They could be asked to find information about the publisher, about Burgos-Debray, or about similar testimonials in English and to discuss what they find in light of Menchú's narrative. The changes Wright made when she translated the title could be pointed out and discussed as well, and the difficulties of translating the work could be explained.

For students whose Spanish allows them to work in both languages, a discussion of the cover and title could be followed by an examination of terms in passages that present particular challenges to the translator. Depending on the extent of their language skills, they could be asked to discuss, for example, the role of *conciencia* in the Spanish and its appearances in English as "consciousness" or "awareness." This type of exercise would no doubt be richer for students who have some

familiarity with Spanish (and should in fact suggest many similar
activities for those with the appropriate language skills). But even
students unable to work in Spanish could be asked to examine the
English text for examples of the experience Menchú points to as the
one that guides her while she talks to Burgos-Debray. *Conciencia*
implies "awareness"—"waking up" in the sense of seeing clearly—
an "illumination" that, when its development is traced through passages selected in Spanish, leads from the raising of a young woman's
consciousness to a complex strategy for bringing to light certain secrets
in order to protect their integrity.[12] Regardless of the language in which
students carry out this exercise, they would confront not only the
difficulties inherent in rendering Menchú's story in English, they would
also need to consider the issue of translation with respect to this central
experience. What is more, once *conciencia* is placed in the context of
Menchú's very deliberate and conscious decision to risk betraying her
people in order to make outsiders aware of their suffering, students
should recognize that their own role within the narrative is one of
potential intruder, for whom Menchú is constantly mediating or
translating from Quiché to Spanish (to English) not only words but
also the very incidents of the story.

Although we did not think of Menchú's narrative in this way until
we had discussed it several times, the more times we read her reminder
that "I'm still keeping my Indian identity secret" (Menchú 1984, 247),
the more we considered her a translator in the widest possible sense
of the word. This means that we have come to view the marketing of
her story, whether in Burgos-Debray's Paris apartment or on the
English-language cover, as absolutely consistent with her decision to
learn Spanish and leave her village. "My name is Rigoberta Menchú,
and here's how I woke up," Menchú might say in the English title
that could be proposed to students as they were encouraged to think
of how she might sound if she were able to cast her story in their
idiom. What might she want from you, they could be asked, how
would she expect you to insert yourselves in her story? How do you
think she might have envisioned you as she gave permission to Wright
to make an English-language translation of her book? How well do
you think Wright has made way for a realization of the "you" Menchú
envisioned?

And how do you think *Wright* envisioned you as she prepared that
translation? students could be queried as the discussion returned,
inevitably, to the English-language version. Why do you think she
placed a first-person pronoun in the title, or made her other adaptations?

Why, for example, is the second person addressed in Wright's version? Who is that "you" in Wright's text?

None of those questions would be answered easily, and some might not be possible to answer at all. By considering them, however, students would be enabled to see Wright, Burgos-Debray, Menchú, and themselves engaged in a collaboration that results not from passivity and transparency on the part of the "translators," but from assertiveness and interchange. They should also realize that to make Wright or Burgos-Debray or Menchú visible is not to "criticize" but to acknowledge them. In the same way, it should be evident that a translator's visibility does not lessen the impact or immediacy of a story for its readers, but actually intensifies that immediacy by compounding an awareness of translation and bringing the act of mediation to light. "Im-mediation" results from the simultaneous distancing and participation that characterize translation directed by *conciencia* as both self-consciousness and conscience as ethical responsibility.

Notes

1. We use "transculturation" thinking of Pérez Firmat's discussion of it with respect to "the Cuban condition": "the word properly designates the fermentation and turmoil that *precedes* synthesis." It is thus "a coinage that denotes transition, passage, process" (1989, 23).

2. See, for example, the work by Lefevere 1984; Venuti 1986; and White 1990; and the articles in Warren 1989.

3. See Warren's "celebration of otherness" (5), or White's description of the translator's identity "split irremediably in two" (231), or Maier's "compact" (628).

4. Among the essays and books we looked at, the following were especially useful: Crapanzano (1984), Watson and Watson-Franke (1985), Frank (1979), Geiger (1986), Patai (1988), and Tedlock (1983). (We use the terms "life history" and "testimony" interchangeably because Menchú employs both "genres" when she "turn[s] her life story" [Burgos-Debray, xiv] into a *testimonio* that bears witness to the "problem of repression, poverty, subalternity, imprisonment, struggle for survival"—all experiences that characterize the *testimonio*, according to Beverley [1989, 14]. See, however, Beverley's discussion of the distinctions between *testimonios* and oral histories [13–14].)

5. A comparable danger haunts the work of interpreters who wish to clearly signal their self-reflexivity with regard to their acts of interpretation; one of the effects of extensive self-reflection on one's "location" is that it can displace the "real" subject of their interpretation. In extreme cases, such self-reflexivity becomes a mode of self-aggrandizement whereby the interpreter mobilizes a host of personal details to keep herself at the "center" of an interpretive "performance." In some instances, self-reflexiveness can be (and

is) deployed not as a way of accounting for one's position, but as a way of explaining it away, a way of exempting oneself.

6. This question, and the discussion that follows, arose simultaneously with the question that frames our discussion of Burgos-Debray's suppression of her presence in Menchú's testimony. We saw them as complementary questions. For purposes of clarity, however, we present them in a linear narrative. But, in a classroom situation, we would encourage both questions to be asked, and discussion around them to proceed simultaneously, in order to minimize the risk of one subjectivity being subsumed under the other.

7. "We live down the street from what I consider to be the prettiest park," one of Carol's former students from a class on Central American politics and poetics wrote to her recently from a university town in the Pacific Northwest, evoking her reading of *Rigoberta Menchú*: "It includes a big rose garden with 300 different types of roses. There is a community garden where neighbors plant corn or beans or whatever side by side. Almost like Rigoberta Menchú's community."

8. White also uses this word to refer to "a set of practices by which we learn to live with difference" (1990, 257).

9. It is odd that Wright should refer to Menchú's "original," since there is no evidence that she had access to the tapes of Menchú's voice from which Burgos-Debray worked.

10. Trinh T. Minh-ha analyzes a somewhat different move where "difference" is invoked to disempower some and empower others: "[L]et difference replace conflict. Difference as understood in many feminist and non-western contexts, difference as foreground in my filmwork is not opposed to sameness, nor synonymous with separateness. Difference, in other words, does not necessarily give rise to separatism. . . . Many of us hold on to the concept of difference not as a tool of creativity to question multiple forms of repression and dominance, but as a tool of segregation, to exert power on the basis of racial and sexual essences. The apartheid type of difference" (1988, 74).

11. Here, it might be useful to consider the reception of Salman Rushdie and his two works about India and Pakistan, *Midnight's Children* and *Shame*, in the West, where they have been read as representative of the "realities" of the subcontinent. Clarke Blaise, for example, describes *Midnight's Children* as "a continent finding its voice" (see Dingwaney, 1992). The same could be said of *Rigoberta Menchú*: the blurb on the back cover packages the book as "one of the few complete expressions of Indian self-knowledge since the Spanish conquest."

12. In Spanish, where *conciencia* is "born," and birth is commonly expressed as a "bringing to light" *(dar a luz)*, this strategy is formulated in the language itself as well as conceptually.

Works Cited

Belsey, Catherine. 1985. "Constructing the Subject: Deconstructing the Text." In *Feminist Criticism and Social Change*, edited by Judith Newton and Deborah Rosenfelt, 45–64. New York: Methuen.

Beverley, John. 1989. "The Margin at the Center: On *Testimonio*" (Testimonial Narrative). *Modern Fiction Studies* 35(Spring): 11–28.

Burgos-Debray, Elisabeth. 1983. *Me Llamo Rigoberta Menchú: y así me nació la concienca.* Barcelona: Argos Vegara.

Crapanzano, Vincent. 1984. "Life Histories: A Review Essay." *American Anthropologist* 86 (December): 953–60.

Dingwaney, Anuradha. 1992. "Author(iz)ing *Midnight's Children* and *Shame:* Salman Rushdie's Constructing of Authority." In *Reworlding: Essays on the Writers of the Indian Diaspora*, edited by Emmanuel Nelson. Westport, CT: Greenwood Press.

Frank, Gelya. 1979. "Finding the Common Denominator: A Phenomenological Critique of the Life History Method." *Ethos* 7(Spring): 68–94.

Geiger, Susan N. J. 1986. "Women's Life Histories: Method and Content." *Signs* 11(Winter): 334–51.

Gómez-Peña, Guillermo. 1989. "The Multicultural Paradigm: An Open Letter to the National Arts Community." *High Performance.* Fall: 18–27.

Gorin, Joe. 1990. "Network News." *Report on Guatemala* 2(3): 14–15.

Lefevere, Andre. 1984. "Translations and Other Ways in Which One Literature Refracts Another." *Symposium* 38(Summer): 127–42.

Maier, Carol. 1989. "Notes After Words: Looking Forward Retrospectively at Translation and (Hispanic and Luso-Brazilian) Feminist Criticism." In *Cultural and Historical Grounding for Hispanic and Luso-Brazilian Feminist Criticism*, edited by Hernán Vidal, 625–53. Minneapolis: Institute for the Study of Ideologies and Literature.

Menchú, Rigoberta. 1984. *I . . . Rigoberta Menchú: An Indian Woman in Guatemala*, edited by Elisabeth Burgos-Debray; translated by Ann Wright. London: New Left-Verso.

Minh-ha, Trinh T. 1988. "Not You/Like You: Post-colonial Women and the Interlocking Questions of Identity and Difference." *Inscriptions* 3–4: 71–77.

Patai, Daphne, ed. and trans. 1988. *Brazilian Women Speak: Contemporary Life Stories* (Collection of Interviews). New Brunswick, NJ: Rutgers University Press.

Pérez Firmat, Gustavo. 1989. *The Cuban Condition: Translation and Identity in Modern Cuban Literature.* Cambridge: Cambridge University Press.

Said, Edward W. 1979. *Orientalism.* New York: Vintage Books.

————. 1985. "In the Shadow of the West." *Wedge: The Imperialism of Representation, The Representation of Imperialism* 7–8 (Winter–Spring): 4–12.

Seiburth, Richard. 1989. "The Guest: Second Thoughts on Translating Hölderlin." In *The Art of Translation: Voices from the Field*, edited by Rosanna Warren, 237–43. Boston: Northeastern University Press.

Sommer, Doris. 1988. " 'Not Just a Personal Story': Women's *Testimonios* and the Plural Self." In *Life/Lines: Theorizing Women's Autobiography*, edited by Bella Brodzki and Celeste Schenck, 107–30. Ithaca, NY: Cornell University Press.

Tedlock, Dennis. 1983. *The Spoken Word and the Work of Interpretation.* Philadelphia: University of Pennsylvania Press.

Vélez, Diana, ed. and trans. 1988. *Reclaiming Medusa: Short Stories by Contemporary Puerto Rican Women.* San Francisco: Spinsters/Aunt Lute.

Venuti, Lawrence. 1986. "The Translator's Invisibility." *Criticism* 28(Spring): 179–212.

Warren, Rosanna, ed. 1989. *The Art of Translation: Voices from the Field.* Boston: Northeastern University Press.

Watson, Lawrence C., and Maria-Barbara Watson-Franke. 1985. *Interpreting Life Histories: An Anthropological Inquiry.* New Brunswick, NJ: Rutgers University Press.

White, James Boyd. 1990. *Justice as Translation: An Essay in Cultural and Legal Criticism.* Chicago and London: Chicago University Press.

II Contexts

Kenneth Burke defines "scene" as the "background of the act, the situation in which it occurred" (1962, xv). He explains that "scene," like other terms in his pentad, are generative and can be used as ratios, for example as scene-act or scene-agent. More recently, critics have explored further complications in terms such as "scene," "context," and "culture." Gloria Anzaldúa, in *Borderlands*, defines the new *mestiza*, the woman, like herself, who lives on the borders between cultures, languages, genres, and sexual identities. Anzaldúa moves us beyond an essentialist conception of culture, gender, race, and language. Similarly, in "Linguistic Utopias," Mary Louise Pratt argues for a linguistics of contact, which acknowledges that cultures are not intact, homogenous groups, but are, instead, heterogeneous and changing.

The six essays in this section focus on various contexts and on how these contexts inform an understanding of students, texts, and theories of teaching and learning. The authors implicitly define "context" in different ways, but each understands contexts as changing.

The first three essays examine broad cultural contexts. Judith Scot-Smith Girgus, a middle-school teacher, and Cecelia Tichi, a university teacher, collaborate to explain that a "generation of students has grown up in the culture of television and live *in, with,* and *through* it." They then argue that features of television can be used effectively in teaching. Mary Savage presents three views from the elementary school context through her interviews with four teachers from the Bronx, each of whom discusses how her own cultural background informs her teaching of students from many other cultures. Norma Alarcón takes a broad historical perspective to analyze changing definitions of "Chicana" and "Chicano" and the resulting political and personal consequences.

The next three authors turn to academic contexts within larger cultural contexts. Reginald Martin gives a brief history of "integrationist" and "separatist" literature before exploring problems in contemporary literary theorists' treatment of both kinds of literature. Robert S. Burton argues that "no matter what our background, we share with authors the experience of 'fragmentation on a global scale.' " He warns that behind the interest in "multiculturalism" lies "a habit of 'othering' or 'differentiating' that threatens to contain, rather than open up, the field of cultural and cross-cultural studies." And H. W. Matalene focuses on his experiences in teaching "The Secret Life of Walter Mitty" to students at Shanxi University, China, to explore how texts, theories, readers, and teachers are culture-bound.

Works Cited

Anzaldúa, Gloria. 1987. *Borderlands/La Frontera: The New Mestiza.* San Francisco: Spinsters/Aunt Lute.

Burke, Kenneth. 1962. *A Grammar of Motives.* Berkeley: University of California Press.

Pratt, Mary Louise. 1987. "Linguistic Utopias." *The Linguistics of Writing: Arguments Between Linguistics and Literature,* edited by Nigel Fabb et al., 48–66. Manchester: Manchester University Press.

5 Teaching in the Television Culture

Judith Scot-Smith Girgus
Horpath Hall School, Nashville, Tennessee
Cecelia Tichi
Vanderbilt University

> I was born in a house with the television always on.
> —The Talking Heads, "Love for Sale," 1986

> TV is the park where we went every day after school.
> —Heidi Stanley, college freshman, 1990

These statements, one a song lyric, the other a student's in-class comment, probably strike dread in the hearts of teachers of English. Committed to the written word, many of us are repelled by the thought of students' habitats filled nonstop with the siren song of television and its images. Committed, moreover, to values of the natural world and particularly appreciative of the idea of the park as a designed recreational space, we may feel horrified by the student's easy assumption that TV could possibly be considered equivalent to outdoor activity, that the screen could be synonymous with—even displace— the park. We might wish to recommend to the student two powerful anti-television polemics, Marie Winn's *The Plug-In Drug* (1977), emphasizing the narcotic quality of TV, and Neil Postman's *Amusing Ourselves to Death* (1985), which argues that television "has made entertainment the natural format for the presentation of all experience" (87).

Perhaps Betsy Byars, a writer of children's books, provides the apparently exemplary, cautionary anti-TV tale in *The TV Kid* (1987), which features eleven-year-old Lennie, child of a single-parent family. Living with his mother in a motel she owns and operates, he is shown to be lonely, bored, failing science—and immersed in television, especially game shows in which he is the fascinated consumer. As the novel opens, he is hosing down a walk, reminded by his mother that his homework must be done:

"Aren't you through yet?" Lennie's mother called. "You've got to do your homework, remember?". . . .

Lennie walked on to the office. As he went inside, he paused in front of the TV.

A game show was on, and there were five new cars lined up on a revolving stage. The winning contestant got to pick one of the cars, and if it started, he got to keep it. Only one of the cars was wired to start.

"It's the Grand Am," Lennie said instantly. He felt he had a special instinct for picking the right box or door or car on shows like this. "I *know* it's the Grand Am."

"Lennie, are you watching television?" his mother called from the utility room.

"I'm looking for a pencil," he called back.

"Well, there are plenty of pencils on the desk."

"Where? Oh, yeah, I see one now."

Lennie was hoping to stall until he could see if it really was the Grand Am as he suspected.

The contestant wanted to try for the Catalina. "No, the Grand Am, the Grand Am!" Lennie murmured beneath his breath. He found the stub of a pencil on the desk. . . .

"Lennie, I meant what I said about no television," his mom called.

"I know you did."

"No television at all until those grades pick up."

"I know."

A commercial came on. "Doc-tor Pep-per, so mis-under-stooooood."

Here we see Lennie resist his mother's directives, immersed as he is in the seductive TV game show. Ultimately, a crisis—a rattlesnake bite that threatens Lennie's life—brings renewed, intimate contact with his mother and with the policeman who rescues him. Watching TV from his hospital bed, Lennie has a TV epiphany, realizing "the people who made television commercials didn't know anything about life. . . . It seemed to him suddenly that every TV person he had ever seen wasn't real. . . . Lennie thought, his own family—just him and his mom— was a hundred times realer than the Bradys or the Waltons or the Cleavers or any other TV family you could name" (108–9). This is the revelation that rescues Lennie from the corruptive fantasies of television and brings him back into the real world. Within moments, he switches off "Let's Make a Deal" and begins work on his science report.

Byars's concluding scenario might gladden any teacher's heart, and instructors in English may naturally assent to its themes, since we are heir to a decades-long history of ingrained anti-TV hostility. The culture of print—our culture, as teachers committed to the written word— has defined its resistance to the technology of television as a war waged for the survival of the mind. In 1951, the newspaper critic Harriet Van Horne complained that "now in the third year of the Television Age, . . . our people are becoming less literate by the minute. . . . Chances are that the grandchild of the Television Age won't know how to read this" (quoted in "Dark (Screen) Future," *Time*, 1951). In 1962, Ashley Montagu referred to "the sterile puerilities which find so congenial a home in the television world." In the name of "good taste," he called for an abatement of its "noisome vulgarity" (1962, 132).

Imagery of narcotic addiction has similarly threaded its way through public discourse on television. "Some people . . . ignore TV because they are afraid of getting hooked," wrote a *Time* magazine journalist in 1968. "What is to be done with parents who are themselves television addicts?" asked a writer in 1964. Television could "become the worst cultural opiate in history, buy and corrupt all talent, and completely degrade the sensibility of the country," another critic had written in the early 1950s (*Time* 1968, 98; Shayon 1964; Willingham, 117).

Even the most recent child-rearing guidance books reinforce the binary division between reading and television. "Parents should show their children that reading is both enjoyable and useful. They shouldn't spend all their time in front of the TV. . . . Are you addicted to soap operas? Do you look forward to Friday nights so you can space out?" (Cutright 1989, 100, 119). "Would [your daughter] insist on watching right up to bedtime if her father was waiting to read the next installment of their bedtime story?" (Leach 1986, 676). "Think about your child's study habits. . . . Does he do his homework in front of the TV?" (Cutright 1989, 75, 129–30).

The vehemence of this rhetoric is clearly indicative of a battle for the mind itself. Essentially, two realms—television and print—have been cast in the adversarial relationships of puerility *vs.* maturity, low culture *vs.* high culture, entertainment *vs.* intellectual engagement, frivolity *vs.* seriousness, contamination *vs.* purity, robotry *vs.* critical imagination, sickness *vs.* health. These are the battle lines that have continued, uncontested, for nearly forty years. The way the argument has been cast suggests that the resolution of the conflict is possible solely through one's maturation. The child held captive by the powerful, popular medium will ultimately renounce TV and embrace the intellectual-imaginative complexity of the printed text. As one analyst observes, "We expect children to like television precisely because they are easily amused and do not know any better, but we also expect them to grow out of it" (Attallah 1984, 225).

At this point, many contemporary instructors in English may protest that for educational purposes we use TV regularly in the classroom, perhaps showing videos of canonical fiction like *The Scarlet Letter* or the BBC Shakespeare, or major historical moments such as special presidential addresses and feats from NASA, including the unforeseen horror of *Challenger.* But aren't teachers who do so stigmatized by colleagues? Doesn't the sight of an instructor wheeling the monitor and VCR cart down the hall elicit the contemptuous thought, "Easy day, pacing yourself out?" In the back of one's mind, one might even think, "bribing the students," or "pandering." Doesn't the teacher with the video equipment run the gauntlet? Perhaps it is not surprising, therefore, that so much current work in media literacy is really a thinly disguised effort on the part of teachers—in the guise of "analyzing" TV "accurately"—to wean students from what they appreciate—TV— to make them dislike it and in the hope that the students will then embrace the print-culture traditions the teacher considers valuable.

The fact, nevertheless, is that a generation of students has grown up in the culture of television and live *in, with,* and *through* it. Life-threatening snake bites to the contrary, they will experience TV as an integral and important part of their autobiographies. It can even be argued that, in the 1990s, TV is an actual environment. To call TV by its slang names of "box" or "tube" is to downsize it to a mere geometric solid, relegated to a minor place in one's personal or cultural space. But "environment" makes television that space itself, an encompassing surrounding, be it park or habitat. Whether we like it or not, the fact is that for students of all levels, TV is a natural and integral part of life. Given these facts, we need to begin to ask, what is the TV environment really like? What traits define it? What characteristics can we expect to find in our students as a result of their TV-era conscious-ness? And how can we work *with* these traits productively and energetically in the classrooms?

We may begin with the issue of TV in the household at a historical moment in which parents are in the work force full time, and when family units themselves assume diverse forms. The household may be comfortable precisely because the "television [is] always on." This is to say that the rhythms of TV may set a regularizing pace, that the sounds of TV are today's natural, comforting sounds of the household, replacing the rattle of pots and pans. Yet nowhere in the child-rearing literature is this point acknowledged. Instead, the characteristic tone is one of admonition and reproach, "Be sure that you and your child don't automatically turn on TV when you get home and leave it on until bedtime, so that it is background noise in your home" (Cutright

1989, 114–15). "The set is *never* switched, or left, on 'to see what's on' or because 'I'm bored' or as background 'company' " (Leach 1989, 677).

Is all this true? It is helpful to hear what students themselves have to say. A college freshman of 1990–91 recalls, "I can remember as a preschooler waiting for *Gumby* and *Harveytoons* to come on at my grandmother's house while she made me a grits-and-eggs breakfast." Another remarks, "Much of what I remember from TV when I was little was spent sharing the blanket with Robin and John, my older brother and sister." Still another: "I only watched shows that gave me a feeling of belonging. For example, I was able to live vicariously through Marsha Brady ["The Brady Bunch"] and experience the family's adventures since I, too, was the oldest girl in my family." One student recalls watching holiday-season TV specials with her father "as we curled ourselves in sleeping bags on a cold winter night."

These statements show the assimilation of TV into the viewer's emotional life and point to the likelihood that, within the culture of television, the viewer's cognitive processes themselves are undergoing change. In fact, it is evident that the contemporary viewer enacts a cognitive process identified by Raymond Williams in the mid-1970s. In *Television: Technology and Cultural Form,* Williams cautioned that analysts of television were misguidedly, anachronistically operating like drama or film critics or book reviewers, approaching individual programs as "a discrete event or a succession of discrete events" (1975, 88). Williams, a British Marxist social analyst with particular interests in the cultural institutions of print, had been a BBC television reviewer between 1968 and 1972, and he became convinced that the forms of broadcasting in the TV age were altering perceptual processes. Prior to broadcasting, Williams observed, "The essential items were discrete. . . . People took a book or a pamphlet or a newspaper, went out to a play or a concert or a meeting or a match, with a single predominant expectation or attitude" (88). The fundamental expectation was of a discrete program or entity.

But increasingly, Williams found, in the era of television broadcasting, the discrete program yielded to a structure far more fluid: "There has been a significant shift from the concept of sequence as *programming* to the concept of sequence as *flow.*" He goes on: "There is a quality of flow which our received vocabulary of discrete response and description cannot easily acknowledge" (93). Conceding that vestigial elements of discrete programs remain intact in the timed units of a "show," he argued nonetheless that the intervals between these units have disappeared. In American broadcast television, the advertisements are incorporated into the whole, so that the segments, ads, trailers, previews, announcements, and so forth become "the real flow, the real 'broadcasting' " (90). Williams calls all this "a new kind of communication phenomenon" that demands recognition (91).

We can get an idea of how this "new kind of communication phenomenon" works by revisiting that opening scene from *The TV Kid*, in which readers participate in Lennie's transit to and from the television world of the game show to that of his mother's demands. We enter Lennie's consciousness directly, moving with him in the halfhearted search for a pencil and then back again, and yet again, to the game show world. We cross and recross to alternative loci. Psychologically, the individual enters the television world, then crosses back for interaction with someone else in the immediate environment, and then recrosses to enter the television world again, this time an entirely different world as the program alternates with the commercial.

This alternation defines the so-called viewer as a figure continuously moving, a sojourner, a figure in transit between different TV worlds. The alternation works in several ways. First, each single channel alternates program and commercial sequences, constantly moving the viewer out of one and into the other (e.g., from a game show to a Doctor Pepper commercial). Ostensible, undivided attention to one channel is really a sojourning in and out of diverse worlds.

As we see, moreover, in the fictional representation of *The TV Kid*, the viewer is also pulled away from absorption in TV back into the surrounding habitat. The search for a pencil, the need to respond to a parent, forces Lennie to cross and recross a cognitive threshold from the habitat to the TV worlds and back again. "I *know* it's the Grand Am. . . . I'm looking for a pencil. . . . the Grand Am, the Grand Am!" As viewer, one may prefer the TV world, but it is not possible to stay there. Others in the habitat claim attention. To meet various sensory demands, the individual must constantly move, adjust, accommodate, engage, withdraw to move again, and so on. And of course, since the mid-1960s, the remote channel changer has made possible a viewer's participation in multiple TV worlds. To flip around the channels, themselves multiplied by the spread of multistation cable television systems, has become a common viewer experience and given new emphasis to televisual "flow."

And there is an activism in teleconscious flow that, until now, has been concealed by the doctrine of TV's narcotic effect. Back in 1954, the speaker of a humorous, anecdotal magazine essay recorded that children were simultaneously involved in two, or even three, activities while watching TV, that the electronic baby-sitter by no means monopolized their attention:

> The children began to play jacks, read the comics, fight, and flip baseball cards while watching. This still kept them roughly on the site of the television set but hardly immobilized. (Whitbread and Cadden 1954, 82)

These very children, we have been told, had previously sat in silent absorption before the likes of "Howdy Doody" and "Super Circus." Yet now they have taken up other activities—conducted simultaneously. Only very recently has the concept of mediated communication entered the design of studies on TV watching, as communications experts acknowledge that decades of experiments, so carefully designed to be "scientific," in fact drastically change, erase, or alter the conditions of the actual television environment. A 1971 study involving twenty families' household TV usage found viewers "engaged in a host of activities while the set was on, reading a newspaper or magazine, talking, sleeping, staring out a window," all phenomena "that regularly occur in natural environments yet are suppressed by researchers" (Anderson 1988, 204).

Another psychological study, involving children as subjects, concludes that they constitute "the lively audience"—the data corroborate the findings from both the twenty American households and the anecdotal observations of the mother whose children fought, flipped baseball cards, and played jacks while watching television (see Palmer 1986). This study finds that, while watching TV, young children play with pets, look after brothers and sisters, play board games, make and build things, play with toys, jump and dance, read, do homework, fight and talk (148–51). "The TV babies really can do their homework, watch TV, talk on the phone and listen to the radio all at the same time," argues a guest columnist in a 1990 *New York Times* editorial. "It's as if information from each source finds its way to a different cluster of thoughts" (Pittman 1990). This columnist, significantly, writes under a *Times* rubric called "Voices of the New Generation," positioning himself as one bred to be a "TV Baby." (Teachers take note: this young man took to the written word to make his point.)

If the culture of TV is that of teleconsciousness, then certain implications must be faced. First, the texts that represent individuals and groups in a setting in which a television set is turned on reveal a new pluralistic state of consciousness in which engagement in the on-screen realm proceeds simultaneously with engagement in diverse activities in the surrounding habitat. Attention shifts to and from the television, including it, but not excluding other activities. In this formulation, thought itself changes, becoming multivalent. The empowerment of the individual becomes a function of the ability to engage in this multicentered thinking. The individual is cognitively functioning in two or more places simultaneously, in affairs of the habitat—or the classroom—and in those of the on-screen world, assigning primary attention alternately to one or the other.

Yet it would be inaccurate to characterize this kind of thought in pejorative terms. It is not a state of distraction or of attention divided, not an either/or state, but one of multiplicity as the mind turns simultaneously to several centers of attention, constantly prioritizing and reprioritizing among them. The onscreen world may be compelling, even deeply absorbing, but only intermittently so as the mind reassigns itself new centers of attention. And this teleconscious state can be attributed to adults as well. The novelist Jill McCorkle describes the father of a teen in these terms:

> I called for my . . . father. He was stretched out on the sofa watching football, the volume of the set turned completely down so that he could hear his album of wildlife sounds. One minute he was at the bowl game, the next he was in a jungle with loud bird sounds, like chekaw chekaw. (1990, 84)

Might we suggest that any number of teachers of English might imagine themselves—ourselves—similarly engaged? Might we hint that there are cognitive practices in which we have engaged but failed to examine?

TV-age consciousness is additionally affected by the remote channel changer, a lifelong instrument of empowerment for students. Temptation to dismiss it as a technology abetting the shortening of the attention span misses the larger point, namely, that the opportunity to move oneself to new centers of attention frees the individual to make choices, act on those choices, to feel a certain degree of autonomy. The individual with a lifelong sense of such decision-making ability has every expectation of carrying forward that personal power to the classroom.

What, then, are the implications of all this for the classroom environment? First, it is important to recognize that the TV-era student finds the fluidity of crossed and recrossed mental foci of the habitat and the on-screen worlds to be mirrored in the cooperative learning situation. Just as the television watcher moves in and out of the on-screen world(s) with a certain cognitive fluidity, so the student working in a cooperative group participates in a cognitive process that allows her or him to move from one point of focus to another. Therefore, the teleconscious student expects to work cooperatively rather than hierarchically or autocratically. And the idea of cooperation in no way conflicts with individual empowerment. The teleconsciously empowered student enters the classroom with a democratic, egalitarian outlook. The student expects to work in the ways congenial to his or her multicentered habits of thought. The most natural pathways to learning in these terms are those which are cooperative in spirit and operation. Functionally, this teleconscious cooperation works laterally in the classroom, meaning that the learning environment is maximally effective whenever students have the opportunity to engage in self-motivated, self-directed work which they then share with others, who in turn share their work with them. Students are empowered in the TV environment, especially in the age of the remote. Peer learning or coaching situations are empowering because they make students responsible for their own learning and involve them in helping others to learn. One way to formulate this kind of work for the students lies in the term "instant publishing," in which work output is presented without delay and yet, as the term "publishing" indicates, retains its formal and literate basis.

Students in this kind of classroom environment assume major responsibilities for presentation of work and for the classroom agenda, deciding in peer consultations who will be responsible for what. Classroom time becomes student time—students are in possession of their thoughts and their output. Ironically, at a cultural moment in which the term "couch potato" derides television watchers for passivity, the fact is that the real couch potatoes are students in the traditional classroom, who merely sit down and listen—passive recipients rather than active learners.

The instructor's role necessarily must shift in the classroom of teleconscious students. Just as the student's role in this era changes from receptivity to activity, from teacher-directed tasks to self- and group-initiated tasks, so too must the teacher undertake a quite deliberate self-redefinition. This is not easy, for it requires shedding some of our most cherished views of ourselves as figures of central authority. In essence, the instructor must relinquish the position of both center and apex of the classroom. For maximal effectiveness with a classroom full of TV-era, teleconscious students, the teacher must become *the facilitator, rather than the director.* The teacher becomes a figure moving among groups of students in a room where several activities are in progress simultaneously. This teacher might first work with a group of students gathered around a computer, then proceed to another group busy with a rehearsal, then move on to a third group who are reading. The sense of motion or fluidity—the flow—within the classroom and, in addition, the elevated noise level necessarily accompanying this decentralized environment will pose no problem for the students. As individuals accustomed to the televisual flow, and as participants in a teleconscious mentality, they will work effectively in such an environment, experiencing the scene as normal. With the opportunity for computer-assisted writing, moreover, they will find composition to be an activity compatible with teleconscious thought. Students writing with word processors can move material around, shift, delete, reenter, and try out new possibilities—all of this akin to the ways in which they have watched TV with the remote, watching segments, moving to others, and, with the VCR, zipping and zapping and reversing for desired repetition.

A word about student group work is much in order here, for the United States is a nation whose individualist traditions tend to militate against collaboration. The frontier values of rugged individualism filter into the classroom in the ethos of individual effort. And while the student must be held responsible for his or her own learning (with anxiety about plagiarism or cheating always hovering at the edges of schooling), the impact of American ideology on education can be found in an unwarranted degree of isolation—isolation of the kind not encountered in the world of work, where team effort is increasingly the norm. This is to say that if the empowered students are those learning from one another, then it is imperative that we learn to set aside our own biases and help students learn in groups. Fortunately, an NCTE publication has addressed this issue; a title of particular interest is *Focus on Collaborative Learning* (1988). Other helpful texts include Elizabeth G. Cohen, *Designing Groupwork: Strategies for the Heterogeneous Classroom* (1986); Nancie Atwell, *In the Middle: Writing, Reading, and Learning with Adolescents* (1987); and Lucy McCormick Calkins, *Lessons from a Child: On the Teaching and Learning of Writing* (1983).

As for the decentralized teacher roving from group to group, that figure may appear to be slighting or even shirking pedagogical duties— until one realizes that this teacher of the teleconscious age has shifted the burden of his or her responsibilities to a preactive role. The work of classroom planning becomes especially crucial for the decentralized teacher. Teacher-as-facilitator is a self-definition mandating substantial preactive behavior on the instructor's part. Yet it is precisely the preactive behaviors that enable one to become the facilitator rather than the more autocratic director.

In this vein, the criteria for administrative supervision must also change, for the on-site measurement of traditional skills in lecture presentation, classroom control, and the like becomes irrelevant. Evaluation of the decentralized teacher's performance requires, instead, an initial preconference at which the teacher explains to a supervisor what has been planned and scheduled and what the objectives of that planning are. Then the classroom visit becomes an occasion on which the supervisor moves through the various study groups, assessing each according to its own goals.

The classroom hour must also be reconceptualized in the era of the teleconscious student. The older idea of the linear forty-or fifty-minute period must give way to a new structure most effectively accommodating the newer generation of students engaged in fluid and multi-centered processes of thought. Just as the contemporary student has experienced segmented time as normal and natural, so too the classroom session can be designed to take educational advantage of cognition reliant on multiple centers of attention, with shorter spans of high-intensity focus. The decentralized class period thus lends itself to segmentation, to subdivision into several learning opportunities. The mini-lessons advocated by Atwell and Calkins are particularly opportune here. It must be said again that students remain fully responsible for their own learning in this model, but it ought to be pointed out as well that, when motivated and self-empowered, they are quite capable of sustained effort, which is readily adaptable to the two-period block often found in the middle-school curriculum. (And this model perhaps continues into homework. One seventh grader reported that her essay, judged superb by the teacher, was drafted and redrafted between intervals of favorite TV programs.)

Teachers of literature have a particular stake in the kinds of reading that students do in the TV age. The widespread lament that reading has declined and, especially, that students resist the classics must be taken very seriously. Teachers, however, may tend to approach this issue in the binary, adversarial model noted earlier, that of TV *vs.* print. The crucial point to recognize is this: it's not that students of the TV culture are not as "good," but that they are different. It is important, therefore, that teachers consider what kinds of reading find favor with students of the TV age, given their acculturation to on-screen visuality and action—just as it is important that we neither dismiss nor condescend to students whom we assume are television oriented and therefore not as sophisticated as those with primary allegiance to print. At the same time, it is essential to understand which kinds of reading meet with resistance and outright puzzlement precisely because they lie outside students' epistemic experience in the TV culture.

Not surprisingly, students of the television age are receptive to texts replete with dialogue and physical and external action. A seventh-grade group, for instance, enthusiastically reads Daphne du Maurier's *Rebecca*, perhaps because of its structural affinity with TV soap opera, while a class of college juniors and seniors similarly appreciates Harriet Beecher Stowe's *Uncle Tom's Cabin*, possibly because its scenes are graphically visual and its plot(s) action oriented—which is to say, compatible with TV.

It is, however, the literature of interior, psychological complexity that puzzles these same students. Ernest Hemingway's *Old Man and the Sea* is found to be uninteresting to the seventh graders because the fisherman protagonist only "talks to his hands" for three days, that is, because there is insufficient action. The college class similarly resists Nathaniel Hawthorne's *House of the Seven Gables* because "nothing happens" until the concluding chapter.

Each English teacher can doubtless extend these divisions, which are important, but not so that we can deplore the resistance of today's students to texts we know to be profound—rather, on the contrary, to enable us to undertake careful preparation in advance, knowing that students will need particular kinds of help and motivation. The degree to which the text lies identifiably outside the TV culture (e.g., the psychological explorations of Hawthorne) is the degree to which the teacher must make the students activists in learning, for instance by distributing study questions and breaking the class into small groups that report to one another both prior to beginning the novel and proceeding through each classroom session on it. The groups, perhaps three or four, will be building bridges from their own experience to the text. One of them might be assigned to consider a philosophical issue they will encounter in the reading, another to consider a topic based on their experience but applicable to a character they are about to meet in the text, a third to ponder a hypothetical situation paralleling one in the reading. Here again, the teacher's preactive planning is vital to the groups' success, and any teacher who has worked with groups in such a manner knows that the planning is an intellectual wrestling match that takes time.

We must be aware, too, that teleconscious students have a different understanding of literary form. Their experience of cognitive fluidity with multivalent centers of attention makes the open form the natural one. They will not demand that narrative exhibit a beginning-middle-end structure and may indeed find the traditional pattern of ascending levels of conflict, climax, and resolution characteristic of literature of another era, one different from their own. They will appreciate the looser, open-ended, and multiple plotted design characteristic of the TV-era fictions (and perhaps also the narrative fluidity of William Faulkner and James Joyce). And after all, since the 1960s, TV itself has exploited its own fluidity in the open structures of "M*A*S*H," "Hill Street Blues," and "L.A. Law," and of the sitcoms whose weekly endings students do not perceive to be conclusions, since the basic conflicts among characters remain unresolved. (The TV-culture students' own writing will, in turn, exhibit these traits.)

Finally, we need to be aware that TV-era writers are already producing a literature that directly references television, exploiting possibilities of the screen itself and basing stories on readers' familiarity with certain programs. Donald Barthelme's "And Now Let's Hear It for the Ed Sullivan Show" (1974) seems to read like a transcript of that variety hour, while T. Coraghessan Boyle's "Heart of a Champion" (1983) operates from the same premise of reader familiarity in its satiric reprise of "Lassie." In *Platitudes* (1988), the novelist Trey Ellis presents a chapter structured on the scanning of the cable stations, while in *The Sportswriter* (1986) Richard Ford uses the TV screen as a way to reveal his characters' thoughts. These are just a few. As David Foster Wallace, another TV-era writer, has said, "Most good fiction writers, even young ones, are intellectuals. . . . And television, its advertising, and the popular culture they both reflect have fundamentally altered what intellectuals get to regard as the proper objects of their attention" (1988, 38–39). This means that the English classroom of the immediate future will need to incorporate the literature of the television culture.

Works Cited

Anderson, James A., and Timothy P. Meyer. 1988. *Mediated Communication: A Social Action Perspective*. Newbury Park: Sage.

Attallah, Paul. 1984. "The Unworthy Discourse: Situation Comedy in Television." In *Interpreting Television: Current Research Perspectives*, edited by Willard D. Rowland, Jr., and Bruce Watkins, 222–49. Beverly Hills, CA: Sage.

Atwell, Nancie. 1987. *In the Middle: Writing, Reading, and Learning with Adolescents*. Portsmouth, NH: Boynton/Cook.

Barthelme, Donald. 1974. "And Now Let's Hear It for the Ed Sullivan Show." In *Guilty Pleasures*, 101–108. New York: Farrar, Straus and Giroux.

Boyle, T. Coraghessan. 1983. "Heart of a Champion." In *Great Esquire Fiction*, edited by L. Rust Hills, 403–9. New York: Viking.

Byars, Betsy. 1976. *The TV Kid*. New York: Viking Press.

Calkins, Lucy McCormick. 1983. *Lessons from a Child: On the Teaching and Learning of Writing*. London: Heinemann.

Cohen, Elizabeth G. 1986. *Designing Groupwork: Strategies for the Heterogeneous Classroom*. New York: Teachers College Press.

Cutright, Melitta J. 1989. *The National PTA Talks to Parents: How to Get the Best Education for Your Child*. New York: Doubleday.

Ellis, Trey. 1988. *Platitudes*. New York: Vintage.

Focus on Collaborative Learning. 1988. Jeff Golub, Chair, and The Committee on Classroom Practice. Urbana, IL: National Council of Teachers of English.

Ford, Richard. 1986. *The Sportswriter.* New York: Vintage.

Leach, Penelope. 1986. *Your Growing Child: From Babyhood through Adolescence*. New York: Knopf.

McCorkle, Jill. 1990. *Ferris Beach: A Novel*. Chapel Hill, NC: Algonquin.

Montagu, Ashley. 1962. "Television and the New Image of Man." In *The Eighth Art: Twenty-Three Views of Television Today*, 125–34. New York: Holt, Rinehart and Winston.

Palmer, Patricia. 1986. *The Lively Audience: A Study of Children Around the TV Set*. Sydney, London and Boston: Allen and Unwin.

Pittman, Robert W. 1990. "We're Talking the Wrong Language to 'TV Babies.' " *The New York Times*. January 24, A23.

Postman, Neil. 1985. *Amusing Ourselves to Death: Public Discourse in the Age of Show Business*. New York: Viking.

Shayon, Robert Lewis. 1964. "Father Television Knows Best." *Saturday Review* (December 5): 42.

Time. 1951, July 30. "Dark (Screen) Future." *Time* 58: 53.

Time. 1968, November 8. "The Videophobes," 98.

Wallace, David Foster. 1988. "Fictional Futures and the Conspicuously Young." *Review of Contemporary Fiction* 8(3): 36–53.

Whitbread, Jane, and Vivian Cadden. 1954. "The Real Menace of TV." *Harper's Magazine* 209(October): 81–83.

Williams, Raymond. 1975. *Television: Technology and Cultural Form*. New York: Schocken.

Willingham, Calder. 1952. "Television: Giant in the Living Room." *The American Mercury* 74 (February): 114–19.

Winn, Marie. 1977. *The Plug-In Drug*. New York: Viking.

6 Multicultural Teaching: It's an Inside Job

Mary C. Savage
Consultant in Multicultural Education
New York City

> I have wasted an incredible amount of energy in my life waiting
> for X to happen. Well—it's an inside job.
> —Meg Christian, *Meg and Chris at Carnegie Hall*

Three years ago, after working as a teacher and administrator in a
small liberal arts college in New England for almost twenty years, I
moved to New York City to learn more about multicultural education.
I worked in elementary schools all over the city and interviewed
teachers individually and in groups to learn how at least some of the
people teaching in multicultural situations think about what they are
doing. Given the fact that the global economy links Americans with
the peoples of the world, all teachers teach in multicultural situations.
Teaching situations in New York City, however, are both obvious and
intense. Teaching here is almost always a matter of teaching people
who are "different." One out of every seven persons living here is an
immigrant; one out of three children entering the public schools speaks
a first language other than English. Only a handful of teachers teach
in neighborhoods where they also live; most do not speak the first
language of the children they teach; almost all teach children who
come from economic classes "different" from their own. Most public
school teachers orient their lives around middle-class values, while
most of their students come from poor and working-class communities.
The bulk of this essay is composed of three interviews with four
teachers who work in the Bronx: Billy Cunningham, Mimi Aronson,
Isabel Beaton, and Ida Rivera. They think of their work not as teaching
literature, but as teaching children. They teach children who live in
an often hostile multicultural world how to make that world safer,
more just, more loving. I am learning that this is an inside job. Even
though each teacher brings to bear on her work professional beliefs
and practices which are powerful and sophisticated, to a considerable

79

degree the approaches they have crafted for multicultural education rely on the fact that they have been able to draw strength from their own cultural backgrounds.

Billy Cunningham and Mimi Aronson work in a section of the Bronx with students from backgrounds which are predominantly black (New York, West Indies, Africa), Latino (Puerto Rico, Dominican Republic, Honduras), Asian (Vietnamese, Laotian), and European (Irish, Italian, Ukranian). Isabel Beaton and Ida Rivera teach in a pre-kindergarten program serving Hunts Point, a section of the South Bronx. Their students come from backgrounds which are primarily Latino and they also teach a handful of students whose primary language is English. Isabel and Ida are more aware, however, of the challenge of teaching in a very poor community.

The Cultural Background of Teachers as a Source for Multicultural Teaching

Billy Cunningham draws much of her theory of teaching from child-hood experiences as the daughter of a mother who worked in a multicultural garment shop and as a student in a school where differences in ethnic origin were honored. These early experiences gave her an appetite for difference and an almost aesthetic delight in culture. She is deeply grounded in values she identifies as gospel, values which encourage her to use what she has to improve any situation. Although Billy does not say so directly, I think her growing up as a black American in a strong, multigenerational family grounds her vision with a matter-of-factness which gives her energy and endurance. Mimi Aronson's impulse is to do something helpful in complicated situations; she needs to be counted among those who work to make a difference. I think of Mimi's work as rooted in Jewish heritage, but she describes her approach as "universal" and is very suspicious of multiculturalism, which she views as promoting stereotyping. In her view, her work is based on faith that people who can understand differences need not fear them, nor do they need to take their fear out on any kind of scapegoat. Both Isabel Beaton and Ida Rivera draw on having grown up in extended families (Italian and Puerto Rican) which have experienced being "minorities" in a dominant culture. They are in the midst of learning how not to consider themselves strangers in a strange land, but to find communal support among the parents with whom they work. They both draw from their Roman Catholic background a sense that they should make a difference in the world and that their sympathy and loyalties should be with those who suffer as a result of the way society is arranged.

Theoretical Orientation

Multicultural Teaching for a Multicultural World

According to Paulo Friere (1981), literacy is the ability to read words so that we can read the world around us in such a way that people become freer and live more fully. In this sense, the context for multicultural education is the fact that our world is so arranged that we affect (and are affected by) people who live all over the globe. The rationale for such education is based on the theory that each of us walks into an already existing arrangement of the physical world and the people in it. Each of us needs to act responsibly in the situation since, as soon as we enter it, the culture there becomes the culture which emerges from the situation as a result of our action in it. (For a view of culture as emerging, see Clifford 1988.) Teachers committed to liberating education also need to act in solidarity with those most harmed by the unjust system which at present sustains global arrangements (Gutierrez 1973).

In my neighborhood, multicultural education takes place in the following physical and cultural context. For the past nine months I have been living in Harlem's central valley, bounded on one side by the Harlem River and on the other by the rocky slope of Morningside Heights and, beyond that, the Hudson. Not too far to the north, the rivers converge in a spot called Spuyten Duyvil, after the boast of a drunken Dutchman that he would cross the convergence in spite of the devil who turned up storms there. All this nearby water is not unusual for New York. The city is composed of islands which contain sixty-five square miles of inland waterways. Abundance of water for drinking, irrigation, power, and transport frames much of the history of New York state. In fact, Europeans were first drawn to the area by the alluringly wide expanse of the Hudson.

The block I live on is a multicultural sort of place: walking down the street I can hear French, Spanish, several African languages, West Indian patois, and English bearing the accents of the southern United States, Brooklyn, Harlem, not to mention the precisely articulated English of my landlady, a nearing-eighty retired journalist, working composer, and black woman who is a Republican to boot. The houses on the street, mostly brownstones with a handful of small apartment houses, are one sign that the block, like Harlem generally, mixes people who reflect different economic conditions and class-based values. Some of the brownstones have been refurbished to their original splendor; others have been cut up into rooming houses; five have been boarded up entirely by the city or other absentee landlords; two of them, the "welfare" buildings, are used to house families and individuals on public assistance until the city finds them more appropriate housing. One of the two has no plumbing. Negotiating all these cultural differences and living in the middle of them is not a subject I learned much about in school.

Across the street from me is the playground of the elementary school, set off by a fence and a low wall. Men whom my landlady calls "the bums" hang out on the wall, in front of which is a hydrant that is open most of the time. The men sitting on the wall use water from the hydrant to mix their drinks, neighbors from down the block come to wash their cars, people from the building without plumbing use it to fill their water jugs and as a place to empty their slop buckets. One day a deranged woman took off all her clothes and washed most of them there before the police came to drive her off.

The always-running water reminds me that for a long time New York has gone far afield to meet its needs for water and water power. As early as 1748, Collect Pond, which supplied water for what is now downtown, was so polluted that even horses would not drink it. Currently, New York City is reviewing contracts for hydroelectric power generated by the Canadian James River Project, which will further devastate the traditional hunting and fishing grounds of the Cree Indians, at the very least by concentrating levels of mercury which make fish poisonous. When Matthew Coon Come, the Cree chief, testified in Manhattan, he reminded New York officials that his "grandfathers have always managed to leave their land as it had been" (Verhovek 1991). This is not an option for those of us living on my block. Given the way our society is structured, we cannot sustain ourselves on the land where we live. We go far afield to meet our needs in ways that affect (and are affected by) the lands and lives of a great many people, most of whom we never meet.

So when I re-envision teaching "English" in my neighborhood school, I think not just about how this "minority" school functions in a "dominant" educational system, not just about how to help children negotiate the cultural and class differences represented on the street, not just about how the culture in the neighborhood can enrich the wider culture. I also consider how all of us on the block, and in the wider society, can live wisely and well within the spider web that connects us with people around the world. And then I panic. Who could know enough to be of some use in this situation?

Liberating Praxis

The panic comes as a result of being overly determined by disciplinary ways of thinking. When my college colleagues and I were designing an interdisciplinary curriculum whose capstone was a problem-solving seminar, we might have said that the problems collocated around the hydrant involved geography, cultural studies, engineering, early childhood education, history, etc. The "inside the English department" equivalent of this talk is an argument about what texts, interpretative paradigms, and interpretative communities we should posit for reading. This kind of disciplined thinking can get out of hand if it is reinforced by years of graduate study and supported by professional organizations and structures which are relatively ignorant of local culture or have blind spots about the global context of local activities (including the way professional activities often drain off local energies). Disciplined knowledge gone awry creates *academentia*, that hardening of the heart and restriction of the imagination you get by degrees, which, when it begins to cure itself, results in the aforementioned panic. (For a definition of academentia, see Daly 1987. For a discussion of academentia and college English, see Savage 1989.) Fortunately, even at our most academented, my colleagues and I knew that situations as we found them in life were undisciplinizable and that the knowledge emerged as we worked in—and as part of—the situations. This kind of knowledge—whether you call it liberating praxis, practical knowledge, or mother wit—is central to multicultural teaching.

Practical knowledge is what helped Isabel Beaton's immigrant Italian grandmother send her children to American schools for the first time. One day she just opened the door and told her son and daughter that the children walking by were going to school and they should follow them. They did, but the children went to a Catholic school which would not let the new students enter. The next day she opened the door again and told her children to follow other children going in the other direction. They did. This school, the public school, accepted them and sent them to a classroom where a teacher yelled the word "crayons" all day long. So began a long and dialogical relationship with the dominant culture which, two generations later, was to inform Isabel Beaton's ability to teach in the South Bronx.

The teachers I interviewed have in common a relatively high proportion of practical knowledge which I find challenging. As a college teacher I was encouraged in habits of thought which placed texts and interpretation and paradigms for interpretation at the center of my inquiry, often at the expense of the students in front of me and certainly in place of the mother wit I brought with me from my own background. These teachers feel relatively freer to draw on the strength of their backgrounds and are impelled to act with, and on behalf of, their students. All four demonstrate a commitment to doing something concrete and helpful within the confines of the situation as it exists and a willingness to learn from others, including students. Under their influence I am trying to re-envision teaching "English" as a way of reading a multicultural world with the graciousness and wisdom necessary for making it a better place in which to live.

So I pass this invitation along. I hope reading these interviews prompts you to touch again the strength that your background provides for the liberating practice you are fashioning in and from the multi-cultural situation in which you find yourself.

What Fades Is What You're Not Around

Wiletha (Billy) Cunningham is a fifth-grade teacher in the North Bronx. In 1988, she wrote a master's thesis called "Creating a Positive Educational Climate to Celebrate Diversity within Unity."

Savage: Your curriculum develops out of the kids and their conflicts— as if you are as concerned with how they act as much as with what they know.

Cunningham: That seems to be a priority for me. More than the disciplines—math and science and so on. Just because the world is so wild and we're supposed to be preparing them to live out there. If we can send a few people out there who have their guidelines drawn clearly, maybe that will help.

Actually—it sounds clichéd—but I really don't think these kids see each other's differences. So it's not difficult to show them how well they get along and to say to them from time to time, "This will probably change as you get older." It's an interesting thing when you say that. When you say, "A time will come when you cling more to people who are like you than you do now. So try to remember what you're learning now. That there's no difference. Remember how much you enjoy playing with kids who are from different backgrounds." And they say, "Why? Why is the time coming? Why is that? Why?" Because they don't see why it has to change.

My sense of it is that as you get older and you go to school and get jobs you come into a sense of your own group. Your sense of your own group develops and what you have in common with your own group increases as you get older. What fades is what you're not around. So you lose that sense.

Also as you get up and up in the grades, high school begins to separate people, you know specializing in this and that. You see the African American students go one way and the groups really do split off from one another and by the time you're in college . . .

And then at work you meet people from other cultures and you may even go to lunch with them but, as soon as you go back to the neighborhood, you're just with the people that you're like. New York neighborhoods are not diversified. Neighborhoods are really polarized, so that elementary school gives you the only real opportunity—and junior high—and high school too if you allow it, but you can get awfully clannish.

My own background? My mother was a seamstress in the garment center. It was a union shop and they had every ethnic group I could imagine. And we went to visit people. They cooked for us—whether it was Carlota, who was Puerto Rican, or Millie and Rosie and Katie, who were Italian, and Iris, West Indian. Just on and on and on.

I went to schools which were all integrated. I can remember Natalie from Estonia and other students. That's when I found out about Latvia and Estonia and Lithuania—in elementary school. We had twins from Jamaica. We had Asian students. The teacher discussed the countries with us and had the students tell us about where they had come from. It was such a nice natural flow. It makes so much sense to me.

I think New York has so much potential that goes completely untouched. We ignore it completely. And it was kind of serendipitous for me to do the thesis when I did it because we had the incident in Bensonhurst and this and that. And they were talking about what can we do about it. And I had been thinking what do about it for years and years. I know how to solve this problem. Teachers do. Right here in this school one of the teachers somehow contacted someone in Chinatown and the class visited Chinatown and then the teacher invited the Chinese students up here. We know how and we do it. But the Board of Ed has to be more active, like in setting visits up across the city.

Savage: In the groups we've been in together I've seen you uplift the level of the discussion to something larger or more positive, often by sharing how comfortable you are in your heritage and family. I wonder how you learned how to do that.

Cunningham: I'm not sure. In the Gospels—and that's part of why I'm open because there's that spiritual background in my family—in the Gospels, there is the parable of the talents. It was always a caution from my grandmother: "Don't bury your talents. If you want more, use what you've got." I would rather not say anything. But sometimes I can hear floundering or superficial stuff and I figure if I'm going to be here and participate, let's at least get it to where we're really touching on some important things.

It's that I really love people. And I would really like to see a time come when we could look at. . . . You know when I look at Lithuanian and Ukranian Easter eggs, it is one of . . . it's just like . . . I can get lost in those. And I would love to have celebrations that were not just around one ethnic group. It seems to me that there's so much power in people if we could ever get to the point of not being divided.

I just think that that's what I try to do in a group. If I hear people not being able to get along, to me it's like—wait a minute, first we have to get along, then we can do whatever else the group has as its goal. But if we're going to fight one another . . .

In terms of my personality, I have to be careful that I don't misunderstand arguing. That's something I've learned from Karen Rosner. Just as I teach Sunday school, she teaches Saturday school at her synagogue. One day we were talking about the things we teach and she mentioned how they get their kids to question things. She brought a book they used. And I opened the book and one of the things it said right away was that they teach arguing.

In my culture, to argue means to be disagreeable and impudent, but in the Jewish culture, to argue means to present yourself well and to stand up for your point. What a cultural difference! And I could see if I had a child from a culture which said arguing was important, when I said something to him in class and he answered me back, I might mistake that for impudence because that's how I read the signals on account of how I've been raised.

And so it's so clear to me that, if we can understand what's underneath the stuff that goes on, we don't have problems with each other; we just have different signals and different meanings. People are so important and there's so much good in people and I think we are missing it to look at things that are so divisive . . .

People are terrific and the stuff that drives us apart is so obvious, if you really think about it. And that's why that's the title of the thesis: "Celebrating Diversity within Unity." That's the key. I think it's the key to stopping obvious things like racism, but I think it's also the key to rebuilding cities.

This Whole Multicultural Thing Bothers Me

Miriam (Mimi) Aronson, a teacher with twenty-seven years' experience, is at present a staff developer in reading and writing. Finding a way to represent Mimi's views about multicultural education was the most challenging task this essay presented. Because disciplinary thinking tends to devalue narrative and process, it is easy to miss the import of Mimi's thinking. Her talk and her teaching are almost all process. Thoughts emerge from experience and in dialogue and are rarely reified.

Mimi's exchange with Chieko Toyoshima, a student in a university language arts class, is illustrative, I think. Chieko, a special education teacher in her forties, grew up in a small seacoast town in Japan and emigrated to the United States when she was a young woman. World War II affected her early schooling, at the very least by making books and paper scarce, but soon she became enamored of books and, in her first years in the United States, she found that reading philosophical works relieved the loneliness of not being able to speak English well. When Mimi introduced Writing Process as a teaching technique in the language arts class, she drew Chieko into an extended discussion of Solzhenitsyn's poem "Campfire and Ants," which describes the frenzy of ants running in confusion back into the burning log from which they had just escaped. In her discussion, Mimi drew a picture of herself as a poor reader of poetry who, nevertheless, connected the poem with her own background—in this case with the horror her uncle experienced when Jewish prisoners ran back into flames ignited by Allied bombing just before Auschwitz was liberated.

The open way Mimi shared her process and experience drew Chieko further into the poem and, in subsequent classes, could have led to the kind of multicultural understanding which emerges as people discover the effect of global events like World War II on personal matters like family histories and habits of reading. Even in the course of the short exchange I quote below, other students were deeply touched as Mimi and Chieko used the poem to open up some of the frenzy Europeans and Japanese experienced in the war. Mimi's view that the key to education is sharing "universal" experiences across "differences" undergirds her ability to share herself and hold pedagogical situations open until mutual understanding begins to emerge.

Aronson: I discovered reading and writing processes fifteen years ago. They came into my heart and soul and changed me as a person. What I see when I go into buildings is teachers who are working very hard, but not getting much. And kids who want to work hard, but don't know how. So now I am trying to teach people that they don't have to work so hard; that learning can be natural, can be open.

Savage: How do you go about finding books and methods to support your work with kids, especially with kids who come from a different background than you do?

Aronson: Basically I bring pieces that I love, ones that make me want to write. What I bring to the kids has to resonate with me. If it's not going to get to me, I don't have time to give it to the kids. And they know that too now. They don't bring me things that don't resonate with them. It's just like going on line. You know: "We're going to go in size spaces—girls over here, boys over here." You say that enough—you're going to get two lines. You say enough—we're going to look at this writing and react to it and write from it and write about it and what did we think and did you do it and how come it looks like that and try this one now. By the time Christmas comes, they're really kind of good at it.

But you have to realize each school is different; each room is different; communities are very different within buildings. It's really just like a home—if you give to kids a lot and nurture a lot, then kids give back and there is happiness and playfulness. If there is no nurturing and you don't give to your kids, then there is this deadening silence.

Savage: There is so much in your approach to education that speaks to me of Jewish culture. But you don't identify that part of you as coming out of Jewish heritage.

Aronson: It is my strongest trait. But I think it's a human trait, across the board. I mean I'm Jewish. I like being Jewish. I am comfortable with Jewish people. I like Jewish thinking. I like Jewish talk. But I don't think I act out of being Jewish.

I didn't like stereotyping, ever. It bothers me when people believe in that. I think it bothers me because I come from a race that was killed because of that categorizing. And it will come again unless I fight to make a difference.

This whole multicultural business bothers me a lot. I think that the more we put out that differences are positive, the more we're fostering the hatred people have in them. People do hate and are frustrated and angry and upset. And rather than saying, "O.K. I didn't make this work, what can I do to change it or do it a different way," they say, "Who can I get? I'm not happy. It's probably the kid. I'll beat her up tonight." That's what people do. And the Jewish person is the best person to beat up.

My uncle, who is an Auschwitz survivor, let me notice that the Holocaust comes again. It has come again and again in six thousand years. And I have to try to defuse as many people from it coming again . . .

Savage: In terms of your school work, how do you see yourself as defusing hatred?

Aronson: Helping teachers see they can be nice to kids. We need to start touching as well as teaching and talking. The way I feel, I'm part of the people who need to support the work of making a difference. I like helping people learn how to think so they don't have to be angry. I really believe, if people think, they don't have to be so angry and they can really figure things out.

Mimi Aronson gave a workshop to a reading and language arts course I taught at a New York college. I mentioned to her my concern that only a few students enjoyed writing. One was in the middle of a novel, but most wrote only for school. More enjoyed reading. A few had formed and reformed their lives around books. But most looked on reading as a chore.

Mimi invited the students to respond in writing to various pieces of literature and music. As the students shared their writing in small groups, Mimi circulated—being amazed and puzzled in turn. Finally she asked Chieko Toyoshima to join her in front of the class so that they could discuss what they had written in response to Solzhenitsyn's piece "A Campfire and Ants."

Toyoshima: I am not an experienced reader. So when I read poems I don't get deep meanings, and that always bothers me. When I read this one I felt that this poem was very action packed. And I told Mimi I liked the poem: it was action packed and dramatic. But I didn't get the most important thing. The meaning. What I didn't get was the ants going into the fire. Since the poet is a political writer, there has to be some meaning in there. About the human condition. About what human beings do in the extreme.

Aronson: I must tell you. I'm a terrible reader; I don't understand poems. So I have the same feelings, but I take another road. I don't care anymore.

Toyoshima: You're getting old.

Aronson: That's it. When I was young I kept trying, but now I know better. I guess I should be able to do it. But now I just follow another way to help my own writing and get to what is important to me. I respond personally to the poem first. And that frees me up to do my own poetry. Because if I believed in my own heart, for me, that I needed to know "the point" all the time I could never write.

Toyoshima: Tell them already.

Aronson: I know. So I wrote about . . .

Toyoshima: About your uncle.

Aronson: My uncle shared a story. He's an Auschwitz survivor and he just started telling stories about that recently. The first one he told me was how the Americans bombed the camp indiscriminately, setting off fires all over. The Jews had been rounded up into the room where they normally had roll call for the ovens. And many of them became so disturbed by the bombing they ran into the fires started by the bombing. This is part of what I wrote:

> All the prisoners rushed into the large hall
> the hall used for roll call,
> the hall used to siphon off those numbers that would never
>   return—
> the hall used to take away their possessions—
> rings, glasses, teeth, cut-thin hair.
> The hall now held what was left of several hundred of Auschwitz.
> Why bomb them? hit these still-barely-alive?
> Exploding bodies and fires igniting the hall.
> Bright, luring flames calling you, inviting you . . .

Toyoshima: After Mimi told me that—I said, "Maybe the ants ran back in the fire because it was mass hysteria and they were enticed into the fire." This whole thing is about insanity; human nature, or whatever.

Aronson: Maybe. I don't know. But I love to see that there are two of us and we come from different places and we come at something differently and yet we became friends tonight. And I like that.

Everything Is Very Intertwined

Isabel Beaton, a teacher, and Ida Rivera, a bilingual program assistant, work together in a pre-kindergarten class which had been supported by Project Giant Step, a New York City initiative to fund high-quality education for "at risk" four-year-olds.

Savage: Isabel, how did you develop your interest in multicultural teaching?

Beaton: I've always taught in situations where the children were black, Hispanic, Italian, like that. So I've always been careful to choose picture books where the children would see themselves or animals. It really helps that so many picture books have animals as characters because then I don't have to be so careful about the overabundance of books with white, blond-haired, blue-eyed children. In the picture books that I read them, in the illustrations I use in the classroom, when I draw people, in the language that I use, I work to create a situation in which they can see themselves and hear themselves and be validated.

I know how I felt—and feel—about always having a model that's not me put before me. I'm not tall; I'm not blond; I don't have long legs; I don't have narrow hips. When I was in fourth grade I tried to take ballet because the Board of Ed was having this thing with enrichment and the ballet person said: "Wide hips and wide feet. You will breed well, but you will never be a ballerina." I was in fourth grade.

When we're talking multicultural, school culture is one of the cultures the children have to be proficient in. The children have to learn school language; they have to learn school behaviors; they have to learn school politics; school economics; they have to learn all those parts of a school culture.

It's sick. What I'm doing is helping preserve the status quo—which bothers me. On the other hand, I don't want the kids to . . . I'm making them Italian. I'm teaching them how to work the system.

Savage: Where does the radical edge of your thinking come from?

Beaton: First of all from being Italian. And living in a situation in which I was in the minority. Then from having a father who lied and a mother who told the truth. And thinking about his need to not be truthful and her need to speak as she saw it. My father never, never admitted—could never admit—that we were discriminated against in any way. In order to live, he had to say the American things and he had to believe them—to the point that he couldn't comfort us in times when we were hurting. Living with the two, always being a little off balance, made me question.

I think it helps very much that I work with four-year-olds. That's another culture too. The culture of the four. It keeps me very respectful because there is so much I don't understand. I so often don't understand them, and they have to figure out five or six different ways of telling me something. So who's patient? They are so proficient. Their language is not really Spanish, it's the language of four. And their language is not really English, it's the language of four. And I have to listen so closely . . .

My Spanish is pretty good. I can get by. But once I had a little girl, Kathy, and she was crying, crying, crying, crying. I thought she wanted to go home; I thought she was homesick. I couldn't figure out what she wanted. All she kept saying was—"Quiero irme. Quiero irme" (I want to go). I tried everything. It's rare I can't comfort a child, but for fifteen minutes she just kept sobbing, "Quiero irme." And I thought: Oh God what is it. She wants to go home. She's sick. It's the first day of school; she's lonesome. I racked my brain until I said, Oh stupid— she means, "I've got to go! I've got to go!" "Al bano? Peepee, Kathy?" "Si, maestra."

I think if we go the route of personal response, we'll figure it out— if we're careful. I get suspicious when people make it so complicated. The more difficult you make reading and writing, the more apprehensive I get. If the student's personal response to a book is completely off the wall as far as you are concerned, you validate it until you can figure out what's going on. He knows what he's talking about. You're the professional so that's your work. This is supposed to be challenging to you, teacher. Figure out what they're trying to say in their writing. And then to go with it.

I can't tell my kids what I'm doing. They're too young for me to sit them down and say, "This is what I'm doing." But a college teacher could. You can be much more aboveboard with adults. Right? You can just say, "You have been underprepared. Somebody . . . Did you guys do your job? I don't know. Did somebody else not do their job? I don't know. But here we are." It's like my kids too. My little ones. They are the ones who are there. So they are the ones I have to teach. Who shows up are the kids that you teach.

Savage: Isabel, when you first started to work here, it seemed to me you were much less comfortable with the parents.

Beaton: Yes. I felt like a stranger in a strange land. I felt alien. I just didn't understand where people were coming from. In the beginning I was very angry with the parents because I felt that what they did was affecting their children so badly, the choices that they make. And then I became angry at the world, at society. But then I knew I couldn't be mad at society either and not eat myself up, so I had to talk myself through that.

I decided to stop being angry and to be joyful at what was happening with the kids and that eased it.

Savage: How did you think beyond your anger?

Beaton: O.K. Christopher. His mother had four children—the two older, Christopher, and the baby. She is young; she is so young. She's an addict. And she supports her habit by prostitution.

But she brought that kid every day. He was in school every day. I was angry for her—for being on crack, for prostitution, but she brought the kid every day. I knew I couldn't greet her with my anger . . .

The baby died from malnutrition. She let the baby die. She brought me the pictures of the baby's funeral. And my heart went out to her. I know it's her fault that that baby died. But she's grieving anyway.

And after I started looking at the parents and saying . . . Options aren't options unless you know they're options. They don't know they have options; they just don't. Or in some people's lives crack is an option, I don't know.

And if I didn't understand the culture. And it's not any other culture—black culture, Hispanic culture. It's just poverty culture; it's abused culture; it's being-kicked-everyday-of-your-life culture; it's not-getting-hugged-culture; it's . . .

She had another baby. We had to celebrate that baby. We had to. And she knows we are still watching Christopher—even though he is in the next grade.

Rivera: Christopher I see in the morning for breakfast so I know he eats. We made sure that that kid went home full and if there was anything left over we gave it to the mother to make sure she would feed them.

And she's not alone. It's not only this child.

Beaton: Everything is very intertwined. And I think we just began to see that. We have to be very intertwined. We have to be intertwined with the mothers and intertwined with the kids. And I can't do that if I'm angry. And I got to liking these people. Some nutty people, but I love them so much.

Rivera: And underneath all that nuttiness, there are really genuine, lovely people.

Beaton: And I know—push comes to shove—they're there. They're gutsy, courageous.

Rivera: They have to be—for the environment they're living in. If they weren't like that they would just be buried.

My Cultural Background as a Source for Multicultural Teaching

The largest lesson I learned from these interviews is that, to respond to the invitation to re-envision teaching "English," I need to refurbish parts of my own cultural background that I gave up as I worked my way up the educational ladder. My own personal inside job has to do with healing a split I experience between the academic world and the world outside and overcoming the feeling that, in order to become a teacher, I had to change class loyalties from the working class to the middle class.

As I look back at my education in English from the perspective of my experience of multicultural education in New York, I am struck by the fact that schooling separated me from much of the richness and variety of the cultures around me. School drained the color from literature and from my imagination. I know this sounds inflated, but I was very serious about reading. Reading was a way to get beyond the confines of the world into which I had been born (an Irish Catholic family in a working-class community of a small industrial city). At the state college I attended, however, my English teachers, mostly youngish men, championed New Criticism and, it seems to me now, were obsessed by stories of other youngish men going through rites of passage. My education teachers, mostly women, drilled us in "professionalism," which then seemed merely petty, but now feels like part of a larger system separating teachers from students. My graduate school classes, like most journals today, were awash with a single color—a polemic over literary theory—which I joined enthusiastically. Critical theory, especially feminism, taught me I had reproduced the assumptions of the dominant society in my own teaching—from the way I selected texts to the way I interacted with students. So I developed critical perspectives from which to reread my own education even as I worked on how to teach. I would probably still be doing this work, happily—since it was very good work, except for an epiphany that occurred one spring.

I was looking for an apartment, reading the ads and frantically asking everyone I knew. Then one Sunday morning when I stepped into a grocery store to pick up the newspaper and a cup of coffee just after I finished my run, I looked down the street and saw hundreds of young college professors stepping into similar stores after their runs. I asked myself what new Sunday morning religion I had joined and realized that, if I kept going as I was going, I would live where the people I knew lived. As a result I would not know many working-class people like the ones with whom I had grown up and not know at all, in a personal, neighborly way, the "marginalized" people who are so central to all that talk in critical theory. I began to feel I wanted more people from different backgrounds in my life. I wanted my color back. So I moved to New York.

Interviewing these teachers reminded me that getting my color back is not solely a question of where I live. It is an inside job. For me, part of that job is healing a split I experienced between academic knowledge and "ordinary" knowledge. I left home for graduate school in Washington, D.C., at great cost. My stepmother, who was dying of cancer, felt very threatened, mostly because she suspected I was about to become loyal to a professional class. She refused to say good-bye and told me to take all my belongings with me. She died in January, just before my first grad school exams, a coincidence which left me feeling I had gained "advanced" study at the expense of my family. That spring, Martin Luther King, Jr., was assassinated and D.C. burst into flames and riot. I remember a black friend, a southern woman in her forties who had marched with King, saying she heard the news of the assassination when a young white man came into the student lounge saying, "Well, they finally got the bastard."

A week later the city was calmer and I went back to my schoolwork. I remember reading *Finnegan's Wake* outdoors in the newly warm spring, cradled in the crotch of a tree on a university quad, while a National Guard jeep, complete with rear-mounted machine gun and gunner, circled every half-hour. Since then I have been trying to put the two experiences together—reading literature and dealing with a city on the brink of collapse.

The question of multicultural literacy is a question of purpose. As Billy Cunningham says, "It's the key to stopping obvious things like racism, but I also think it's the key to rebuilding cities." Working here in the city is also helping me heal the separations which drained the color from my life. Here I am learning that rebuilding cities begins with getting my own color back.

This is my story which I have related. If it be sweet, or if it be not sweet, take some elsewhere, and let the rest come back to me.

Works Cited

Clifford, James. 1988. *The Predicament of Culture: Twentieth-Century Ethnography, Literature, and Art.* Cambridge: Harvard University.

Daly, Mary. 1987. *Webster's First New Intergalactic Wickdary of the English Language.* Boston: Beacon.

Friere, Paulo. 1981. *Education for Critical Consciousness.* New York: Continuum.

Gutierrez, Gustavo. 1973. *A Theology of Liberation: History, Politics, and Salvation.* Maryknoll, NY: Orbis.

Savage, Mary C. 1989. "Writing as a Neighborly Act: An Antidote for Academentia." *ADE Bulletin* 92(Spring): 13–19.

Verhovek, Sam Howe. 1991. "Cree Chief Asks New York to Drop Hydroelectric Plan." *The New York Times*, October 1, B4.

7 Chicana Feminism: In the Tracks of "the" Native Woman

Norma Alarcón
University of California, Berkeley

In 1992, as Spain prepares to celebrate the quincentenary of "the discovery," contemporary Chicanas have been deliberating on the force of significations of that event. It took almost four hundred years for the territory that today we call Mexico to acquire a cohesive national identity and sovereignty. Centuries passed before the majority of the inhabitants were able to call themselves Mexican citizens. As a result, on the Mexican side of the hyphen in the designation "Mexican-American," Chicanas rethink their involvement in Mexico's turbulent colonial and postcolonial history, while also reconsidering, on the American side, their involvement in the capitalist neocolonization of the population of Mexican descent in the United States (Barrera, Muñoz, and Ornelas 1972).

In the 1960s, armed with a post-Mexican-American critical consciousness, some people of Mexican descent in the United States recuperated, appropriated, and recodified the term *Chicano* to form a new political class (Acuña 1972; Muñoz 1989). Initially, the new appellation left the entrenched middle-class intellectuals mute because it emerged from the oral usage in working-class communities. In effect, the new name measured the distance between the excluded and the few who had found a place for themselves in Anglo-America. The new Chicano political class began to work on the hyphen, eager to redefine the economic, racial, cultural, and political position of the people. The appropriation and recodification of the term Chicano from oral culture was a stroke of insight precisely because it unsettled all of the identities conferred by previous historical accounts. The apparently well-documented terrains of the dyad Mexico/United States were repositioned and reconfigured through the inclusion of the excluded in the very interiority of culture, knowledge, and the political economy. Thus, the demand for a Chicano/Chicana history became a call for the recovery and rearticulation of the record to include the stories of the race and class relations of the silenced against whom the very notions of being Mexican or not-Mexican, being American or not-American, and being a citizen or not a citizen had been constructed. In brief, the call for the story of Chicanas and Chicanos has not turned out to be a "definitive" culture as some dreamed. Rather, the term itself, in body and mind, has become a critical site of political, ideological, and discursive struggle through which the notion of "definitiveness" and hegemonic tendencies are placed in question.

Though the formation of the new political Chicano class was dominated by men, Chicana feminists have intervened from the beginning. The early Chicana intervention is seen in the serials and journals that mushroomed in tandem with the alternative press in the United States in the 1960s and 1970s. Unfortunately, much of that early work by Chicanas often goes unrecognized, indicative of the process of erasure and exclusion of racial ethnic women within a patriarchal cultural and political economy. In the 1980s, however, there has been a reemergence of Chicana writers and scholars who have not only repositioned the Chicano political class through a feminist register, but who have joined forces with an emergent women-of-color political class that has national and international implications (McLaughlin 1990).

In the United States the 1980s were, according to the Ronald Reagan administration, the decade of the "Hispanic"—a neoconservative move assisted by the U.S. Census Bureau (Giménez 1989) and the mass media to homogenize all people of Latin American descent. This resulted in the occlusion of their heterogeneous histories of resistance to domination, in other words, their counterhistories to the more commonly disseminated histories of invasions and conquests. At the same time, in the 1980s, a more visible Chicana feminist intervention gave new life to a stalled Chicano Movement (Rojas 1989). In fact, in the United States, this rejuvenation through feminist intervention appears to be the case among most racial ethnic minority movements. By including feminist and gender analysis in the emergent political class, Chicanas reconfigured the meaning of cultural and political resistance and redefined the hyphen in the name Mexican-American (Anzaldúa and Moraga 1981; Alarcón 1989, 1990).

To date, most women writers and scholars of Mexican descent refuse to give up the term Chicana. Despite the social reaccommodation of many as "Hispanics" or "Mexican-Americans," it is the consideration of the *excluded*, as evoked by the name Chicana, that provides the position for multiple cultural critiques—between and within, inside and outside, centers and margins. Working-class and peasant women, perhaps the "last colony," as a recent book announces (Mies, Bennholdt-Thomsen, and von Werlhof 1988), are most keenly aware of this. As a result, when many a writer of such a racialized cultural history explores her identity, a reflectory and refractory position is depicted. In the words of Gloria Anzaldúa:

> She has this fear   that she has no names   that she has
> many names   that she doesn't know her names
> She has this fear   that she's an image   that comes and
> goes clearing and darkening   the fear that she's the dreamwork
> inside someone else's skull . . . She has this fear that if she digs
> into herself   she won't find anyone that when she gets
> "there"   she won't find her notches on the trees . . . She
> has this fear that she won't find the way back (1987, 43)

The quest for a true self and identity, which was the initial desire of many writers involved in the Chicano Movement of the late 1960s and early 1970s, has given way to the realization that there is no fixed Chicano identity. "I," or "She" as observed by Anzaldúa, is composed of multiple layers without necessarily yielding an uncontested "origin." In the words of Trinh T. Minh-ha, "Things may be said to be what they are, not exclusively in relation to what was and what will be (they should not solely be seen as clusters chained together by the temporal sequence of cause and effect), but also in relation to each other's immediate presences and to themselves as non/presences" (1989, 94). Thus, the name Chicana, in the present, is the name of resistance that enables cultural and political points of departure and thinking through the multiple migrations and dislocations of women of "Mexican" descent. The name Chicana is not a name that women (or men) are born to or with, as is often the case with "Mexican," but rather it is consciously and critically assumed and serves as a point of re-departure for dismantling historical conjunctures of crisis, confusion, political and ideological conflict, and contradictions of the simultaneous effects of having "no names," having "many names," not "know(ing) her names," and being someone else's "dreamwork." However, digging into the historically despised dark (prieto) body in strictly psychological terms may get her to the bare bones and marrow, but she may not "find the way back," to writing her embodied histories.

The idea of plural historicized bodies is proposed with respect to the multiple racial constructions of the body since "the discovery." To name a few, indigenous (evoking the extant as well as extinct) tribes, criolla, morisca, loba, cambuja, barcina, coyota, samba, mulatta, china, and chola come to mind. The contemporary assumption of mestizaje (hybridism) in the Mexican nation-making process was intended to racially colligate a heterogeneous population that was not European. On the American side of the hyphen, mestizas are non-white, thus further reducing the cultural and historical experience of Chicanas. However, the mestiza concept is always already bursting its boundaries. While some have "forgotten" the mestiza genealogy, others claim an indigenous, black, or Asian one as well. In short, the body, certainly for the past five hundred years in the Americas, has been always already racialized. As tribal "ethnicities" are broken down by conquest and colonizations, bodies are often multiply racialized and dislocated as if they had no other contents. The effort to recontextualize the processes recovers, speaks for, or gives voice to women on the bottom of a historically hierarchical economic and political structure (Spivak 1988).

It is not coincidental that, as Chicana writers reconstruct the multiple names of the mestiza and Indian women, social scientists and historians find them in the segmented labor force or in the grip of armed struggles. In fact, most of these women have been (and continue to be) the surplus sources of cheap labor in the field, the canneries, the maquiladora border industries, and domestic service.

The effort to pluralize the racialized body by redefining part of their experience through the reappropriation of "the Native Woman" on Chicana feminist terms marked one of the first assaults on male-centered cultural nationalism on the one hand (National Association for Chicano Studies 1989), and a patriarchal political economy on the other (Melville 1980; Mora and del Castillo 1980; Córdova et al. 1986; Ruiz and Tiano 1987; Zavella 1987).

The Native Woman has many names also—Coatlicue, Cihuacoatl, Ixtacihuatl, among others. In fact, one has only to consult the dictionary of *Mitología Nahuátl*, for example, to discover many more that have not been invoked. There are those who long for the "lost origins," as well as those who feel a profound spiritual kinship with the "lost"— a spirituality whose resistant political implications must not be under-estimated, but refocused for feminist change (Allen 1988). But for many writers the point is not to recover a lost "utopia" or the "true" essence of our being. The most relevant point in the present is to understand how a pivotal indigenous portion of the mestiza past may represent a collective female experience as well as "the mark of the Beast" within us—the maligned and abused indigenous woman (Anzaldúa 1987, 43). By invoking the "dark Beast" within and without, which many have forced us to deny, the cultural and psychic dismemberment that is linked to imperialistic, racist, and sexist practices are brought into focus. These practices are not a thing of the past either.

One has only to recall the contemporary massacres of the Indian population in Guatemala, for example, or the continuous "democratic" interventionist tactics in Central and South America, which often result in the violent repression of the population.

It is not surprising, then, that many Chicana writers explore their racial and sexual experience in poetry, narrative, essay, testimony, and autobiography through the evocation of indigenous figures. This is a strategy that Gloria Anzaldúa uses and calls "La herencia de Coatlicue"—The Coatlicue State. The "state" is, paradoxically, an ongoing process, a continuous effort of consciousness to make "sense" of it all. Every step is a "travesia," a crossing, because "every time she makes 'sense' of something, she has to 'cross over,' kicking a hole out of the old boundaries of the self and slipping under or over, dragging the old skin along, stumbling over it" (Anzaldúa 1987, 48, 49). The contemporary subject-in-process is not just what Hegel would have us call the *Aufhebung*—that is, the effort to unify consciousness "provided by the simultaneous negation and retention of past forms of consciousness within a radical recomprehension of the totality" (Warren 1984, 37), as Anzaldúa's passage also suggests. The complex effort to unify, however tenuously, Chicanas' consciousness, which is too readily viewed as representing "postmodern fragmented identities," entails not only Hegel's *Aufhebung* with respect to Chicanas' immediate personal subjectivity as raced and sexed bodies, but also an understanding of all past negations as communitarian subjects in a doubled relation to cultural re-collection, and re-membrance, and to our contemporary presence and nonpresence in the sociopolitical and cultural milieu. All of which together enables both individual and group identity as oppressed racialized women. In order to achieve unification, the Chicana position, previously "empty" of meanings, emerges as one that has to "make sense" of it all from the bottom, through the recodification of the native woman. As such, the so-called postmodern decentered subject, a decentralization which implies diverse multiply constructed subjects and historical conjunctures, insofar as she desires liberation, must move towards provisional solidarities especially through social movements. In this fashion one may recognize the endless production of differences to destabilize group or collective identities on the one hand, and the need for group solidarities to overcome oppressions through an understanding of the mechanisms at work, on the other (McLaughlin 1990; Kauffman 1990).

The strategic invocation and recodification of "the Native Woman" in the present has the effect of conjoining the historical repression of the "noncivilized" dark woman—which continues to operate through "regulative psychobiographies" of good and evil women such as that of Guadalupe, Malinche, Llorona, and many others—with the present moment of speech that counters such repressions (Spivak 1989, 227). It is worthwhile to remember that the historical founding moment of the construction of mestiza and mestizo subjectivity entails the rejection and denial of the dark Indian Mother as Indian, which has compelled women to often collude in silence against themselves and to actually deny the Indian position even as that position is visually stylized and represented in the making of the fatherland. Within these blatant contradictions the overvaluation of Europeanness is constantly at work. Thus, Mexico constructs its own ideological version of the notorious Anglo-American "melting pot," under the sign of mestizo and mestiza. The unmasking, however, becomes possible for Chicanas as they are put through the crisis of the Anglo-American experience where ("melting pot") whiteness, not mestizaje, has been constructed as the Absolute Idea of Goodness and Value. In the Americas, then, "the Native Woman" as ultimate sign of the potential reproduction of *barbarie* (savagery) has served as the sign of consensus for most others, men and women. Women, under penalty of the double-bind charge of "betrayal" of the fatherland (in the future tense) and the mother tongues (in the past tense), are often compelled to acquiesce with the "civilizing" new order in male terms. Thus, for example, the "rights" of women in Nicaragua disappear vis-à-vis the "democratizing" forces of the United States, the Church's "civilizing-of-women" project, and traditional sexisms notwithstanding Sandinista intentions (Molyneux 1985). In this scenario, to speak at all, then, "the Native Woman" has to legitimize her position by becoming a "mother" in hegemonic patriarchal terms, which is often impossible to do unless she is "married" or racially "related" to the right men (Hurtado 1989). As a result, the contemporary challenge to the multiple negations and rejections of the native racialized woman in the Americas is like few others.

For Chicanas, the consideration of the ideological constructions of the "noncivilized" dark woman brings into view a most sobering reference point: the overwhelming majority of the workers in maquiladoras, for example, are "mestizas" who have been forcefully subjected not only to the described processes, but to many others that await disentanglement. Many of those workers are "single," unprotected within a cultural order that has required the masculine protection of women to ensure their "decency," indeed to ensure that they are "civilized" in sexual and racial terms. In fact, as Spivak and others have suggested, "The new army of 'permanent casual' labor working below the minimum wage—[are] these women [who today] represent the international neo-colonial subject paradigmatically" (Spivak 1989, 223). These women (and some men) were subjected to the Hispanic New World "feudal mode of power," which in Mexico gave way to the construction of mestizo nationalism, and were also subjected to an Anglo-American "feudal mode of power" in the isolation of migrant worker camps and exchange labor, which in the United States gave rise to Chicano cultural nationalism of the 1960s. In the 1990s these women now find themselves in effect separated in many instances from men who heretofore had joined forces in resistance. Though work in the fields continues to be done with kinship groupings, the "communal mode of power" under the sign of the cultural nationalist family may be bankrupt, especially for female wage-workers. Although, of course, the attempt to bring men and women together under conservative notions of the "family" continues as well. In this instance "family" may be a misnaming in lieu of a search for a more apt name for communitarian solidarity.

Whether it be as domestic servants, canners, or in the service industry in the United States, or as electronic assemblers along the U.S./Mexican border, these "new" women-subjects find themselves bombarded and subjected to multiple cross-cultural and contradictory ideologies. There exists a maze of discourses through which the "I" as a racial and gendered self is hard put to emerge and runs the risk of being thought of as "irrational" or "deluded," as these women attempt to articulate their oppression and exploitation. In the face of Anglo-European literacy and capitalist industrialization, which interpellates them as individuals, for example, and the "communal mode of power" (as mode of de-feudalization) (Spivak 1989, 224), which interpellates them as "Mothers" (the bedrock of the "ideal family" at the center of the nation-making process, despite discontinuous modes of its construction), the figure and referent of Chicanas today are positioned as conflictively as Lyotard's "differend." She is the descendant of native women who are continuously transformed into mestizas, Mexicans, émigrés to Anglo-America, "Chicanas," Latinas, Hispanics— there are as many names as there are namers.

Lyotard defines a differend as "a case of conflict, between (at least) two parties, that cannot be equitably resolved for lack of a rule of judgment applicable to both arguments. One side's legitimacy does not imply the other's lack of legitimacy" (Lyotard 1987, xi). In appropriating the concept as a metonym for both the figure and referent of the Chicana, for example, it is important to note that, though it enables us to locate and articulate sites of ideological and discursive conflict, it cannot inform the actual Chicana/differend engaged in a living struggle as to how she can seize her "I" or even her feminist "We" to change her circumstances without bringing into play the axes in which she finds herself in the present—culturally, politically, and economically.

The call for theories elaborated based on the "flesh and blood" experiences of women of color in *This Bridge Called My Back* (Anzaldúa and Moraga 1983) may mean that the Chicana feminist project must interweave the following critiques and critical operations: (1) multiple cross-cultural analyses of the ideological constructions of raced "Chicana" subjects in relation to the differently positioned cultural constructions of all men and some Anglo-European women; (2) negotiation of strategic political transitions from cultural constructions and contestations to "social science" studies and referentially grounded "Chicanas" in the political economy who live out their experiences in heterogeneous social and geographic positions. Though not all women of Mexican/Hispanic descent would call themselves Chicanas, I would argue that it is an important point of departure for critiques and critical operations (on the hyphen/bridge) that keep the excluded within any theory-making project. That is, in the Mexican-descent continuum of meanings, Chicana is still the name that brings into focus the interrelatedness of class/race/gender and forges the link to actual subaltern native women in the U.S./Mexico dyad. (3) In negotiating points one and two, how can we work with literary, testimonial, and pertinent ethnographic materials to enable "Chicanas" to grasp their "I" and "We" in order to make effective political interventions? This implies that we must select, in dialogue with women, from the range of cultural productions those materials that actually enable the emergence of I/We subjectivities (Castellano 1990).

Given the extensive ideological sedimentation of the (Silent) Good Woman and the (Speech-producing) Bad Woman that enabled the formations of the cultural nationalist "communal modes of power," Chicana feminists have an enormous mandate to make "sense" of it all as Anzaldúa desires. It requires no less than the deconstruction of paternalistic "communal modes of power," which is politically perilous since often it appears to be the "only" model of empowerment that the oppressed have, although it has ceased to function for many women, as development and postindustrial social research indicates. Also, it requires the thematization and construction of new models of political agency for women of color who are always already positioned cross-culturally and within contradictory discourses. As we consider the diffusion of mass media archetypes and stereotypes of all women which continuously interpellates them into the patriarchal order according to their class, race (ethnicity), and gender, the "mandate" is (cross-culturally) daunting. Yet, "agent-provocateurs" know that mass media and popular cultural production are always open to contestations and recodifications which can become sites of resistance (Castellano 1990).

Thus, the feminist Chicana, activist, writer, scholar, and intellectual has to, on the one hand, locate the point of theoretical and political consensus with other feminists (and "feminist" men) and, on the other, continue with projects that position her in paradoxical binds, for example by breaking out of ideological boundaries that subject her in culturally specific ways and not crossing over to cultural and political areas that subject her as "individual/autonomous/neutralized" laborer. Moreover, to reconstruct differently the raced and gendered "I's" and "We's" also calls for a rearticulation of the "You's" and "They's." Traversing the processes may well enable us to locate points of differences and identities in the present to forge the needed solidarities against repression and oppression. Or, as Lorde and Spivak would have it, locate the "identity-in-difference" of cultural and political struggle (1984, 1988).

Acknowledgments

I would like to thank Gloria Anzaldúa, Rosa Linda Fregoso, Francine Masiello, and Margarita Melville for their reading and comments on this essay. Responsibility for the final version is, of course, mine.

Works Cited

Acuña, Rodolfo. 1972. *Occupied America: The Chicano's Struggle Toward Liberation.* San Francisco: Canfield Press.

Alarcón, Norma. 1989. "Traddutora, Traditora: A Paradigmatic Figure of Chicana Feminism." *Cultural Critique* 13(Fall): 57–87.

———. 1990. "The Theoretical Subject(s) of *This Bridge Called My Back* and *Anglo-American Feminism.*" In *Making Face, Making Soul*—Haciendo Caras: *Creative and Critical Perspectives by Women of Color,* edited by Gloria Anzaldúa, 356–69. San Francisco: Spinsters/Aunt Lute.

Allen, Paula Gunn. 1988. "Who Is Your Mother? Red Roots of White Feminism." In *The Graywolf Annual Five: Multicultural Literacy,* edited by Rick Simonson and Scott Walker, 13–27. Saint Paul: Graywolf Press.

Anzaldúa, Gloria. 1987. *Borderlands/La Frontera: The New Mestiza.* San Francisco: Spinsters/Aunt Lute.

Anzaldúa, Gloria, and Cherríe Moraga, eds. 1983. *This Bridge Called My Back: Writings by Radical Women of Color.* New York: Kitchen Table, Women of Color Press.

Barrera, Mario, Carlos Muñoz, and Charles Ornelas. 1972. "The Barrio as an Internal Colony." In *People and Politics in Urban Society,* edited by Harlan Hahn, 465–98. Urban Affairs Annual Reviews, vol. 6. Los Angeles: Sage Publications.

Castellano, Olivia. 1990. "Canto, locura y poesía: The Teacher as Agent-Provocateur." *The Women's Review of Books* 7(5): 18–20.

Córdova, Teresa, et al. 1986. *Chicana Voices: Intersections of Class, Race, and Gender.* Austin: Center for Mexican American Studies.

Giménez, Martha. 1989. "The Political Construction of the Hispanic." In *Estudios Chicanos and the Politics of Community,* edited by Mary Romero and Cordelia Candelaria, 66–85. Austin: National Association for Chicano Studies.

Hurtado, Aída. 1989. "Relating to Privilege: Seduction and Rejection in the Subordination of White Women and Women of Color." *Signs: Journal of Women in Culture and Society* 14(4): 833–55.

Kauffman, L. A. 1990. "The Anti-Politics of Identity." *Socialist Review* 1: 67–80.

Lorde, Audre. 1984. *Sister Outsider: Essays and Speeches.* Trumansburg, NY: The Crossing Press.

Lyotard, Jean-Francois. 1987. *The Differend: Phrases in Dispute,* translated by Georges Van Den Abbeele. Minneapolis: University of Minnesota Press.

McLaughlin, Andrée Nicola. 1990. "Black Women, Identity, and the Quest for Humanhood and Wholeness: Wild Women in the Whirlwind." In *Wild Women in the Whirlwind: Afra-American Culture and the Contemporary Literary Renaissance,* edited by Joanne M. Braxton and Andrée Nicola McLaughlin, 147–80. New Brunswick, NJ: Rutgers University Press.

Melville, Margarita B., ed. 1980. *Twice a Minority: Mexican American Women.* St. Louis, MO: C. V. Mosby.

Mies, Maria, Veronika Bennholdt-Thomsen, and Claudia von Werlhof, eds. 1988. *Women: The Last Colony.* London: Zed Books.

Minh-ha, Trinh T., 1989. *Woman/Native/Other: Writing Postcoloniality and Feminism.* Bloomington: Indiana University Press.

Molyneux, Maxine. 1985. "Mobilization Without Emancipation: Women's Interests, the State, and Revolution in Nicaragua." *Feminist Studies* 11(2): 227–54.

Mora, Magdalena, and Adelaida R. Del Castillo, eds. 1980. *Mexican Women in the United States: Struggles Past and Present.* University of California, Los Angeles: Chicano Studies Research Center.

Muñoz, Carlos. 1989. *Youth, Identity, Power: The Chicano Generation.* London: Verso.

National Association for Chicano Studies. 1986. *Chicana Voices: Intersections of Class, Race, and Gender.* Editorial Committee, Teresa Córdova, chair. Austin: Center for Mexican American Studies.

Rojas, Guillermo. 1989. "Social Amnesia and Epistemology in Chicano Studies." In *Estudios Chicanos and the Politics of Community,* edited by Mary Romero and Cordelia Candelaria, 54–65. Austin: National Association for Chicano Studies.

Ruiz, Vicki L., and Susan Tiano, eds. 1987. *Women on the U.S.-Mexico Border: Responses to Change.* Boston, MA: Allen and Unwin.

Spivak, Gayatri C. 1988. "Can the Subaltern Speak?" In *Marxism and the Interpretation of Culture,* edited by Cary Nelson and Lawrence Grossberg, 271–313. Urbana and Chicago: University of Illinois Press.

————. 1989. "The Political Economy of Women as Seen by a Literary Critic." In *Coming to Terms: Feminism, Theory, Politics,* edited by Elizabeth Weed, 218–29. London: Routledge.

Warren, Scott. 1984. *The Emergence of Dialectical Theory: Philosophy and Political Inquiry.* Chicago: University of Chicago Press.

Zavella, Patricia. 1987. *Women's Work and Chicano Families: Cannery Workers of the Santa Clara Valley.* Ithaca, NY: Cornell University Press.

8 Current African American Literary Theory: Review and Projections

Reginald Martin
Memphis State University

Several historically and pedagogically important events happened to literature written by blacks and the black-authored criticism of that literature in the 1960s. First, during the 1960s, the "integrationist" literature from black authors of criticism and prose that predominated in the late 1940s and throughout the 1950s was both shouted down and effectively transformed by the proponents of "separatist" writing by black writers for a black readership. I think here especially of the many black literature professors and black commercial journalists who labored during the late 1940s, 1950s, and early 1960s to show how much Gwendolyn Brooks's *Annie Allen* (1949) was like T. S. Eliot's *The Wasteland* (1922) or labored to show how similar in content, structure, style, theme, and intent Ralph Ellison's *Invisible Man* (1952) was to James Joyce's *Portrait of the Artist* (1916). This kind of critical and comparative paradigm was *completely* disrupted by the black nationalist and literary separatists of the 1960s.

The separatists argued that there *had* to be "uniquely black" ways of judging and "seeing" literature and that not a trace of this method could be effectively implemented in a system that compared writing by blacks to the writing of the very white "oppressors" the blacks were writing against. This separatist movement in the black criticism of black-authored texts was especially ironic in the late 1950s and early 1960s, as prominent black writers such as Lorraine Hansberry and James Baldwin argued for the "universality" of their own writings, as well as those of other blacks, while at the same time insisting on some uniquely black messages and indexes in their texts. But Hansberry and Baldwin saw no reason to eschew comparisons between their works and the works of a Lillian Hellman or a William Faulkner. Equally ironic, as black characters began to have prominent parts in the works of white authors, such as Jean Genet's *The Blacks: Or a Clown Show* (1960), the portrayals (and there really were not that many) became almost completely positive, in Genet's case even to the extent of making all the blacks completely good and all the whites completely bad. Nat Turner in William Styron's *The Confessions of Nat Turner* (1967), where the major black character is neither good nor bad because he is deranged, is a warped oddity in the history of publishing in this country. It has already earned its own book-length response in *Black Writers Respond to William Styron's Nat Turner* (1971).

Be that as it may, at this pivotal time, certain black authors such as Hansberry (just before her untimely death) and Brooks (before her radical conversion at the Black Writers Conference in 1970 at Fisk University) continued to exact their craft as they saw fit, ignoring the swelling tide of separatist criticism, while others such as Ellison stopped their creative work altogether and concentrated on their prose works, and some black authors ceased publishing completely. After *Black Fire* (1968), edited by LeRoi Jones and Larry Neal, the forceful rhetoric and politically timely message of separatist criticism (and its many later offshoots) was to rule until Henry L. Gates's overwhelmingly influential discussion of the syncretic use of Euro-Anglo-based critical ideas, such as metatextuality, in his introduction to *Black Literature and Literary Theory* (1984). And for reasons known only to himself, Gates has now made a turn that in many ways would align him with some of the early separatists by insisting that signification is an original African-based trope in his most recent book, *The Sign and the Signifying Monkey* (1989).

What we find now in the works of black *and* white critics of African American literary theory are solid proponents of both these schools of thought: those who argue convincingly that *only* critically identified black "windows" should be used to look at black-authored creative works (many feminist critics make the same argument for women's writings) and those who argue, agreeing with both Georges Poulet *and* Trudier Harris, that the battle by black academics has been to have *more* tools applied to black-authored texts, not *fewer*. Proponents of this latter idea would argue (a) that if more critical tools are used, even though those tools may be of European origin, then black-authored works stand a better chance of being examined, and thus read, taught, and, eventually, inserted into the canon; and (b) that not only is a syncretic approach to the criticism of black-authored texts more viable in gaining acceptance for those texts in Anglo academies, but also that such an approach to the literature rhetorically mirrors both the structure of the literature and that immensely syncretic group we (for the social moment) now call "African Americans." Thus, we understand the "unique cultural product" (literature) better as we also come to know the "unique" cultural group better. Such "in-group" knowledge shared by the exogamous mainstream the syncretists deem as important and "good."

Conversely, the black literary separatists would agree with Henry Highland Garnett in his original 1843 "Address" that it "takes the slave to understand the problems of the slave" and the minute "outsiders" begin to judge the "deeds" (texts) of the slaves, they do so with cultural blinders and malice aforethought. Thus, it is especially important that the in-group share only among themselves and judge only themselves by their own indexes. I think, here especially, of the similar arguments in the early 1980s writings of Amiri Baraka in the pages of *Black American Literature Forum* (1982) and in Alice Walker's *In Search of Our Mothers' Gardens* (1983), which asserted a similar theme, admittedly with different subjects and intentions. The dangers in the arguments of both the syncretists and the separatists are important to note.

If one fully takes the approach of the syncretists, one runs the usual, and by now historically tiresome, risk of overwhelming all "windows" and indexes that might be argued to be "uniquely black" by continually referring to (and deferring to) the gargantuan volume of Soviet-, Euro-, and Anglo-American literary critical thought. In such practices there is the imminent danger of "uniquely black" indexes becoming more and more amalgamated until there is no more (positive) difference. In plainer terms, what once may have been acknowledged to have been a black contribution to literature or literary theory may become simply a white, or an "American," contribution. (Analogously, think of Nancy Reagan in 1981 at a White House celebration of the arts expounding on Benny Goodman being one of the "founders" of jazz as Dizzy Gillespie rolled his eyes and gasped for breath in the background. Mrs. Reagan was merely responding to jazz as a unique "American" art form, but she was also forgetting to mention that jazz and its founders were also uniquely black.) The syncretists do not admit it, but such an occurrence *would* be acceptable to them, as at the root of all of their syncretic arguments lies the *mainstream* idea that there ought to be one vast canon of equally great texts based only on *critically agreed upon* merit. The syncretists believe that such a "matrix" canon would be better than the limiting "mainstream canon" with which we now work.

The syncretists also believe that a matrix canon would be better than a plethora of "mini-canons" running wild and unrestrained in each academy and actually teaching students very little about writing or the historical development of literature—one academy here for working-class, heterosexual white male authors of the 1930s, one here for rich, white, atheistic lesbian authors of the 1970s, one over there for late-1980s homosexual black male Catholic authors, and one located somewhere near Berkeley, California, for androgenous, Jewish-mulatto literature of the coming millennium. Finally, the syncretists believe also that a matrix canon by its very syncretic nature would be infinitely more representative of black-authored texts and would assure the inclusion of these texts. Here the separatists would begin to laugh— loudly.

Critically agreed upon merit, the separatists would argue, can come only from critics with power, power that will be more than likely derived from the cultural climate of the times. Exactly how will the black syncretists help to construct a "matrix canon" that is inclusive of black authors if these black critics are educationally and politically estranged from black culture and its unique cultural products such as black-authored texts? Further, exactly *how* do these syncretist critics propose to start their process in the cultural climate of the times (reexamine the original 1987 proposal for Stanford's core curriculum in literature) that denies the literary merit of most black-authored texts. You'll be lucky, the separatists will continue to shout, to find training in a graduate school that even includes any black-authored texts or criticism to begin to contemplate. And after that, with most of the mainstream critical faculties still promoting only the study of the "deeper structures" of a text, and black colleges falling into fiscal disarray all around you, you'll be lucky to get a job.

Of course, something the separatists will not admit is that their assertions on cultural climate and the dearth of proper training and job opportunities would even more so apply to them and their "less acceptable" ideas. Further, they could never be brought to admit that their exclusive critical practices are just as bad or good as mainstream exclusionary critical practices. And as they continue to narrow their critical circle, they begin to speak only to themselves. The sentiment of Houston Baker's old poem resurfaces again and again in the background of both these schools' flailings: "No matter where you travel, you still be black" (1979).

It seems to me that both of these schools have been effectively tempered by research outside the discipline of literary theory that they either do not know about or have effectively ignored. As a critic myself, I do acknowledge that the power of esoteric, specialized criticism (and critics) has become so enormous in the academies that literary theory *can* afford to ignore other disciplines, ignore even other specialized "schools" within the discipline of literary criticism. But irrespective of the reasons why such a critical moment is a fact, the powerful body politic of what is specialized "theory" today (it can change again the minute a new generation of critics needs to make tenure) can and often does ignore other important ideas, even when the empirical and documented research of other disciplines or other critics in the sphere of literary theory clearly make most of what we say, at best, trivial. We are often trivial because we are both powerful and arrogant for the critical moment, and we forget the very impetus of Western criticism in the first place: to help *someone* understand *something* about a text or author better, in some readable and useful way. My impression from keeping up on many of our journals is that few critics would even recognize my above paraphrase from Horace's "The Art of Poetry." So caught-up are they in the latest "poststructuralist moment" from the Continent that, between their own multitudinous publications, they have time to read only tertiary and badly derivative critical works, never the primary. The primary text I mention below is only one example of a text extratextual to the body politic of literary theory whose findings should earn it a place in our critical canon, as it conclusively undermines most of what we believe about the "Western arts tradition"; there are many more such primary texts in strict linguistic areas, the sociology of knowledge area, and group psychology research areas.

The very belief that anything Europe has offered in the study of literature is "new" and "uniquely European" (or white) is blasted into critical shards by the linguistic, textual, and archeological research published in 1987 by Martin Bernal in the first of his promised four-volume series, *Black Athena: The Afro-Asiatic Roots of Classical Civilization, Volume I: The Fabrication of Greece, 1785–1985* (please note the ending year of the first volume). While Bernal *does* add new information and new paradigms to what black historians have been saying at least since John G. Jackson's *Ethiopia and the Origins of Civilization* (1939), the core of his thesis has been stated again and again by black historians and linguists such as Jackson, Chancellor Williams, Ivan Van Sertima, Asa Hilliard, and, especially, George M. James, author of *Stolen Legacy* (1954): that the civilized ancient world was both in origin and development black, and that it was left to "ancient" Europe to co-opt (without reference or royalties) on a large scale the arts— including the literary arts—of the blacks. The publication of *Black Athena* makes a difference because, first, it strikes the critical and objective tone of the traditionally "objective historical" text. The evocation of such a text paradigm is of the utmost importance when one is not only trying to revise history, but is also trying to undo one of the stronger tenets of the sociology of knowledge which states that most traditional adherents to an idea would prefer not to have that idea disrupted by a "more true" idea.[1] Secondly, because Bernal is *not* black, he will not have his research immediately silenced. The success of Bernal's first volume was so tremendously positive that his second volume, *Volume II: The Linguistic and Archeological Evidence* (1991), is already under back order although it has not even been officially published.

Coinciding and (I believe) purposely dovetailing on the success of *Black Athena* is St. Clair Drake's *Black Folk Here and There* (1987–1990), which, astoundingly, provides linguistic and archeological evidence that even Bernal missed. The revisionist, yet empirical and objective power of these two texts, and others like them from other disciplines, is why I earlier stated that the discipline of literary theory could greatly profit, and in fact increase its powers, if it would pay more attention to other disciplines and less attention to only its own echoes. Consider the true earth-shaking importance of Bernal's work to the current body of literary theories.

Clearly, our critical ideas must be rethought in every genre of American literary theory if our Greek and Roman models are merely derivative. If the corpus of largely European-based criticism we normally think of is, in fact, not white-based but black-based (remember, neither Parmenides nor Aristotle left Greece to study in Norway but in Egypt, reappearing later with their "new" literary critical knowledge in mid-sixth and fourth centuries B.C.), then reactionary arguments about "unique black indexes" in response to "oppressive white indexes" seem not only moot, but self-contradictory.

Nevertheless and obviously, various unique modes of literary expression and various unique critical responses to those texts did historically arise in the United States. "Unique" African American literary critical themes are as valid for examination as are the "unique" Agrarian critics' ideas, and no one says that the Agrarians should not be studied simply because they were initially a small group of cultural conservatives who wanted to turn the study of literature into intrinsically what it is not: a scientific method. I find that the Agrarians' ideas are worthy of study if for no other reason than the fact that its later emanation, the New Criticism, still cuts such an enormous swath across the American critical landscape and our ideas of "valid" ways to judge a literary work of art. Similarly, the study of African American literary theory and its postulations on unique indexes may illuminate in unique ways.

Notes

1. See Frank G. Martin, "The Egyptian Ethnicity Controversy and the Sociology of Knowledge," *Black Economics Review* (1982): 35–40. In this fascinating study, Martin conclusively shows that the inability of scholars and society in general to acknowledge the true ethnicity of the Egyptians is simply an act of intellectual and "in-group" defiance which coincides precisely with the major tenet of the sociology of knowledge school: that a new idea, no matter how valid or "proven," is unwelcome when its acknowledgment would disrupt the major beliefs of the in-group.

Works Cited

Baker, Houston. 1980. *Black American Literature Forum* 22(8): 23–29.

Baraka, Amiri. 1982. "Afro-American Literature and Class Struggle." *Black American Literature Forum* 16(2): 21–35.

Bernal, Martin. 1987. *Black Athena: The Afro-Asiatic Roots of Classical Civilization. Vol. I: The Fabrication of Ancient Greece, 1785–1985*. New Brunswick, NJ: Rutgers University Press.

————. 1991. *Vol. II: The Archaeological and Documentary Evidence*. New Brunswick, NJ: Rutgers University Press.

Brooks, Gwendolyn. 1949. *Annie Allen: Poems*. New York: Harper.

Drake, St. Clair. 1987–1990. *Black Folk Here and There: An Essay in History and Anthropology* (vol. 1–2). Los Angeles: Center for Afro-American Studies, University of California.

Eliot, T. S. 1966. "The Wasteland." In *The Collected Poems of T. S. Eliot*. New York: Viking.

Ellison, Ralph. 1952. *Invisible Man*. New York: Random.

Garnett, Henry Highland. 1970 [1843]. "An Address to the Slaves of the United States." In *Afro-American Writing*, edited by Amy Harrison, 79–85. New York: Garland.

Gates, Henry Louis, ed. 1984. *Black Literature and Literary Theory*. New York: Methuen.

————. 1989. *The Sign and the Signifying Monkey*. New York: Doubleday.

Genet, Jean. 1960. *The Blacks: Or a Clown Show*. New York: Grove.

Horace. 1978. "The Art of Poetry." *The Collected Works*. New York: Bantam.

Jackson, Darwin, ed. 1971. *Black Writers Respond to William Styron's Nat Turner*. New York: Bantam.

Jackson, John G. 1939. *Ethiopia and the Origin of Civilization*. New York: Blyden Society.

James, George M. 1954. *Stolen Legacy*. New York: Philosophical Library.

Jones, LeRoi, and Larry Neal, eds. 1968. *Black Fire: An Anthology of Afro-American Writing*. New York: Morrow.

Joyce, James. 1978 [1941]. *Portrait of the Artist as a Young Man*. In *The Portable James Joyce*, edited by Malcom Cowley. New York: Viking.

Martin, Frank G. 1982. "The Egyptian Ethnicity Controversy and the Sociology of Knowledge." *Black Economics Review* 10(3): 35–40. Normal: Illinois State University Press.

Styron, William. 1967. *The Confessions of Nat Turner.* New York: Random, NAL.

Walker, Alice. 1983. *In Search of Our Mothers' Gardens.* San Diego: Harcourt.

9 Talking Across Cultures

Robert S. Burton
California State University at Chico

"Multiculturalism" became more than just a buzzword during the 1989–90 academic year. While NCTE geared up to run its annual Summer Institute on the topic of "Cross-Cultural Criticism" (using for its subtitle the question "How Can I Teach Literature That I Don't Already Know?"), at least five major academic journals in the field of literature and cultural studies devoted special issues to multicultural literature (*Modern Fiction Studies*, Spring 1989, "Narratives of Colonial Resistance"; *Performing Arts Journal*, Spring 1989, "The Multiculturalism Issue"; *Ariel*, October 1989, "Post-Colonial Literature"; *PMLA*, January 1990, "African and African American Literature"; and *College English*, November 1990, "African-American Criticism"). Clearly, the shared emphasis has done much to awaken English studies to the increasingly prized multicultural voices in circulation. At the same time, I want to suggest that what also lies behind this surge of interest is a habit of "othering" or "differentiating" that threatens to contain, rather than open up, the field of cultural and cross-cultural studies. In other words, both the question behind the Summer Institute and the intentions behind publishing special journal issues devoted to multicultural literature highlight and emphasize the "otherness" and the apartness of this body of literature from the so-called mainstream tradition. No matter how noble or innocent this approach may be, it seems to be another version of what Edward Said calls "Orientalism": of stressing the exotic otherness of a culture and thereby separating it from your own (uncontaminated) body. As Said has argued, this approach sanctions value judgments about the inferiority of the "other" culture, culminating in "statements about the Oriental mentality, the inscrutable Oriental, the unreliable and degenerate Oriental, and so forth" (1984, 223).

Is it not better to recognize that we already *know* much about multicultural literature and the experiences that inform it? Of course,

I do not mean that by living in Western society we automatically assimilate the multicultural voices and visions of writers such as Salman Rushdie, Bessie Head, or Alice Walker; nor do I wish to slip into easy, "we-are-the-world" type generalizations that the mass media frequently and willingly endorse; but I do insist that, no matter what our background, we share with these authors the experience of "fragmentation on a global scale." We live in a world that the cultural anthropologist James Clifford describes as "increasingly out of place" (1988, 6), where one feels "a pervasive condition of off-centeredness in a world of distinct meaning systems" (9). It is difficult, indeed self-defeating, to think of oneself or one's society as pure or absolute anymore, Clifford argues, when the society around us is increasingly hybridized and intercultural. Perhaps, at a rather mundane level, peeking into a refrigerator or a closet or randomly scanning TV channels can bear Clifford's argument out, as it might indicate the stew of influences and backgrounds that circulate, seemingly naturally and unnoticed, in our everyday life. Indeed, as I write this essay, I am inevitably swamped by a feeling of "off-centeredness in a world of distinct meaning systems" on several levels: as an Englishman in California's Central Valley, immersed in a climate and a landscape unknown to me for the first twenty-five years of my life; as a teacher trying to be both polished performer and puzzled participant when teaching classes on Toni Morrison, Hanif Kureishi, Bharati Mukherjee, et al.; as an employee on a campus where red-brick buildings and gleaming classrooms stand over what was once the site of a Maidu Indian settlement, and so on.

I am suggesting, then, that the multicultural voices currently being published to great acclaim are highly articulate and powerful versions of our own voices: displaced, fragmented, off-centered, yet attempting to attain wholeness and completeness. Jamaican-born writer Michelle Cliff speaks of her "struggle to get wholeness from fragmentation while working within fragmentation, producing work which may find its strength in its depiction of fragmentation" (1988, 60). And Salman Rushdie has said, in response to criticism from both Muslims and Westerners against *The Satanic Verses*: "What is being expressed is a discomfort with a plural identity. And what I am saying to you—and saying in the novel—is that we have got to come to terms with this. We are increasingly becoming a world of migrants, made up of bits and fragments from here, there. We are here. And we have never really left anywhere we have been" (1989, 114).

Our intentions, I think, as teachers and scholars should be, like Cliff's and Rushdie's, to acknowledge the "bits and fragments" of our world experience and, like Clifford's, to celebrate "[a] modern 'ethnography' of conjunctures, constantly moving *between* cultures" (1988, 9). Perhaps instead of trying to give polished, critical assessments of Bessie Head, Salman Rushdie, or Alice Walker, we could appreciate and share the strategies used by them as they articulate their feelings of displacement and attempt to become whole through the process of writing. The ideal classroom situation, then, might be one where, instead of asking what makes Salman Rushdie or Bessie Head different from ourselves, we eagerly examine and learn from the choices they made as they composed their polished yet plural and displaced selves. Admittedly, when I have tried to do this with Rushdie's *Midnight's Children* or Head's *A Question of Power* (in an upper-division course on multicultural literature), students initially seem to be puzzled and put off by Rushdie's excessive playfulness and Head's tortuous psychological probings. But instead of placating students with trite "background" information about the Indian independence movement or the status of women in Botswanan society, I prefer to have the students immerse themselves in this feeling of confusion and displacement and, like the authors, to articulate that experience with honesty either through their own creative writing or through a more formal exercise in expository writing.

From this, a legitimate question follows: How can we, as teachers, hope to "empower" our students if we expose them to seemingly confusing and despairing gestures such as these? Isn't it more productive and beneficial to the students, this line of inquiry goes, if we simply help them to become whole, giving them a sense of control or power over the texts that we bring into the classroom? Don't our students need to be empowered to buy self-confidently into the American dream and thereby attain heightened status, particularly with a good job?

Although I am sympathetic to this line of argument, I am also deeply skeptical of the notion of "empowerment" as it has sometimes been applied to cross-cultural studies and the teaching of writing. First, it assumes that someone (normally the teacher) actively possesses a certain "power" that can then be transferred to a passive consumer (normally the student) who then becomes magically "empowered." Second, it assumes that having "power" is inherently a positive value. However, isn't it fairly obvious that people with power have potential to cause considerable damage to others? In his 1980 manifesto for empowerment, *Writing with Power*, Peter Elbow unashamedly admits, without a trace of irony, that by encouraging empowerment in the student writer's voice he is "[i]n effect . . . saying, 'Why don't you shoot that gun you have? Oh yes, by the way, I can't tell you how to aim it' " (1981, 310). Frankly, I am not cheered by such a prospect, especially when Elbow goes on to suggest that, given the dangers involved, you should "practice shooting the gun off in safe places. First with no one around. Then with people you know and trust deeply. Find people who are willing to be in the same room with you while you pull the trigger" (310).

Perhaps the important question to ask when we talk of "empowerment," then, is what are we empowering our students to do? If we are encouraging them to buy into the American dream, then I am nervously skeptical; if we are urging them to feel complacent and comfortable about their superiority over foreign cultures, then I remain skeptical; if we are asking them to experiment wantonly with loaded guns, then my skepticism turns to unambiguous opposition.

As Robert Pattison argues in *On Literacy* (1982), a significant danger with current literacy programs is that they simply pass on the power of the status quo by teaching specialized, often bureaucratic, skills; this has very little to do with deepening the consciousness of students or cultivating what Alice Walker calls "an awareness and openness to mystery" (1983, 252). Worse, Pattison continues, "Established American literacy, with its emphasis on mechanical skills and its assertion of the limitations of language, thwarts man's desire to feel himself fully represented in words" (1982, 203). Perhaps by encouraging students to represent in words a deepening of consciousness and openness to mystery, we can stimulate an awareness of the fragmentation and displacement in their own lives and improve their ability to appreciate and articulate, as many multicultural writers already do, such fragmentation.

I trust I am not foolish enough to think, however, that I have at all times avoided wielding the loaded gun of "false empowerment" or refrained from ever giving my students the loaded gun. I have tried to use power responsibly; like most teachers, I am annoyed with myself when I talk too much in class or get drawn into giving easy definitions or making simplistic categorizations about works of literature. In a multicultural literature class that I teach regularly, I have seen how student access to a false sense of power can potentially be dangerous when I ask for group presentations on a country and culture whose literature we are examining at the time. Early on in the semester I organize the class into small groups of three or four students and designate a particular culture to each group; then, on a prearranged day, each student in the group is responsible for giving short five-to seven-minute presentations on one of a variety of topics related to the readings and the culture (from a brief overview of mythological heroes in that culture to an appreciation of its religions or its architecture, and so forth). I originally established this assignment, believing it would give students a valuable opportunity to be responsible for another culture and thereby to re-present it, in all its popular and sophisticated manifestations, to the rest of the class. By becoming, in effect, ambassadors for that culture, they would compose their own narratives about it. Furthermore, because I do not evaluate these presentations (the rest of the class does), the presenters are not obliged to address their information exclusively to me.

Even though presentations are often respectful and stimulating (music and food go down particularly well), sometimes a student or an entire group will resort to facile lectures on the culture by assuming a pose of authority and claiming control over it with a string of absolutes and generalizations about an author's life, a leader's politics, or a country's current state of affairs. I do not like this abuse of authority, but I do not denounce it when I see it happen in the classroom because I trust that the audience knows when a presenter is being overly reductive. Further, I think that the presenter knows when he or she has resorted to ethnocentric generalizations. Not until you stand in front of a classroom, with a full seven (or seventy!) minutes of time to occupy, do you reach into your storehouse of knowledge only to find, perhaps, empty clichés and simple platitudes which you try to cover up as smoothly as possible. We have all been in this situation, and if we are honest with ourselves, we have realized afterwards how ignorant and unprincipled we were. Criticizing students for such a presentation might arouse their fear and resistance, in effect consolidating their ignorance and possibly even moving them to further biases and prejudice. Instead, I do not comment on the presentations in the hopes that the presenters, and the class audience, will think through the merits and limitations of each talk.

The danger, then, of asking students to become ambassadors for a culture was that it placed them in a position of considerable authority that was easily abused. I had wanted to make students "responsible" for a culture and even though most, I believe, used that responsibility sensibly (coming to possess their author, leader, country, or national dish in a way that we all possess role models by pinning them on our walls, refrigerators, or office doors), the idea of reducing a given culture to the status of an exotic or estranged "other" was still tempting for several presenters.

A similar, yet more reflexive, activity for a multicultural course is described by Greg Sarris in an essay from *College English*, "Storytelling in the Classroom: Crossing Vexed Chasms" (1990). In the first class meeting of his American Indian literature course, he recounts a story that had been passed down to him by his Pomo elders. During the next several class meetings, he then asks his students, in groups, to retell the story in their own words and to be self-conscious about their strategies for retelling. The purpose, he explains, is to let students "see how they are approaching the story and begin to explore unexamined assumptions by which they operate and which they use to frame the texts and experiences of another culture" (1990, 169). The larger plan behind Sarris's essay, and behind his teaching practice, is to get students to "talk across . . . the spaces between their world and that of an American-Indian text" (171).

Getting a student to talk back to a text, or across the spaces between the text and the reader, and encouraging the continual realignment of a student's framing devices as he or she negotiates the text are surely admirable activities for any literature class, but especially so for a multicultural literature class where, as I have argued, it is easy to make dangerous and distorting distinctions between "self" (the uncontaminated reader) and "other" (the "foreign" text). I suspect that the predominant tendency in our classrooms is still to encourage students to contain and consume multicultural narratives in an uncritical and unselfconscious way. We like to think we are producing students who become "rational" and "enlightened" by this magical "empowerment."

I want to finish by briefly examining selected examples of multicultural literature where the authors themselves seem *very conscious* of ways by which their narratives continue to be appropriated and consumed by so-called enlightened and empowered Western readers. In several postcolonial novels a fairly standard type or character is often invoked who speaks on behalf of such enlightened literacy as a deliberate form of control and closure.

This happens conspicuously in Chinua Achebe's *Things Fall Apart* (1959) where the novel "closes" with the British District Commissioner (responsible for the administration of Nigeria) surveying the tragic suicide of the African protagonist, Okonkwo, and planning in his own mind the book that he will write on the series of events that have led up to Okonkwo's death:

> The story of this man who had killed a messenger and hanged himself would make interesting reading. One could almost write a whole chapter on him. Perhaps not a whole chapter but a reasonable paragraph, at any rate. There was so much else to include, and one must be firm in cutting out details. He had already chosen the title of the book, after much thought: *The Pacification of the Primitive Tribes of the Lower Niger.* (1959, 191)

The irony, of course, is fairly obvious: Achebe's novel has been devoted to Okonkwo's complex and nonlinear story enriched by its embedded oral-based stories. The District Commissioner, who appears only on the periphery of this story, has nevertheless attempted to distill it into a single paragraph. Okonkwo's story is therefore pacified and controlled by the Commissioner's "power"—a combination of his skills with literacy (his ability to capture the series of "native" events with well-chosen words) and with the gun (the guardian and enforcer of "justice") that he brings to Africa.

The further irony is that our history textbooks and our teaching methods may still accord with the District Commissioner's paradigm. Similarly, our mass media may still be in the paradigm presented in R. K. Narayan's *The Guide* (1958), where a similar episode "closes" the novel. A California TV personality called James J. Malone suddenly appears at the novel's end to interview the Indian protagonist, a swami whose Gandhi-like fast on behalf of rain in a drought-ridden Indian village has caused much concern and celebration across the continent and world. Like the District Commissioner in Achebe's novel, Malone looks for ways to reduce, through rational explanation, the swami's mysterious power over his followers; in asking questions such as "Can fasting abolish all wars and bring world peace?" he seems set on receiving a string of one-word answers that merely affirm his preconceptions. Malone's attempts to be an invisible presence in the Indian village as he asks these questions (he insists, "I won't disturb you . . . I won't disturb you . . . I wouldn't hurt your customs" [216–18]) seem merely to be further examples of "othering" and "differentiating" strategies. In fact, his presence is far from invisible: clumsily, he sets up his interviews, organizes the background lighting, and even asks for a stand-in once he realizes that the swami is too feeble-looking to have any appeal on TV.

I want to finish with one more postcolonial example: Nadine Gordimer's *Burger's Daughter* (1979). Gordimer, like Achebe and Narayan, closes her novel with the inclusion of a Western perspective towards her predominantly non-Western story. For most of the novel the reader identifies with Rosa Burger as she struggles to compose a whole and unified self amid the pieces and fragments of identities that impinge on her: as a daughter to a celebrated member of the Communist party in South Africa, as a lover of a free-floating and wealthy white liberal, as a nurse at Baragwanath Hospital, where she helps to treat the victims of the 1976 Soweto uprisings, and as an increasingly active opponent of the Pretorian government, which eventually has her imprisoned. The novel closes with her letter from

jail delivered to a family friend in the south of France: the letter,
Gordimer writes, "bore the stamp of the Prisons Department in Pretoria
but this aroused no interest in the handsome postman who stopped
in for a Pernod when he delivered the mail, because he could not
read English and did not know where Pretoria was" (361). Furthermore,
what finally prevents the letter's recipient, Madame Bagnelli, from
fully understanding and appreciating the letter is that one of its crucial
lines has been censored by the South African prison authorities. The
novel's last sentence, ominously, reads: "Madame Bagnelli was never
able to make it out" (361).

My fear is that we are blinded by the same combination of
ethnocentrism and ideological censorship so that we are not able to
"make out" what is issuing from non-Western countries and that this
inability, in turn, is deafening us to the multicultural voices amongst
us. Surely, Achebe, Narayan, and Gordimer plead with us not to be
like the French postman, the American James J. Malone, or the English
District Commissioner—not to look for easy closure when looking at
non-Western texts and cultures. "The foreigner is within me, hence
we are all foreigners," declares Julia Kristeva (1991, 192). The point is
that we must now find better ways to talk across the spaces between
readers, texts, and cultures. We might find that we are not so much
talking to "the other" as we are to parts of ourselves that have lain
undiscovered and unarticulated.

Works Cited

Achebe, Chinua. 1959. *Things Fall Apart.* New York: Fawcett.

Cliff, Michelle. 1988. "A Journey into Speech." In *The Graywolf Annual Five:
    Multicultural Literacy,* edited by Rick Simonson and Scott Walker, 57–62.
    Saint Paul: Graywolf Press.

Clifford, James. 1988. *The Predicament of Culture: Twentieth Century Ethnog-
    raphy, Literature, and Art.* Harvard: Harvard University Press.

Elbow, Peter. 1981. *Writing with Power: Techniques for Mastering the Writing
    Process.* New York: Oxford University Press.

Gordimer, Nadine. 1979. *Burger's Daughter.* London: Penguin.

Kristeva, Julia. 1991. *Strangers to Ourselves,* translated by Leon S. Roudiez.
    New York: Columbia University Press.

Narayan, R. K. 1958. *The Guide.* London: Penguin.

Pattison, Robert. 1982. *On Literacy: The Politics of the Word from Homer to the
    Age of Rock.* Oxford: Oxford University Press.

Rushdie, Salman. 1989. Interview in *Newsletter on Intellectual Freedom* 38:
    106–14.

Said, Edward. 1984. *The World, the Text, and the Critic.* London: Faber.

Sarris, Greg. 1990. "Story-telling in the Classroom: Crossing Vexed Chasms." *College English* 52: 169–84.

Walker, Alice. 1983. *In Search of Our Mothers' Gardens*. New York: Harvest/ Harcourt Brace Jovanovich.

10 Walter Mitty in China: Teaching American Fiction in an Alien Culture

H. W. Matalene
University of South Carolina, Columbia

Roland Barthes once remarked of narrative that it "is simply there like life itself . . . international, transhistorical, transcultural." Elaborating for Barthes, Hayden White goes on to say that "we have relatively [little] difficulty *understanding* a story coming from another culture, however exotic that culture may appear to us. [For] as Barthes says, 'narrative . . . is *translatable* without fundamental damage' in a way that a lyric poem or a philosophical discourse is not" (1981, 1–2).

The error of Barthes's international, transcultural, translatable view of narrative has been apparent to Laura Bohannan (1966), John F. Povey (1972), Bruce Pattison (1972), J. R. Gladstone (1972), Albert H. Marckwardt (1978), Catherine Wallace (1986), Peter Strevens (1987), and many others, who, lacking the innocence of the celebrated European theoretician, have seen narrative from the perspective of the low-prestige ESL classroom. In the fall of 1982, having just begun teaching American fiction at Shanxi University in the People's Republic of China, I, too, learned how culture-bound narrative is. Peng Jian, the leader of the third-year class, came up to me perplexed about the next assignment, which he and his classmates, with characteristic diligence, had already read. I quote him exactly: "We can *translate* the story," he said, never having heard of Barthes or White, "but we cannot *understand* it." And he asked, "Why did the author write the story?" At the question, I had a moment of icy terror. But I finally saw that Peng Jian could not imagine a set of cultural and historical circumstances to which the writing of such a story might be a possible response, and within which the behavior of the story's characters might make sense. Hence, to my own astonishment, I came to devote four classroom hours, a whole week, to presenting a classic American short story only 2,500 words long—"The Secret Life of Walter Mitty," by James Thurber.

124

I had assigned the story, which might seem an unduly sexist and culturally chauvinistic choice, first, because it was one of the few I *could* assign, not having grasped before leaving South Carolina how hard it would be to find a decent collection of American fiction in a provincial Chinese university and then get copies of the chosen texts into the hands of three hundred students. But chiefly, I assigned "The Secret Life of Walter Mitty" because the Four Modernizations were much in the air at Shanxi University in 1982. Thurber's story speaks directly to the pursuit of happiness and self-esteem through science and industrialization—the agonizing project of self-transformation on which one of the world's proudest peasant civilizations has been bent ever since her military humiliations at the hands of the British in 1842, and of their Japanese imitators in 1895.

In asking me why Thurber had written "The Secret Life of Walter Mitty," Peng Jian had put his finger squarely on the chief problem that Chinese university students have with American fiction. For the best of them, translation only becomes a problem when authors, often in passages of dialogue, shift to colloquial idioms or change spellings to represent dialect. I made a point of glossing such matters as soon as we came upon them. But as Peng Jian knew, translating is not necessarily understanding. He was asking me to describe American culture as I know it: to tell the class all the things that no American critic of Thurber would ever dream of telling a roomful of American readers of "The Secret Life of Walter Mitty." Some of these nuggets of American criticism he might be able to find in the Shanxi University library, where, in 1982, the collection was still being recatalogued and reshelved in the wake of the Cultural Revolution. But Peng Jian knew that memorizing what American critics think the American laity need to know in order to grasp an American author still leaves a Chinese— even if fluent in English—far from knowing what that American author counts on readers to know if they are to respond as he or she might hope. In the terms that Reed Dasenbrock has borrowed in this volume from Donald Davidson, Peng Jian had encountered the inadequacy of his classmates' "prior theory" to the task of interpreting Thurber. The few for whom the "site of learning" was between them and Thurber's text felt their "interpretive charity" toward Thurber threatened. Their leader, Peng Jian, was asking me for additional information that might permit the construction of a "passing theory" powerful enough to both save their sense of themselves as charitable interpreters and to account for the merely translatable mysteries of Thurber's story.

Those mysteries are instantly apparent. For instance, as "The Secret Life of Walter Mitty" opens, Thurber plunges his readers into one of the now-famous daydreams of heroism that constitute the secret life of the little bourgeois named in the title. As he drives "on toward Waterbury," Walter Mitty pushes the car "up to fifty-five" while he imagines that he is a navy commander flying a "huge . . . eight-engined . . . hydroplane" through a gathering storm (1945, 34). To me, this bit of setting is instantly, but almost subliminally, meaningful. When Thurber's story was written just before World War II, I was a child in New York City, sometimes spending weekends with school-mates whose families had country retreats in Connecticut, near places like Waterbury, which (in those days) was not yet fully tied-in to the great Megalopolis by parkways, turnpikes, and interstate highways. I can close my eyes and see what going fifty-five on Mitty's road to Waterbury was like. I imagine farms, hills, village storefronts and gas stations; autumn-tinted woods flashing by on either side of the winding, two-lane country road, divided by its solid and broken lines, that lay open before Mitty's rushing car. Fifty-five, then, was not yet the tame, gas-saving speed limit that American drivers on the interstates have come to disdain since the OPEC petroleum crisis of 1973. It was too fast, as Mitty's terrifying wife reminds him. Of her, more later. Right now, my point is that because I have led a relatively privileged, originally Northeastern, beginning-to-belong, American life, Thurber's mention of "Waterbury" places Mitty for me not only geographically, but socially and historically. He is a denizen of nascent suburbia—the very personification of "bourgeois." Hence, cued by the mention of "Waterbury," I begin to see why the story was written.

But what could going "fifty-five" on the road to "Waterbury" mean to Peng Jian, who passed his childhood in China during the Great Proletarian Cultural Revolution? He is the son of one of my Shanxi colleagues, important enough, I am sure, to have been chauffeured about Taiyüan (the seat of the province's government and university) with his father, on special occasions, in one of the university's Shanghai sedans. But he has probably never driven an automobile himself. Even if he guesses that "fifty-five," idiomatically, means "fifty-five *miles per hour*," and even if he converts miles to kilometers so that he can visualize a speed almost twice that of a modern Chinese express train, the Waterbury road he imagines cannot help being very different from the one Thurber counted on readers of the *New Yorker* to envision in 1940. I will be lucky, as a teacher, if Peng Jian's imagined road to Waterbury happens to pass a white, New England church he once saw on a postcard or in a paperback from the Cultural Attaché at the U.S. Embassy in Beijing. More likely, Peng Jian's road will be lined with willows, through which (across fields hoed by a thousand hands) appear the rammed-earth walls of Shanxi villages. His road will be crowded with pedestrians, cyclists, occasional trucks and buses. There will be convoys of young men (faces turned from the blowing dust) straining against shoulder harnesses, pulling the winter's fuel into town. On his way to Waterbury, Peng Jian's Mitty will pass dozens of staring, turbaned peasants perched atop donkey carts heaped high with cabbages. To get through to town, his driver must sometimes pull way over to the left, leaning on the horn to intimidate the oncoming and warn those about to be run down. Fifty-five on Peng Jian's imagined road, as my teacher's imagination imagines it, would be positively genocidal. Mitty is enormously privileged to be on this road in an automobile at all. His ride could never be a chore of settled, middle-class life from which one might plausibly escape into day-dreams. Even for Walter Mitty, there would be real adventure on the road to Waterbury that Peng Jian might visualize as he reads—translating but not understanding.

And what about the "huge . . . eight-engined . . . hydroplane" of the first daydream? In Mitty's day, Americans like Howard Hughes were, indeed, experimenting with prototypes of such flying juggernauts. But modern China has not yet entered Mitty's day. My family and I enjoyed but one domestic flight in China; but it was a moment much like many others for us, when the plane (a venerable Russian copy of the DC-3) finally wobbled to a stop, going "pocketa-pocketa-pocketa" just like all the mystifying mechanical marvels in Walter Mitty's secret life, beside the one-room terminal building outside Taiyüan (a city of two and a half million people). But routine though our arrival may have been to us, it was something of a milestone in the life of the young colleague in English dispatched by the foreign language de-partment with a car and chauffeur to fetch us safely back within the walls of Shanxi University. He was a university graduate in his mid-twenties, yet never until that instant had he been face to face with a real airplane. He had, of course, seen many pictured airplanes; but it was clearly something else again for a child of Shanxi Province actually to be able to walk out on the tarmac and feel China's future fold him in beneath one of its competent, aluminum wings. Machines that go "pocketa-pocketa-pocketa," representing competencies alien to his own linguistically competent mind, embodied my young Chinese colleague's hopes for a richer life under the Four Modernizations. Such machines were not mysterious, alienating threats to his worth as a person, as they are to Mitty and to the many creatures of the American suburb, office, and library who have seen themselves in Mitty ever since Thurber put him on paper.

My point has been, simply, that if (after translating it) Chinese students are to begin understanding American literature, they must have a great deal of help. I went to China expecting to have to find my way across a considerable cultural and ideological gulf. My teaching there benefited immeasurably from the six-week orientation to China's language, culture, and history which my family and I were given by our colleagues in Chinese studies at the University of South Carolina and by the Shanxi scholars then studying on the Columbia campus. But only when I got to China and actually began taking in her sensations, sometimes savoring and cherishing them, and sometimes (as the Chinese themselves do) struggling to scrub them off, hawk them up, and spit them out—only then did I begin to anticipate the kinds of things I would need to dwell upon to help Chinese students achieve "interpretive charity" with a selection of American short stories.

In my Shanxi classes, what mattered about me was not whatever erudite "exam-knowledge" I possessed about the events, personalities, and -*isms* of American literary history. What really mattered was the fact that I was the only person in the room with a knowledge not based entirely on Chinese television and *The People's Daily* of the differences between China and America. Most of my four hours on Mitty went into explaining differences of material culture, and attitudes toward material culture—making it clear that mental imagery and expectations picked up along the road back to Shanxi University from the Taiyüan airport are simply not transferrable to Thurber's road to Waterbury.

I tried also to anticipate and illuminate differences between an ability to respond to English mastered in a language classroom in China and an ability to respond to English picked up, from birth, in America's homes, streets, schools, workplaces, and public media of information and entertainment. For instance, I doubted very much that many of my students would be smiling inwardly, as I was, upon finishing Thurber's opening sentences:

> "We're going through!" The Commander's voice was like thin ice
> breaking. He wore his full-dress uniform, with the heavily braided
> white cap pulled down rakishly over one cold gray eye. "We can't
> make it, sir. It's spoiling for a hurricane, if you ask me." "I'm not
> asking you, Lieutenant Berg," said the Commander. (34)

Having grown up on real American conversations and John Wayne movies, I can sense parody here right away. I can hear and see clichés of colloquial usage and popular culture running amok. The more I think about a "voice like thin ice breaking," the crazier it seems. Is the simile saying that the Commander and his crew are "on thin ice"? Or that the Commander's decision, at last, "breaks the ice"? Or that the decision was "like thin ice breaking" because it seemed to the crew to be committing them to a cold and watery grave? Or that, more literally, the Commander's voice really did have the sickening crackle of "thin ice breaking?" In my American ear two clichés and a variety of inept metaphors fight each other to a semantic draw here, leaving me without a clear meaning but alerting me that something funny is going on. This did not happen in ears that had heard only Chinese classroom English, stiff and formal, tending toward British pronunciations and usages. What, after all, is funny about the plight of an officer and his crew whose only remaining hope is to risk going "though the worst storm in twenty years of Navy flying" (34) before it becomes totally impossible?

Then, there is the matter of the Commander's appearance. In the People's Liberation Army (PLA) of 1982, there were officers and enlisted personnel, but finer discriminations of rank were still frowned upon, and one had to look closely at all the red-starred caps and green fatigues with red collar tabs to see who was who. Officers were distinguished only by having four pockets on their jackets instead of two. By PLA standards, all Western military people are dreadful fops to begin with, and it was therefore necessary for me to explain, in a Shanxi classroom, the absurdity of a navy commander on duty in a crisis—not at a parade or a social gathering—who affects a "full-dress uniform" while blithely violating the regulations for wearing his cap. Thurber counts on his readers to know that general officers in the American military may be indulged in idiosyncratic wearings, and even in customized redesignings of the uniform, from the private's shirt in which Grant received Lee at Appomattox Courthouse to George Patton's riding habit and nickel-plated revolvers in Mitty's own epoch. But American readers will surely smile at a mere field-grade officer, like the navy commander of Mitty's first daydream, who takes the dress regulations so lightly.

As for the "cold gray eye" over which Commander Mitty's heavily braided cap is raked, there is something funny about it too. The "cold gray eye" is a cliché in American English. But a gray eye of any temperature is a great rarity among the twenty-two million people of Shanxi Province. And then there is the old wheeze of "I'm not asking you, Lieutenant Berg." Can this be serious? Again, something funny is going on in Thurber's first sentences that a Chinese translator with no understanding of American life simply cannot "get."

And how about the names? Should I count on my Shanxi class to hear that there is something vaguely British or Irish about "Mitty," a name Thurber has coined, or to know that "Berg," a real name, sounds German or Jewish? China is, of course, bent on tolerating national minorities of her own, though the Han Chinese have historically been terrible racists, looking upon Europeans, for instance, as "long-nosed foreign devils." But (apart from the plight of American blacks, pitied in propaganda, but privately despised in China, just as they often are here) what can I expect my students to know about the relative prestige in American society of a national origin such as that suggested by the name "Berg"?

Its name tells nothing about the social standing of a Chinese family of the dominant Han nationality. There are surprisingly few names for all the millions of Han families. They speak, for instance, of China's "Hundred Great Names," meaning the hundred-odd monosyllables that mark a family as belonging to the Han nation; and in asking the name of a stranger who is visibly a Han Chinese, they have always asked (since long before Communism), regardless of the stranger's visible social status, "What is your *worthy* surname?" Things are clearly different in America. To me, sensing what's in American names, at least for the frequently anti-Semitic Northeastern WASPs and their emulators to whom the *New Yorker* chiefly addresses its stories and advertisements, it is meaningful that Commander Mitty talks *down* to somebody named "Berg."

And the names continue to be meaningful throughout Thurber's story. In the second daydream (34–35), where the world-famous surgeon Walter Mitty saves "the millionaire banker, Wellington McMillan, . . . a close personal friend of Roosevelt," Mitty takes over in the operating room from two Waterbury doctors, and from two famous specialists, "Dr. Remington from New York and Mr. Pritchard-Mitford from London." I know that millionaire bankers seldom thought highly of Franklin Roosevelt, whom they were far more likely to regard as a class traitor. And I know, as my Shanxi students did not, that "Remington" is best-known in America as a brand name for small firearms and ammunition. To me, therefore, "Dr. Remington" suggests that Walter Mitty imagines this specialist, like a rifle, as having greater range, accuracy, and impact than either of the local sawbones, Renshaw and Benbow, possess.

Furthermore, because I have lived in England and studied British culture, I can see Mitty's status-conscious, WASP imagination so transfixed with Things British as to look with contempt on Americans less accomplished in anglophilia than he takes pride in being himself.

For instance, he knows that British surgeons, unlike ordinary physicians, are called "Mister"—not "Doctor." And he can imagine himself one-up in anglophilia even on the great Remington, who is such a parochial Yankee dolt that he calls Pritchard-Mitford simply "Mitford"—thus failing to respect the snobbish, class implications of hyphenated English names, as most Americans noting this peculiarity also probably would. In fact, I have heard the English themselves joke about people with names like "Rice-Pudding." The names tip me off that Mitty's secret life is dominated by the emulative, anglophile pop culture of his day, in which, for instance, the great male dancer was still the apparent WASP playboy, Fred Astaire, and no "ethnic" working-class dancer like a John Travolta or a Gregory Hines could yet expect to star in a film (though a "Bojangles" Robinson might do a cameo appearance in one).

Along with America's fascination with machinery, the emulative anglophilia of American popular culture is Thurber's theme in "The Secret Life of Walter Mitty." It is no accident, therefore, that in the third daydream (36), when he escapes from American brand names like "Kleenex" and "Squibb's," Mitty's anglophilia arms him with the huge, obviously British, Webley-Vickers 50.80 automatic pistol. Mitty is now on trial for the murder of one "Gregory Fitzhurst," evidently a wronger of beautiful women, the prefix of whose name suggests to me, but not to the speaker of Chinese classroom English, that he is something of a bastard—or, to insult Fitzhurst with a rough Chinese equivalent of "bastard," a "son of a turtle."

As for Thurber's treatment of women, nothing much bothered my Chinese students. Mitty's shrewish wife was merely an amusing foreign aberration. Once, at a meeting of Shanxi University's English Club, American divorce rates became the topic, and my wife and I were amazed at a request that we entertain the gathering by improvising a skit representing a "typical" American marital quarrel. We declined, not entirely from shyness about our histrionic abilities.

John F. Povey's account of the response to Mrs. Rip van Winkle in his ESL class reminds me very much of my Shanxi students' response to Mrs. Walter Mitty:

> "If this story were told in your country, would it come out roughly the same in its characters and motivation?" [Povey] questioned. "No," said the Latin Americans, "Our women are satisfied with their position at home, and we have no stories of this henpecking." . . . There were several other responses from students in the same tone. "A Chinese wife is obedient to her husband. Wives in Taiwan don't take part in social activities at all." (1972, 190)

The same goes for mainland China as we experienced it in 1982. Wives did not attend the many official banquets to which my family and I were invited, and on our one officially arranged visit to a peasant household, the men sat down with us and our escorts and translators, while the women came and went between us and another building where they cooked some twenty dishes and ate what was left when we had finished. After all, Confucius said that "women and people of low birth are very hard to deal with. If you are friendly with them, they get out of hand, and if you keep your distance, they resent it" (1938, 216–217).

Much of the best in recent Asian American literature has been written by women such as Maxine Hong Kingston, Betty Bao Lord, and Cathy Song about the subordination of women in Chinese culture, which Communism has not succeeded in legislating away. But the colonizing West cannot take credit for making Chinese women, at last, feel this subordination as pain. Its pathos has been a theme in China's own literature since *The Book of Odes,* long before Confucius; and with or without the pain, the subordination goes on.

In the end, humiliated by his wife as usual, Thurber's hero enters his secret life for a last time:

> He put his shoulders back and his heels together. "To hell with the handkerchief," said Walter Mitty scornfully. He took one last drag on his cigarette and snapped it away. Then, with that faint, fleeting smile playing about his lips, he faced the firing squad; erect and motionless, proud and disdainful, Walter Mitty the Undefeated, inscrutable to the last. (37)

In China, whether by the Guomindang or the Communists, political executions have been handled somewhat differently. And I talked about this difference too. In this last resort of philosophical conviction, this ritual of sacrifice to sanctify ideology, the True Believers in China are thrust to their knees before another, who then blows their brains out from behind with a pistol. A bill may be sent to victims' families for the cost of the bullet.

In 1982, the Cultural Revolution was over. The Gang of Four were gone. Mao Zedong was dead. For the time being the executions occasionally announced on the big bulletin board in downtown Taiyüan were of common criminals. Still, the so-called Ten Years of Chaos between 1966 and 1976 remained on everyone's mind at Shanxi University. Everyone told stories of persecution and martyrdom; everyone hoped that bygones were bygones, but when I was in Taiyüan no one was yet positive that China's quest for Communism would not again turn to human sacrifice.

That was before "June Fourth," as some of those students, now in the United States, refer to the Tienanmen massacre of 1989. In 1919, it had been "May Fourth," in 1925 "May Thirtieth," in 1935 "December Ninth," and we could go on at some length listing the bloody dates in China's long history of student activism against imperial, nationalist, and communist governments (Spence 1991, 117–23, 183–86; Snow 1983, 100–105). I therefore want to close by reflecting upon the trouble my Shanxi students had not only with Mitty, but with stories by Sherwood Anderson, Conrad Aiken, and Ernest Hemingway in which the protagonists were rebellious young people.

They wanted to know why these other stories were written, too. Essentially, they were acknowledging that they had grown up Chinese and that "interpretive charity" toward characters who were growing up American was hard to develop. Despite their Marxist veneer, they came from Confucian, not Oedipal families. They grew up in a culture in which the old age of another is an automatic sign that deference is appropriate and that kind, paternal wisdom is to be expected in return. Reading Anderson, Aiken, and Hemingway, my Shanxi students had trouble conceiving that there was a culture in which unfocused disregard for well-meaning parents, teachers, and other authority figures might seem like "normal" adolescent behavior and need not be felt as criminal, insane, or simply inconceivable.

It may easily be imagined that teaching in such a culture is an absolutely irresistible experience. Following their hearts' custom, a busload of students and colleagues came to the Taiyüan railroad station to see my wife and daughter and me off, pressing their palms against ours on the other side of the glass when we had boarded the train. I shall never forget it.

But China's Confucian way of reading its generation gap has never been without problems. Long before Communism, as Jonathan Spence and many others have shown, China's changes of dynasty have been savage indeed; and the reading of Western literature during the past century has played a part in the Chinese Revolution (Spence 1981; 1990, 302–303, 473, 570, 623). If one wishes to teach American literature to young people in China, then, one must remember how much closer to the "real world" the literary classroom is in China than it is here in the United States. Among other things, Mao Zedong was a poet and critic—a reader of translations of Mill, Montesquieu, Rousseau, and even Herbert Spencer (Spence 1990, 303). Literate China reads the art and criticism of the literary intelligentsia, wants to be told what it means, and alludes to classic literature constantly in public, political discourse. Literate America does not do this. Ronald

Reagan's speech writers trusted us to recognize the words of Clint Eastwood, but I am not holding my breath until I hear unidentified phrases from Gwendolyn Brooks or Michael Harper in an address by an American presidential candidate.

Moreover, wanting to be told what a text means is not the same as wanting to discover—for oneself, and in dialogue with any other reader who cares to discuss the matter—the "passing theory" that seems to work best on this text at this sitting. In Reed Dasenbrock's terms, "the scene of learning" for Chinese students tends to be between them and "The Master"—not between them and the text of which their teacher is simply, for now, a better credentialed reader. In the Confucian *Analects,* saying after saying and book after book, the scene of learning is between Confucius and his students—not between his students and the passages from history or *The Book of Odes* about which The Master speaks. And no matter how hard I tried, some twenty-five hundred years after Confucius, I found it almost universally impossible to shift the scene of learning from the students' involvement with me to the students' involvement with the texts I assigned.

In class, for instance, apropos of Hemingway's "Soldier's Home," I could not get anyone to do anything but praise the patriotism and valor of Harold Krebs, the protagonist. No one would talk about the fact that World War I has emptied Krebs of feeling and purpose. So I talked about it. And on my way back to the Foreign Experts' Building for lunch, I was accosted, one-on-one, by an agitated young PLA officer who wanted to know why American intellectuals hate soldiers. "I think it is a fine thing to be a soldier and defend one's country," he said.

To be allowed to interpret literature in a culture where, for thousands of years, "passing theories" about classic texts have not only been produced and learned, but enforced and obeyed, is to be given a tremendous judicial responsibility. It is to be handed a potential power over life and death that few American English teachers can imagine and that no one in my acquaintance has ever knowingly sought by becoming an English teacher.

In 1982, I was too naïve to sense that I had that power—that I was teaching bright, friendly, patriotic young people new ideas for which to kill and be killed by Deng Xiaoping's soldiers. I should have known. But I had gone to China to see for myself if Communism was as bad as the American capitalist state and press had always claimed. Unaware that I was being recorded, I was merely surprised when an official of the provincial Bureau of Higher Education who had never been in my classroom complimented me on my teaching, some of which he had heard on tape. And I was merely amused when I heard from the campus grapevine that my students were being told in their required political meetings to "be polite to Professor Matalene, but beware the sugar-coated bullets of imperialist ideology that lie hidden in his readings and lectures."

Until "June Fourth," I had wanted very much to go back to Shanxi and see how my old students were getting along under the Four Modernizations. But there was no sugar on the bullets of "June Fourth." And an old Shanxi friend now studying democracy in the United States—a rising young party member now in his thirties, who has been junketed all over the world with Taiwanese money to meet with "June Fourth" leaders in exile—assures me that those who raised the Statue of Liberty in Tienanmen Square are all Chinese to the core: that if they want power, they must expect to take the paternalist role of The Master; that their loyalties are to persons rather than to institutions for the changing, interpretation, and enforcement of laws; and that there is not one genuinely democratic soul among them.

There will no doubt be theoretically sophisticated readers of these pages who will accuse me of not having come to grips with my own cultural chauvinism. They will charge me with failure to privilege the Chinese "other," at least for the sake of argument and insight into myself. A few, innocent of history, may even feel that I have "bashed" the last, best hope that a whole new culture, peaceful, plentiful, and just, may yet be deduced, administratively, from the abstractions of Marxism. I would end with three reminders for such readers. First, large-scale cultural change is not a matter of academic play—of Derridean deconstruction's willing suspension of common sense. As Henry H. H. Remak has put it, speaking of the problems of Old World immigrants to the New World, "You have to remain something before and until you become something else" (1984, 77). Then, I would remind such readers that the most committed and dedicated "China-bashers" since 1949 have been the Chinese themselves and that the bashing has been of millions of bodies and not just of concepts and feelings. There is a "revolution," I think, inherent in capitalism's contradictions; its color, however, is not red, but green. The time must come when best-practice technology will have to be judged not by accountants, but by epidemiologists, ecologists, and engineers. And finally, I would recommend to my critics the shock of teaching fiction in China. I am betting that, after my accusers' return, we will renew, together, the favorite conversation of all the foreign experts I met there: the conversation about whether you think what has happened to you is even remotely like what I think has happened to me.

136   H. W. Matalene

Works Cited

Bohannan, Laura. 1966. "Shakespeare in the Bush." *Natural History* 75(August-September): 28–33.

Confucius. 1938. *The Analects of Confucius,* translated by Arthur Waley. New York: Vintage Books.

Gladstone, J. R. 1972. "Language and Culture." In *Teaching English as a Second Language: A Book of Readings,* 2nd ed., edited by Harold B. Allen and Russell N. Campbell, 192–95. New York: McGraw-Hill.

Marckwardt, Albert H. 1978. *The Place of Literature in the Teaching of English as a Second or Foreign Language.* An East-West Center Book. Honolulu: University Press of Hawaii.

Pattison, Bruce. 1972. "The Literature Lesson." In *Teaching English as a Second Language: A Book of Readings,* 2nd ed., edited by Harold B. Allen and Russell N. Campbell, 195–98. New York: McGraw-Hill.

Povey, John F. 1972. "Literature in TESL Programs: The Language and the Culture." In *Teaching English as a Second Language: A Book of Readings,* 2nd ed., edited by Harold B. Allen and Russell N. Campbell, 185–91. New York: McGraw-Hill.

Remak, Henry H. H. 1984. "European Romanticism and Contemporary American Counterculture." In *Romanticism and Culture: A Tribute to Morse Peckham and a Bibliography of His Work,* edited by H. W. Matalene, 71–95. Columbia, SC: Camden House.

Snow, Edgar. 1983. *Edgar Snow's China: A Personal Account of the Chinese Revolution Compiled from the Writings of Edgar Snow.* New York: Vintage.

Spence, Jonathan D. 1981. *The Gate of Heavenly Peace: The Chinese and Their Revolution, 1895–1980.* New York: Viking Press.

———. 1990. *The Search for Modern China.* New York: Norton.

Strevens, Peter. 1987. "Cultural Barriers to Language Learning." In *Discourse Across Cultures: Strategies in World Englishes,* edited by Larry E. Smith, 169–78. New York: Prentice-Hall.

Thurber, James. 1945. "The Secret Life of Walter Mitty." In *The Thurber Carnival,* 34–37. New York: Harper.

Wallace, Catherine. 1986. *Learning to Read in a Multicultural Society: The Social Context of Second Language Literacy.* Oxford: Pergamon Institute of English.

White, Hayden. 1981. "The Value of Narrativity in the Representation of Reality." In *On Narrative,* edited by W. J. T. Mitchell, 1–23. Chicago: University of Chicago Press.

III Texts

Teachers of literature once considered "the text" a stable artifact. They talked about it as an autonomous creation whose meaning could be decoded by careful explication. They also talked about certain individual texts as part of an approved arrangement, the canon, whose meaning contained the great tradition of Western thought.

Recent critical debates have questioned the usefulness of such talk. Robert Scholes in *Textual Power* argues that instead of teaching autonomous texts we need to teach *textuality*, the notion that "every poem, play, and story is a text related to others, both verbal pre-texts and social subtexts, and all manner of post-texts including [our] own responses" (1985, 20). And Catharine Stimpson speaks for a growing number of teachers when she argues that the static, immobile canon must be reconstructed with new texts that reveal "a multiplicity of traditions carrying on together—sometimes harmoniously, sometimes not" (1988, 28).

Although the seven essays in this section approach the issue from different perspectives, each asks us to rethink our understanding of texts. What texts should we teach? How should we teach them? And in what ways must we connect them to the larger matrix of culture?

The first three essays examine the value of contextual knowledge to an understanding of individual texts. Sandra Jamieson suggests that an author creates an interpretative community as "a model for her reader and for the actual community the writer appears to seek." She goes on to demonstrate how "ruptures" in three African American texts alert readers to expand their contextual knowledge. Chauncey A. Ridley explains how the knowledge of African mythology and African American folklore can help readers contextualize the apparently outrageous violence in Toni Morrison's *Beloved*. Pancho Savery analyzes the history and politics of African American music, particularly bebop, to reveal the cultural subtext at work in James Baldwin's "Sonny's Blues."

The next three authors introduce us to new texts, encouraging us to see how their inclusion enriches our understanding of the crosscurrents within our culture. David Leiwei Li asserts that the exclusive focus on Maxine Hong Kingston's *The Woman Warrior* as "the ultimate representative of Asian American creativity" disregards "the fundamental relatedness of ethnic literary production." In his review of the poetry, fiction, and drama written by other contemporary Asian Americans, he explores the recurring theme of "filiation and affiliation." Renny Christopher points out that the emerging canon of literature on the Vietnam war is almost exclusively "male . . . [and] Euro-American." Because the war was a "shared historical experience," she argues that we need to balance our understanding by reading Vietnamese American texts. Suzanne Evertsen Lundquist examines the strategies Egyptian novelist Naguib Mahfouz uses to recreate and reinterpret Jewish, Christian, and Islamic sacred texts in his engaging narrative *The Children of Gebelawi.*

The last author investigates the text of Native American writer Leslie Marmon Silko. Patricia Riley suggests that Silko's experiments with writing and storytelling revise our traditional understanding of the text. She traces the cultural history of "mixed bloods," then turns to *Ceremony* to illustrate the tension between interpreter and informer in Silko's status as "storyteller."

Works Cited

Scholes, Robert. 1985. *Textual Power: Literary Theory and the Teaching of English.* New Haven: Yale University Press.

Stimpson, Catharine R. 1988. "Is There a Core in This Curriculum?" *Change* 20(March-April): 26–31.

11 Text, Context, and Teaching Literature by African American Women

Sandra Jamieson
Colgate University

Deborah McDowell's call for a textual and contextual approach to literature by African American women precipitates a pedagogical dilemma for many teachers of cultural and cross-cultural literature: classes we once devoted simply to texts must now also teach their historical and cultural contexts, and finding a satisfactory balance is not easy. Traditional academic training would have us adopt the position of "informed interpreters," but, as Reed Way Dasenbrock observes in "Teaching Multicultural Literature" (Chapter 3, this volume), such a strategy is neither pedagogically practical nor theoretically desirable in this case. If we place an overemphasis on context, we will render the text more radically "other" and thus less accessible as literature, leaving an opening for the sociological readings Robert Stepto describes (1979). But if we reject the role of "expert," we leave our students with insufficient context, which will inevitably produce misreadings and prevent them from entering into the interpretive community of the text, encouraging them, instead, to ignore differences and understand these texts purely in relation to their own lives. The difficulty of creating a balance can seem overwhelming.

Dasenbrock argues that we do not need to look outside of the text for contextual knowledge. Instead, we must trust the writer to give us the assistance we need; however, this would seem to imply a unified "author" entirely in control of her text and a cultural context which permits her to be honest about her intentions and meanings. As Mary Poovey shows in "Cultural Criticism" (Chapter 1, this volume), such assumptions limit the possibilities of cultural criticism. But the text can assist us if we modify Dasenbrock's advice with Poovey's insistence that we "ask how race, gender, class, and ethnicity *work*—how they produce and disrupt meanings" and explore the "traces this larger social formation produces on individual texts." A focus on both explanation and disruption allows us to develop a method in which the text itself determines how much context we must teach.

Novels by African American women writers frequently fail to provide the contextual assistance that Dasenbrock finds in African novels. And this failure frequently occurs at what turns out to be key moments in the text. Indeed, one could argue that key moments in these texts are almost always marked by the absence of the informaiton or explanation readers would need to make sense of them. These ruptures seem to call for the application of contextual information, especially as prior to the ruptures the texts have taught us how to attend to their patterns and rhythms so that we will be sharply aware of the interruption and thus "hear" the call for context. Thomas Cassidy argues that Janie's story to Pheoby in *Their Eyes Were Watching God* serves to "create the very community [in Eatonville] which the telling of the story assumes as a prerequisite" (1990, 238). But I would expand this observation to apply to many texts by African American women, and it is precisely this ability to create the interpretive communities required by their texts through those texts themselves which allows them to teach us how to balance text and context.

Many African American women's novels center upon a woman telling her story to a textual audience, usually to explain an event which can only be evaluated when its entire history is known and understood. As the woman tells her story, she teaches her listener how to understand it, and in so doing creates an interpretive community which is then a model for her reader and for the actual community the writer appears to seek. Approaching these texts as the fictional interpreter does—using the information provided by the text to help us understand it and expanding our contextual knowledge when we do not understand—renders the texts accessible to us and indicates what contextual knowledge is required. The moments when our interpretation fails occur when the text either suddenly ceases to explain an event or assertion or seems to overexplain it. Expanding our historical and cultural knowledge in response to these ruptures in the text will enable us to both understand them and explore what they reveal about the communities and identities constructed in and by the text. Harriet Jacobs's *Incidents in the Life of a Slave Girl: Written by Herself* (1987), Zora Neale Hurston's *Their Eyes Were Watching God* (1978), and Toni Morrison's *The Bluest Eye* (1972) provide excellent examples of how such an interpretive and pedagogical strategy can be used to read and teach texts from a variety of historical moments.

The slaves who escaped to the North in the mid-nineteenth century faced the double task of creating identities for themselves as "free" people and of creating communities within which to celebrate that freedom. Harriet Jacobs appears to have found her new home in the North considerably less free than she had imagined, and her "new" identity as active subject in control of her destiny much less accepted. Although she found patronage and support in the community of women abolitionists, her letters describing her "racial outrage," "distrust and disillusionment" with Harriet Beecher Stowe and Cornelia Willis, and her general "lack of courage to meet the criticism and ridicule of educated people" reveal that she was not entirely at ease there (Yellin 1985, 265–68). In *Incidents,* as William Andrews observes, she addressed these lacks by creating both model characters with whom her white northern readers could identify, and failed discursive relationships which they could strive to avoid. These provide teachers of cultural and cross-cultural literature warnings about textual interpretation and lessons about how we should approach the text.

Jacobs's direct address to her "reader" is her most obvious connective strategy. Her recitation of her preadolescent history is flat and seems to exist only to introduce her story; however, it reveals the differences between her two mistresses and their similar hypocrisy. The "reader" is clearly "recognized" as more humane than either mistress, and Jacobs establishes a conspiratorial relationship with "her" asserting that "could you have seen . . . could you have heard . . . could you have witnessed that scene as I saw it, you would exclaim, *Slavery is damnable*" (1987, 23). Her constant repetition of the phrase "I know of a slave who . . ." strengthens this relationship as she shares the secrets of slavery with us.

Constructed thus, the "reader" is assumed by the text to have the heart of an abolitionist. "She" too would entrust "her" baby to an escaped slave to thwart the slave catchers, as does the first Mrs. Bruce. "She" would also hide "Brent," even from an unsympathetic spouse, as does the southern "wife of a slave holder" (in what is, ironically, the only functioning interracial community in the text). If the reader is male, he approaches her text as a "respectful friend" like the Reverend Jeremiah Durham, rather than with "idle curiosity" or "contempt" (Andrews 1986, 250). But with this emphasis on respect, the reader must beware that good intentions do not cause her to act "on the slave's behalf" but against the slave's wishes, as does the second Mrs. Bruce in purchasing "Linda Brent" rather than allowing her to be her own agent of freedom.

It is this issue of agency which really forms the heart of Harriet Jacobs's story of "Linda Brent," and it is thus the issue which precipitates the major rupture in the text. The reader may be able to join the abolitionist community and react with appropriate horror at the victimization of women by the slave system, but could she accept the ex-slave as a subject with free agency and listen to her story? Moreover, could she grant the ex-slave authority over her own story? (The power of this question is revealed by the fact that it was not fully answered within critical circles until Yellin's research in the 1980s.)

After presenting herself as a helpless victim of Dr. Flint, Jacobs "switches the gender network" (Tate 1989, 109) and recounts her seduction of Mr. Sands, assuring us that "I knew what I did, and I did it with deliberate calculation" (54). This admission is accompanied by explanations of her lack of practical alternative, appeals to the reader to understand her situation, and many statements of regret. However, she also asserts that "the slave woman ought not to be judged by the same standards as others" (56), seeming to imply less regret than her protestations would have us believe. An indication of the significance of this event is Jacobs's excessive delay in relating it. After she describes Flint's whisperings, she is clearly preparing to tell us something: she speaks of her longing for someone to confide in and her inability to tell her grandmother who was "very strict on such subjects" (29) but, having built up to a fuller confession, she exclaims "my heart is so full, and my pen is so weak" (30) and changes the subject. She then includes four chapters describing "incidents" of the victimization inherent in slavery before she can return to the confession she seemed ready to make at the end of chapter five.

We can only understand the significance of her reticence, excessive apology, and interrupted narrative when we place this confession in its sociohistorical context. Thus, this is the moment in our classes when we need to provide additional information for our students. Claudia Tate stresses that it was "indeed radical, revolutionary autonomy for a woman to record [such an act of seduction] in a public document, irrespective of her social status" (1989, 109). Jacobs had cause to fear the reaction of her audience. Andrews explains that "women abolitionists tried to fire the moral indignation of their northern sisters by showing how the chattel principle had denied the slave-woman her rightful status in antebellum America's 'cult of True Womanhood'." However, their emphasis on "piety, purity, submissiveness and domesticity" led to their "reinforcement of those tenets" (1986, 241–42). These were tenets that Jacobs challenged on several levels: by seducing Sands, by appropriating Flint's letter-writing strategy and effectively manipulating him, by leveling her gaze on the community from her hidden location and, finally, as possessor of the gaze, by revealing these "secrets" and writing her own story in which she is active subject rather than passive, victimized object.

If we look back to the rupture in the narrative between chapters five and ten with this knowledge, we begin to understand the centrality of Jacobs's confession. We also see a new significance in the failed confession scenes in those interim chapters. Andrews argues that from the "trembling awe and shame" causing her to conceal the truth from Aunt Marthy, Jacobs's female readers are warned of the impediments to a free discursive relationship when "all that stood between them, in effect, was the white female reader's moral pedestal" (250). The attempt to enlist the support of Mrs. Flint provides a second challenge to the reader. Will she

> allow herself to become a discrete, isolated entity, dependent on men, for the sake of bearing male secrets with discretion? Or would she use her hard-won discernment and discretion to separate herself from patriarchal control so as to cherish and foster the confidences that maintained the sub rosa women's community? (Andrews 1986, 256)

To accept Jacobs's secret agency, the reader she imagined must unite with the women of the text against patriarchal structures. Today, the reader must understand how those structures functioned in the 1860s before she or he can understand both the rebellion and the desperation inherent in Linda Brent's actions.

At the end of *Incidents*, Brent finally "muster[s] sufficient courage" to tell her story to her daughter. She says "my pent-up feelings had often longed to pour themselves out to someone I could trust" (189), just as later she would fearfully pour them out to us. The structure of her confession to Ellen appears to be exactly that of *Incidents* itself: "I recounted my early sufferings in slavery, and told her how nearly they had crushed me. I began to tell her how they had driven me into a great sin" (188), but Ellen interrupts, revealing that she already knows, and forgives her mother unconditionally. Brent says, "she hugged me closer as she spoke, and I thanked God that the knowledge I had so much dreaded to impart had not diminished [her] . . . affection" (189). Significantly, Ellen's interruption occurs at precisely the point that Jacobs interrupts her narrative in the text: at the moment when she would reveal Brent's great sin of agency. The embrace of understanding between mother and child is the same embrace Jacobs desires from her readers once she has explained the whole story to us—but first we have to understand the context of her "great sin."

Zora Neale Hurston adopted a similar strategy in *Their Eyes Were Watching God*, where the event that Janie must explain is also one in which she exercised agency. As Janie returns to Eatonville, the people sit "in judgment" of her on their porches (1978, 10), just as a few days earlier a jury had more formally sat in judgment. In both instances they "look into . . . [her] loving Tea Cake . . . [to] see whether it was done right or not" (17, 274), but remain distant, causing Janie to wish they would "come kiss and be kissed" so that she could "sit down and tell 'em things" (18). Pheoby, her "kissin'-friend," does come and she then becomes the "ideal audience, who . . . mirrors back to her friend a faith in her power of agency" (Pryse 1985, 12) allowing Janie to tell her story to Pheoby and the reader. As the two women are embraced by the "kissing young darkness," now also part of the community of listeners (Cassidy 1990, 213), we remember Ellen's embrace of Linda Brent.

The mention of Tea Cake so long before we meet him indicates his importance in the story, and indeed, as Mary Helen Washington points out, from the moment when Tea Cake acknowledges the "privelege tuh tell yuh all about mahself" the story becomes his rather than Janie's (Washington 1987, 243). As we follow Janie through her life, we see an increase in agency from simply leaving her first husband, to publicly humiliating (and metaphorically killing) her second, and literally killing her third. However, her story justifies these first two actions while the third would seem, at least superficially, to have been unavoidable and undesirable—as the judge and jury concluded.

In the Everglades, Janie learned to "tell big stories" (Hurston 1978, 200), and this skill saves her life when she must speak for herself in court. In telling her story "she had to go way back to let them know how she and Tea Cake had been with one another. . . . She sat there and told and when she was through she hushed" (278). The story she tells to the court thus appears to be structured in exactly the same way as the story she tells Pheoby, preceded by "'tain't nothin' lak you might think. So 'tain't no use in me telling you somethin' unless Ah give you de understandin' to go 'long wid it" (19), and ending with a "finished silence" (285).

This issue of understanding appears frequently in the narrative, especially during the time "on the muck," but it is *mis*understanding that Janie fears more than death as she sits in the court room, and it is misunderstanding that caused the anger of both black communities. Janie is afraid that her listeners will conclude that "she didn't want Tea Cake and wanted him dead" (279), and thus she tries to explain the context of her actions.

Her story of life on the muck reveals the complexity of her situation and suggests why she feared being misunderstood. Indeed, this complexity has produced fierce debate among contemporary scholars about how we should interpret Tea Cake's behavior (best summarized by Jennifer Jordan, 1988). If Tea Cake is "the bee to her blossom," the realization of her childhood dream, he is also abusive and Janie's love is described as "self-crushing" (Hurston 1978, 192). Hurston tells us at the beginning that for women "the dream is the truth. Then they act and do things accordingly," calling into question the "truth" of Janie's dream relationship with Tea Cake as does the sentence preceding it: "Women forget all those things they don't want to remember, and remember everything they don't want to forget" (9). Janie seems to forget the similarity between the deaths of Tea Cake and Joe: both could have been saved by early medical attention, both accuse Janie of maliciously causing their affliction, and both die in conflict with Janie as she regains control of her life. She also seems to forget the similarities between all three of her marriages: each husband ceases to ask her opinion and requires her to be submissive, each physically abuses her, and each effectively silences and objectifies her. What she remembers is the sense of community amongst the migrant workers in the Everglades. Although she stresses her satisfaction with her life, she turns her gaze on the violent, sexist, and "color struck" nature of the community, as well as the harsh Jim Crow laws and general racism outside of the muck. (Hurston already addressed these issues in "Color Struck: A Play. Fire!!" [1926] and would return to them in "The 'Pet' Negro System" [1943], "Crazy for this Democracy" [1945], and other essays.) In these respects the muck community is not significantly different from Eatonville and, like it also, the inhabitants make the best of their situation by celebrating life, language, and each other. We can only understand the tension between what Janie remembers and what she forgets when we turn our attention to the historical and cultural context of this novel. Thus, once again, the text has indicated where we need to pause and provide our students with additional information.

Hurston's anthropological studies of African American folklore produced a wealth of "lying tales" and "big stories" and a love for the people whose stories these were, "in an era when many educated and cultured blacks prided themselves on removing all traces of their rural black origins, when a high-class 'Negro' virtue was not to 'act one's color' " (Washington 1982, 15). Thus her work was generally rejected by the community of African American writers which was focusing its attention on the "tragically colored" and, as Robert Hemenway shows, missed the complexity of her arguments (1977, 240–43). In addition, Paula Giddings (1985) shows that in its failure to either romanticize or reject black folk culture, *Their Eyes Were Watching God* fell outside of the two main political positions within the larger black community at the time of its publication. Hurston did not join W. E. B. Du Bois in the call for some self-segregation which eventually led to his resignation from the NAACP (211), but neither did she accept "assimilationist" black leaders who she claimed had "quit the race via the [white person's] tea table" (Hemenway 1977, 238). Her critique of the racism of northern liberals was generally suppressed, although few seemed to be ready to hear it anyway, especially when it sounded like praise for the South (286–300). Giddings argues that most of the more than 400,000 African Americans who migrated north in the 1930s were ready to accept the doctrine of upward mobility that became so prominent in the 1940s and to reject their roots in the rural South. In this they were encouraged by white business interests seeking to "prop up Blacks so that they would be in a position to aid the economy by consuming its goods" (238). Thus, Hurston would have been justified in fearing that by killing Tea Cake, the representative of black culture and community, and returning to her position of economic security and status in Eatonville, Janie would seem to be asserting the values of the latter and rejecting the former. Indeed, this is exactly what both black communities in the text accuse her of, and each time Janie tells her story she tells it in response to this suspicion.

Any such misunderstandings are resolved when we read Janie's story as Pheoby does. Following Pheoby's lead, the reader can grow "ten feet higher from jus' listenin' tuh" Janie (Hurston 1978, 284). But that reader is also encouraged to change things where they are unequal, participate fully, and learn from the story that "you got to *go* there tuh know there" (285). Janie has known Tea Cake's world, and "the kiss of his memory made pictures of love and light against the wall" (286). Those pictures are her dream, and this Tea Cake—the Tea Cake who was passionate, celebrated black culture, and invited Janie to join him in these things—is the one she wants to keep alive. Although she desired escape from the "mad dog" of Tea Cake's sexist rage and jealousy, she wants those judging the relationship to understand that it was only these patriarchal aspects that she wanted dead, not Tea Cake himself or the "folk" culture he represented.

Tea Cake's attitudes about work and money differentiate him from Logan Killicks and Joe Stark (as Susan Willis [1987] and others point out); however, his appropriation of their patriarchal attitudes leads to his downfall. The similar destructiveness of the values and standards of beauty determined by patriarchal white society concerns many African American women writers today. The communities portrayed by Toni Morrison are for the most part default communities which would not exist in a nonsexist, nonracist society. Their inhabitants are determined by the same patriarchal and "color struck" forces as Hurston's, but they are not saved by a folk tradition, and thus communal power assumes a negative character, as Barbara Christian (1985) has demonstrated. In many ways Morrison charts the results of the death of the black culture Tea Cake represented. A discussion of the context described above will help our students understand the complexity and importance of this distinction.

As Claudia narrates the story of Pecola's "unbeing" in *The Bluest Eye*, she adopts the tone of one reminiscing to another member of the community, and we thus become a part of that community. As such, we have access to the clues the text provides to assist our understanding. We read the "Dick and Jane" primer she quotes from and recognize the power of its normative agenda and the subsequent alienation of those of its intended readers who are African American children. We stand outside with her and look at the disused storefront in which Pecola lived. Then we listen to the histories of Pauline and Cholly Breedlove as if this will explain away the rape. However, at the end Claudia tells us that we are part of the community that caused Pecola's descent into madness: we are all responsible. Thus we enter into an interpretive community with the narrator on another level, as we come to understand and share her guilt for the thing that must be explained.

As readers we are no longer positioned as white abolitionist women conspiring with a narrator against the racist patriarchy, or as black or white women celebrating the victory of positive black communal values over negative patriarchal forces. In this case, we are positioned either as members of a small black or a larger white hegemonic community, both of which were established on the back of Pecola and precipitated her destruction. Not only are we implicated in her madness because of "all of our waste which we dumped on her and which she absorbed" (159), but we are also beneficiaries of that destruction. Claudia reminds us that

> we were so beautiful when we stood astride her ugliness. Her simplicity decorated us, her guilt sanctified us, her pain made us glow with health, her awkwardness made us think we had a sense of humor. . . . We honed our egos on her, padded our characters with her frailty, and yawned in the fantasy of our strength. (159)

The interpretive community that Pecola/Morrison creates for us is thus one in which the members learn to understand the consequences of their lives and accept responsibility for their privileges.

The event we must understand in order to fully realize our role in this is the particular moment of Pecola's loss of self. And as with the other works we have seen, that moment is indicated to us by its radical difference from the rest of the text in its refusal to explain itself. Although we have seen Pecola wishing herself invisible as her parents fight, the significant moment is when that invisibility is confirmed by an outsider—Mr. Yacobowsky. Our attention is drawn to this scene because it is the first of only two present-tense narratives in the novel (the second reveals Pecola talking to "herself" at the end). As Pecola walks to the store to buy candy, we glimpse her world and her negotiation of it. With her we feel the "promise and delicate security" of the coins in her shoe and see the "familiar and therefore loved images" of the yellow-headed dandelions. She appears to select her candies, "Mary Janes," for their taste, which she lovingly imagines. However, after her experience with Yacobowsky, the store owner, we see that it is more complex than that: in response to his gaze, the candies become an image of what Pecola is not—what Yacobowsky's inability to see her has indicated she should be. Thus, finally, "To eat the candy is somehow to eat the eyes, eat Mary Jane. Love Mary Jane. Be Mary Jane" (43).

What Pecola sees reflected in the white man's eyes is "a vacuum where curiosity ought to lodge. And something more. The total absence of human recognition" (42). She sees the same lack of recognition in the eyes of many others: the children who tease her out of "contempt for their own blackness" (55); Maureen Peel, who taunts her with her own light skin (61); Geraldine, who calls her "nasty little black bitch" (75); and Mrs. Breedlove, who ignores her to tend to the white child (87). When someone does finally "see" her, it is Cholly, who notices that she looks "whipped" and, overcome by frustration, rapes her. The fact that she is not Mary Jane overshadows all of her interactions and confirms her self-hatred. The fact that they are not Pecola allows the other characters to affirm themselves. These failures to "see" Pecola function like the failed confession scenes in *Incidents*, as a warning to black and white readers about the consequences of such blindness. But it is the interruption of the past-tense structure of the novel with this present-tense sequence which indicates a moment when we need to pause and try to explain what the text does not. Morrison/Claudia shows how the other characters came to hate themselves and believe themselves ugly as a result of similar racist blindness and cultural alienation, but the fact that the narrative of Pecola's experience is written in the present tense indicates that although this text is set in 1941, we are dealing with more than simply one child's loss of self: the event is timeless and is still occurring. In order to understand this connection and its full significance, we must look at both the historical and the textual context of *The Bluest Eye*.

The historical moment we occupy as we realize our place in the interpretive community of the text is the 1960s, and it would appear that the novel returns to 1941 to trace the beginning of attitudes Morrison perceived in her own time. The year 1941 obviously has multiple significances in U.S. history. It represented the end of an era as the nation hovered on the brink of a war which would bring profound changes to American culture, and at first we might feel the need to explain this in all of its complexity. However, it is more revealing to explore the selection of 1941 in a text written in the late 1960s in terms of Executive Order 8802, which prohibited employment discrimination in the "defense industry or Government because of race, creed, color, or national origin." This order was issued by President Roosevelt to prevent the July 1 march on Washington by hundreds of thousands of African Americans organized by A. Philip Randolph's Brotherhood of Sleeping Car Porters. Although it seemed to have significant ramifications, in fact it produced only superficial changes and did not prevent "widespread discrimination" (Franklin 1969, 578–80). It thus demonstrated that the problem of hegemonic racism could not be solved purely by "equal rights" legislation—a demonstration whose implications had still not been fully internalized in the 1960s but which the "Dick and Jane" extracts amply reveal.

Giddings cites the onset of World War II as the moment when the psychological manipulation of race and gender reached new heights. The industrial expansion of the period created a need for new markets, and the increased employment of African Americans in industry produced a new pool of potential consumers, so, Giddings claims, "a formidable array of propaganda" was developed to revive the attitudes of the "cult of true womanhood" and "promote the accumulation of material goods." But first, "Blacks[' and] women's sense of self had to be whittled away before they could become postulants at the altar of the 'new religion'" (242). Thus Pauline Breedlove comes to hate herself as she watches the movies of the 1930s, and Pecola begins to desire the blue eyes of the Shirley Temple mug and the Mary Jane candies. The positive possibilities of black culture and identity were skillfully destroyed and replaced by the materialist desires of the women from "Mobile. Aiken. From Newport News" (Morrison 1972, 67) who control the "dreadful funkiness of passion . . . nature . . . [and] human emotions" (68) and are unable to see beyond appearances.

As we begin to understand how the ideology which established the white, middle-class, nuclear family as normative frames and determines our relations despite legislation promising to "end discrimination," we can return to Pecola's desire to "be Mary Jane" (43). The fact that the scene is written in the present tense, like the quotes from the primer which frame and structure the text, indicates that our own failure of vision continues to create "Pecolas." Thus, the contextual knowledge which *The Bluest Eye* has prompted us to provide enables our students to trace the complex influences of education and consumerism on Pecola's identity formation and its continued impact in the present. By selecting Claudia to tell Pecola's story, Morrison provides a model reader who "reads" the consequences of a lack of community and self-love. And by positioning her readers as members of Claudia's community, she creates an interpretive community which both "sees" Pecola and recognizes its complicity in her destruction. However, this recognition can only occur when readers understand the specific sociohistorical context of the moment of Pecola's "unbeing." Thus, the text calls on us to provide that context.

Interpreters, listeners, and narrative interruptions function similarly in other works by African American women. For example, in Gloria Naylor's *Linden Hills* (1986), we enter Willa's interpretive community to "read" the lives that her predecessors had inscribed on their bodies and their few personal possessions. The textual disjuncture between life on the hill and Willa's experience in the basement forces us outside the text to sociological studies of black communities modeled on white patriarchal society. Likewise, in Alice Walker's *Temple of My Familiar* (1989), the apparently unconnected characters suffer because they ignore their mothers and their past before we, and Suwelo, learn to listen to Miss Lissie. As the characters learn their racial and familial histories, the juxtaposition of their stories demands an exploration of the racial and interracial tensions marking the context of this novel.

This complex relationship between the interpretive communities established by the texts and the contextual knowledge required to understand them can serve many functions as we teach literature by African American women. While we may wish that our students would come to literature with the requisite historical and cultural knowledge, their lack of it necessitates that we teach them to carefully attend to each text in order to discover what they must learn before they can interpret its tensions. Such a pedagogy allows us to integrate our teaching of text and context without removing our focus from the literature. But perhaps a greater benefit is that it encourages the students to take a more interactive approach to reading and engaging in cultural studies because their own reading both reveals what they need to learn and provides a purpose for learning it.

Works Cited

Andrews, William L. 1986. *To Tell A Free Story: The First Century of Afro-American Autobiography, 1760–1865.* Urbana: University of Illinois Press.

Cassidy, Thomas. 1990. "Desire and Representation in Twentieth Century American Realism." Ph.D. diss., SUNY Binghamton.

Christian, Barbara. 1985. *Black Feminist Criticism: Perspectives on Black Women Writers.* New York: Pergamon.

Franklin, John Hope. 1969. *From Slavery to Freedom: A History of Negro Americans.* New York: Vintage.

Giddings, Paula. 1985. *When and Where I Enter: The Impact of Black Women on Race and Sex in America.* New York: Bantam.

Hemenway, Robert E. 1977. *Zora Neale Hurston: A Literary Biography.* Urbana: University of Illinois Press.

Hurston, Zora Neale. 1978. *Their Eyes Were Watching God.* Urbana: University of Illinois Press.

————. 1979. "The 'Pet' Negro System" and "Crazy for this Democracy." In *I Love Myself When I Am Laughing ... And Then Again When I Am Looking Mean and Impressive: A Zora Neale Hurston Reader,* edited by Alice Walker. Old Westbury, NY: Feminist.

Jacobs, Harriet A. 1987 [1861]. *Incidents in the Life of a Slave Girl: Written by Herself.* Cambridge: Harvard University Press.

Jordan, Jennifer. 1988. "Feminist Fantasies: Zora Neale Hurston's *Their Eyes Were Watching God.*" *Tulsa Studies in Women's Literature* 7: 105–17.

McDowell, Deborah. 1989. "Reading Family Matters." In *Changing Our Own Words: Essays on Criticism, Theory, and Writing by Black Women,* edited by Cheryl Wall, 75–97. New Brunswick, NJ: Rutgers University Press.

Morrison, Toni. 1972. *The Bluest Eye.* New York: Pocket.

Naylor, Gloria. 1986. *Linden Hills.* New York: Penguin.

Pryse, Marjorie. 1985. "Zora Neale Hurston, Alice Walker, and the 'Ancient Power' of Black Women." In *Conjuring: Black Women, Fiction, and Literary Tradition,* edited by Marjorie Pryse and Hortense J. Spillers, 1–24. Bloomington: Indiana University Press.

Stepto, Robert B. 1979. "Teaching Afro-American Literature: Survey of Tradition." In *Afro-American Literature: The Reconstruction of Instruction,* edited by Dexter Fisher and Robert B. Stepto, 8–24. New York: Modern Language Association.

————. 1979. *From Behind the Veil: A Study of Afro-American Narrative.* Urbana: University of Illinois Press.

Tate, Claudia. 1989. "Allegories of Black Female Desire; or, Rereading Nineteenth-Century Sentimental Narratives of Black Female Authority." In

Changing Our Own Words: Essays on Criticism, Theory, and Writing by Black Women, edited by Cheryl Wall, 98–126. New Brunswick, NJ: Rutgers University Press.

Walker, Alice. 1989. *The Temple of My Familiar*. San Diego: Harcourt.

Wall, Cheryl A., ed. 1989. *Changing Our Own Words: Essays on Criticism, Theory, and Writing by Black Women*. New Brunswick, NJ: Rutgers University Press.

Washington, Mary Helen. 1982. "Teaching *Black-Eyed Susans:* An Approach to the Study of Black Women Writers." In *All the Women Are White, All the Blacks Are Men, But Some of Us Are Brave: Black Women's Studies*, edited by Gloria T. Hull, Patricia Bell Scott, and Barbara Smith, 208–17. Old Westbury, NY: Feminist.

——————, ed. 1987. *Invented Lives: Narratives of Black Women, 1860–1960*. Garden City, NY: Doubleday.

Willis, Susan. 1987. *Specifying: Black Women Writing the American Experience*. Madison: University of Wisconsin Press.

Yellin, Jean Fagan. 1985. "Texts and Contexts of *Harriet Jacobs' Incidents in the Life of a Slave Girl: Written by Herself*." In *The Slave's Narrative: Texts and Contexts*, edited by Charles T. Davis and Henry Louis Gates, Jr., 262–82. Oxford and New York: Oxford University Press.

12 Sethe's "Big, Bad" Love

Chauncey A. Ridley
California State University, Sacramento

Part I

Inspired by the historical account of Margaret Garner, an escaped slave who attempted to kill her children rather than allow them to be returned to slavery, Morrison's *Beloved* imaginatively examines Garner's infanticide as a form of uncompromising maternal love in conflict, certainly, with white racists but, more emphatically, with the segregated community of black ex-slaves in Ohio. The vernacular basis of her conflict with the black community is the subject of this article.

By vernacular expression, I mean those "arts native or peculiar to a particular country or locale." More specifically, I want to insist that verifiable traces of West African myth, religion, and aesthetic criteria that early slaves could hold in memory and transmit orally have survived in the oral traditions of expression that segregated black communities have developed in America, and these traces distinguish traditional African American vernacular expression from other American traditions of expression.

Morrison has stated that in *Beloved* she places the emphasis on the "minds of the slaves," African descendants who have been socially segregated their entire lives and descended from parents who, for generations, have been segregated.[1] Therefore, since Morrison's body of work clearly attests to her dismissal of the condescending assumption that the trauma of captivity, economic deportation, and enslavement somehow reduced slaves to a *tabula rasa*, the black community's predominant intellectual influences are Pan-African in *Beloved*. Specifically, vernacular "badness" is a secular adaptation of an ancient West African belief system according to which the community of ex-slaves in Ohio not only anticipate, quite accurately, some calamity about to befall Sethe and all in close proximity to her, but condemn her infanticide, attempt to permanently expel her from their community, then finally, reintegrate her.

I am not suggesting that *Beloved* does not extend a powerful and satisfying range of human drama and emotion to even its most casual readers. I am suggesting that levels of meaning specific to the Pan-African vernacular tradition are constitutive of the novel's complete artistic performance and available to those readers willing to research and contemplate the specific Pan-African vernacular resources of great African American literary texts. Not even one's own tradition can be obtained without labor; therefore one teaching a truly multicultural course of study should not resent the need to bring to African American literature at least the equivalent scholarly effort one applies to eluci-dating the specific Western traditions informing works such as *The Oresteia, Beowulf,* or "The Wasteland." Pan-African lore and authori-tative analyses of its idiom, values, and aesthetics are available in most moderately sized college and university libraries, and the effort of researching them involves no more than what is required of African American undergraduates who must become articulate in Western traditions before receiving their bachelor's degrees.

Sethe's "bad" response to the Fugitive Slave Law is the bloody outgrowth of her "big" love, a love more uncompromisingly committed, self-sufficient, and autonomous than any other represented in *Beloved.* When abandoned by the community of ex-slaves in Ohio and cornered by the slave hunters, Sethe defends her autonomy and self-sufficiency with outrageous violence, the most salient feature of traditional tales of "badness." "Big love" is not an expression frequently found in oral folklore, but it is one form of a larger impulse toward the uncompro-mising individual autonomy mythologized in Pan-African religious secular lore, an impulse that in all "bad" lore inevitably results in violence. I will explain Sethe's uncompromising "big" love before more fully clarifying the bloody "badness" which, according to the vernacular lore, is one of the most typical and potentially disastrous results of uncompromising black autonomy.

Even before Sethe kills Beloved, the community finds her guilty of a form of pride that precedes disaster, the uncompromising "pride" (Morrison 1987, 171) of a "used to be slave woman" who resolves to keep her children away from what she "know[s] is terrible" (165). A slave's outrageous claim to such a "big" love trespasses on the prerogatives of the slave-owning status quo who, even to the point of breaking up slave families, legally own and control a slave's children. The law allows slaves only to love "small, grass blades, salamanders, spiders, woodpeckers. . . . Anything bigger wouldn't do. A woman, a child, a brother—a *big love* [my emphasis] like that would split [a slave] wide open." "Loving small" connotes not only a slave's love turned to small things with no cash value for the master, but also for loving a spouse, child, or friend "just a little bit . . . so when they broke its back or shoved it in a croaker sack . . . you'd have a little love left over for the next one" (45). Paul D knows that even his postbellum freedom is deficient until he gets to "a place where you could love anything you chose—not to need permission for desire— well now, *that* was freedom" (162). Lacking *that*, slaves, even at Sweet Home or in Ohio, must learn to love small—temporarily, fatalistically, without commitment—or risk being "split wide open" by the legal violence of the slave system.

Sethe has never learned to love "small." As a young girl, she was owned by a master who fostered in his slaves the illusion of autonomy by encouraging them to initiate their own solutions to problems encountered in their duties, to work one day a week off the plantation called Sweet Home for personal wages, to use these wages to buy their freedom, and to marry whom they choose. Sethe chooses her first husband, Halle, on the basis of his capacity to love his mother "big" enough to buy her freedom with five years' worth of his Sundays.

Halle's achievement seems to attest to a relatively benign system of slavery in which a slave earns human status through capitalistic initiative. Thus, Halle joins one of the central slave oral and literary traditions depicting figures, such as Olaudah Equiano, who by working extra, learning to read, and learning how to calculate their earnings eventually acquire enough money to buy freedom. However, emphasizing the difference between Halle and Equiano reveals that Morrison's novel is a story of "big, bad" love and not simply one of individual capitalistic initiative. Halle and Sethe insist upon not only living but loving as free, committed individuals.

The economics of slavery and the ideology of racism so ruthlessly sever black love and family ties that not even Equiano's efforts can overcome the "man in the middle" (Equiano 1987, 29); the slave trader who turns Africans into property sleeps between Equiano and his sister on their final night together, representing the slave system's repression of black family ties.

When Sethe and Halle marry and have three children their first three years of marriage, the impossibility of Halle's working enough Sundays to free them all begins to expose the violence beneath the benign surface of Sweet Home. The plantation's decline into difficult financial straits intensifies this threat, since selling the children would raise capital. So Halle and Sethe plan to escape. Their "big love," their claim to a family unity that supercedes the slave owner's legal economic interests, makes them outlaws. If slaves like Equiano must be determined and ingenious to live as free individuals, slaves must be outlaws to love as free, committed individuals, a condition that will eventually demand "badness" of them.

Propagated orally for centuries in traditional toasts, boasts, epic verses, and narratives, mythologized "bad" men and women use outrageous violence to defend outrageous claims to uncompromising self-definition, autonomy, and beyond these, to status, power, and privileges. Thus, they directly affront slave institutions that assume legal power to determine the meaning and destiny of African descendants, and they meet the slave system's relentless violence with their own violence.

First transcribed from John Little's 1857 oral slave narrative published in *A Northside View of Slavery*, "bad nigger" was originally a term owners used for slaves who would not readily submit to slave discipline. Alan Dundes suggests that the slaves quickly realized that what was bad for slavery was good for them, so they began to use "bad" subversively to mean good (Dundes 1973, 581). In a legal context in which a slave's efforts to maintain the most basic forms of human autonomy and self-sufficiency—resisting rape, defending loved ones, and collecting wages for labor—were usually punished as crimes, this vernacular irony apparently allowed slaves to praise defiant slaves while safely appearing to acquiesce to the slave owner's condemnation of the defiance. Even more radically, this irony gives expression to the slaves' dismissal of the values represented by "good," "legal," and "moral" as received from "good, Christian" slave owners. If "good nigger" denoted a perfect slave, then "bad niggers" were likely to be regarded as far more dignified, although more dangerous.

Within this hypocritical context, all slaves who achieved any sort of moral consciousness needed, either overtly or covertly, to seek and define moral values for themselves. However, the slave who openly expressed such autonomy would be one prepared to confront the slave system's full legal violence, a violence implicit at every level of social contact between whites and blacks and the true basis upon which slavery was predicated and sustained. Therefore, to avoid outright confrontations with this violence, a slave's conscious moral integrity had to remain a subversive activity.

However, "bad" figures, although not always moral (and certainly not always amoral), are always confrontational. They represent a moment at which black moral autonomy can no longer remain secret, when the slave must make an overt *claim*, take hold of a destiny she has defined for herself, and confront the inevitable legal violence. "Bad" men and women do not trick, retreat, or accommodate. They meet violence with violence. Through them, segregated black communities vicariously lay "outrageous claim" to a destiny which is not a white person's burden but which is autonomously and self-sufficiently their own.

In placing Sethe in the same category as the likes of Stagolee or Willie George King, I realize that I am laying aside some important moral distinctions. Many "bad" men and women are more vicious and exploitative than courageous and self-sufficient. Laying aside these distinctions allows the salient features common to the wider range of "bad" lore to emerge.

All "bad" men and women are prepared to use violence to maintain uncompromising control over defining themselves and their destinies; this autonomy presumes a *status* from which slaves are legally excluded. Remember that Sixo is killed for forgetting that "definitions belonged to the definers, not the defined" (Morrison 1987, 190). Stagolee is certainly asocial for shooting the family man, Billy Lyons; John Henry certainly stands in the way of progress and profit in his fatal contest against the machine. Yet slaves and free blacks in oral lore who "jump bad" in defense of loved ones against whites are no less criminals according to slave law. However sympathetic their motives, their specific crime is less important than the more radical "crime" of African American autonomy and self-sufficiency in a context of slave and racist law. Black autonomy threatens the entire structure of exploitation, and generations of black singers and storytellers have valorized "bad" men and women not because they are, by any consistent standard, moral, immoral, or amoral, but because they are personally capable of sensational violence to maintain their autonomy and self-sufficiency. This valorization occurs only at a distance, though, because the black communities depicted in the tales consistently abandon "bad" heroes at precisely the climactic moment of confrontation between "bad" figures and the racist law. After their deaths, the communities immortalize these figures in ritual retellings of their exploits. Despite some similarities, this tradition is not to be confused with Euro-American outlaw traditions, including Robin Hood or Billy the Kid. Traditionally a sacrificial theme which Morrison reworks into a redemptive one, "badness" is specific to the social conditions of black Americans, and it is an adaptation of the sacred beliefs of West Africans.

Although "bad" women appear with less frequency than "bad" men—such as Railroad Bill, Stagolee, John Henry, Jean Toomer's Tom

Burwell, Richard Wright's Bigger Thomas, and Claude Brown's "Man-child"—they occur with equal force and insistence. Among them are Lucy, Willie George King, numerous unnamed slave mothers of the oral tradition, Zora Neale Hurston's Big Sweet, Margaret Walker's Kissie Lee, Alice Walker's Sofia, and Morrison's Sula, Pilate Dead, and Sethe. Like their male counterparts, they represent secular adaptations of ancient West African sacred beliefs concerning the limits of a mortal's social and metaphysical autonomy. Some of these West African beliefs are mythologized in the lore and ritual devoted to the sacrificial divinity, Sango, the divine African precursor to secular African American "bad" women and men.

The Sango myth is what John W. Roberts (1989), in *From Trickster to Badman*, ignores when he insists that "bad niggers" could not be regarded as heroic by a slave community composed of former West Africans. According to Roberts, most West African societies shared a "deep structural" craving for "harmony and order," a craving which was of practical use to their American descendants for whom "harmony and solidarity" provided protection against Jim Crow laws (Roberts, 205). He contends that, since "bad" figures placed "status above their own well-being and that of their fellow sufferers," the slave communities must have "realized that it was not in their best interests to promote such behavior as heroic" (176). However, Westcott and Morton-Williams are more inclusive and correct in pointing out that most West African cultures, strongly penetrated with Yoruba beliefs, also recognize that a "balanced dualism that permeates all Yoruba religions and cosmological assumptions . . . order, for the sake of renewal and development must be broken. . . . Mankind, without the promptings of *will* [my emphasis] would cease to strive and society and culture would stagnate" (Westcott and Morton-Williams 1962, 33). This salutary willfulness would predictably be embodied in heroes whose actions would illegitimately disrupt the established social and divine order.

Their communities and, consequently, the lore created around the heroes regard them ambivalently; though a community may be momentarily exhilarated by the disruption of an oppressive order, its concern very quickly reverts to the overriding need for harmony, solidarity, and self-protecting order, all of the aspects of social stability that Roberts mentions. At this moment, the hero whose self-legitimizing "promptings of the will" cannot be governed becomes an enemy of community and therefore a sacrificial victim. However, the Yoruba philosophy of balanced dualism provides for a ritualization of this sacrifice whereby the community can simultaneously embrace the "promptings of the will" that regenerated the culture when the old order had stagnated. Thus, in response to outside threats, the community can reenact the ritual in hopes of appropriating the hero's salutary traits while containing within the ritual the potential for internal disruption that must accompany such traits.

Dispersed throughout the Americas and the Caribbean by the West African diaspora, this sacred figure is known as Sango throughout West Africa; Shango in Trinidad, Grenada, and Sao Luiz; Xango in Recife, Belem, and Rio; and Chango in Cuba and Bahia. He is one embodiment of the balancing spiritual and social antithesis to the "harmony" emphasized by Roberts. Born a mortal, Sango is obsessed with godlike autonomy and self-sufficiency. As a young man, he usurps the throne from his older brother who was "too mild for the war-like spirit of the age and tamely suffered the encroachments of provincial kings" (Lawal 1970, 15). As king, Sango ruthlessly defeats the invaders in a series of bloody wars whereby he unifies the West African city-states under his imperial rule. Not content with the gods' aid, he has usurped their power to achieve his ends, ordering his magician to steal one power by which the gods control human destiny, the power to hurl "thunderstones" (sometimes identified as meteors and sometimes as lightning bolts). In all versions of this lore, once the invaders have been routed, his subjects immediately turn their attention to community commerce, stability, and solidarity, yet Sango cannot change with the times. He starts wars against his own generals, whose power and achievements appear to rival his own. Consequently, his subjects abandon him when divine forces exact retribution for his crime of overreaching the stable social and metaphysical stations to which he was born. After his death, though, he is deified by the community which had sacrificed him. Thus, as in "bad" lore the community can enact rituals whereby it hopes to appropriate his will, power, and resourcefulness while containing his internal disruptiveness.

Sango beliefs, which valorize a mortal for illegitimately usurping divine status, predisposed West Africans to create tales in praise of secular "bad" figures who usurp the secular status of whites by assuming their power of self-definition and self-determination. Like Sango, "bad" figures are community heroes and sacrificial victims. At the moment that these heroes face their gravest dangers—the forces of racist law and custom—their communities abandon them; then, once they are dead and white violence has expended itself, their communities mythologize and immortalize them. Comparative mythologists may detect Western parallels in such figures as Alexander, Blake's Satan, or Goethe's Faustus. For claiming autonomous control of human destiny, which overreaches their received social and spiritual status, not only do they endanger themselves, but the gods' retribution endangers all in close proximity to the willful malefactor. Therefore, their communities must ritualistically sacrifice them. Yet, paradoxically, they are also very special heroic archetypes, symbolizing their communities' sense of themselves as comprised of venturesome, resourceful, fiercely independent people.

Part II

As a lover, Sethe is the "baddest" figure in the novel. Paul D, who accutely observes that "more important than what Sethe had done [murder her child] was what she claimed," tells her, "Your love is too thick" (Morrison 1987, 164). Since it is legal and moral for slave owners to separate slave families and lovers for economic reasons; since it is legal and moral to steal a slave mother's milk; since slave hunters ride up to Sethe and Baby's house, 124, "looking righteous" for having god and law on their side, then a slave's "thick," committed love is a dangerously outrageous claim.

In planning his family's escape from slavery, Halle becomes an outlaw, yet his "big" love does not evolve into "bad" love because, at the inevitable moment of confrontation, he is unable to meet violence with violence. Seeing white men milk his wife's breasts, he is paralyzed when a desperate leap into "badness" is called for. Maintaining his claim to "big love" demands a leap beyond subversion into outraged, outrageous violence. Sethe's discovery of his failure disgusts her; her first impression of his capacity to "love big" has been so irrevocably reduced that she can no longer respect him, and her discovery of his consequent madness registers as nothing more than another emotional burden she must bear alone.

Alone, driving herself with the resolution to "get her milk to her children," she escapes Sweet Home while in painful labor with her child, Beloved. Long before she hears of Halle's fate, Sethe attains her Pyrrhic victory over the slave hunters to whom the Ohio community of ex-slaves has sacrificed her. Though in awe of her exploits, the community of ex-slaves resent "her outrageous claims, her self-sufficiency" (171), for they are guilty of "loving small." Stamp Paid, the Ohio community's representative, earned his name while still a slave when he allowed his wife to become the concubine of his master's son. Since Stamp "did not kill anyone" (184), he bears his name as a public confession of his disgrace. Stamp's spitefulness toward Sethe is unworthy of his better qualities, but envy and shame get the better of him.

Not only envy but a very practical, realistic fear repels the black community. According to folk wisdom, "badness" intensifies white supremacist rivalry, sparking outbreaks of white vigilante violence which, subject to no legal restraint or redress, often escalate out of control, victimizing all blacks in the proximity of the malefactor. The research of Lawrence Levine, Eugene Genovese, and John W. Roberts documents the dynamics of such local pogroms. In their discussions of "bad" lore, however, they address neither the practical sacrificial structure of this lore nor the likelihood that this structure's correspondence with Sango lore evinces that early slaves may have perceived the dynamics of this violence in terms of the ancient West African belief systems that inform secular "bad" lore. Sango's story teaches that the power of the lightning bolts will destroy anyone close to the mortal who unlawfully wields it. In many versions, the gods redirect one of Sango's stolen thunderstones, destroying Sango's city and family. Sethe claims a power to protect and rear her children, over-reaching the legal prescription that slaves "love small." Her claim to this power threatens to intensify white supremacist rivalry which, subject to no institutional restraint or redress, threatens all who are near her, so the black community sacrifices her to the slave hunters. To briefly summarize my findings up to this point, before Sethe commits child murder, her "outrageous claims, her self-sufficiency" not only shame the black community guilty of "loving small," but they threaten to attract the lightning bolts, and so the community abandons both Baby and Sethe, sacrificing her to white violence.

The community's resentment against Sethe has been building since the day she arrived at 124, reaching its climax after her mother-in-law, Baby Suggs, indulges herself in a celebration of Sethe's and her children's successful escape. Baby's celebration begins spontaneously when Stamp Paid honors the grandmother's good fortune by enduring scrapes, cuts, and insect bites to bring her some nearly inaccessible wild blackberries that "tasted like church." Stamp's effort recalls to her the love and labor of her missing son, Halle, who had bought her freedom with five years' worth of Sundays. Rising to the occasion, Baby becomes the catalyst for a miracle: this one pail of blackberries becomes a feast for ninety. This communal miracle combined with Sethe's miraculous escape place Baby and her family, as always, "at the center of things [in the community]. . . . Giving advice; passing messages; healing the sick, hiding fugitives, loving, cooking loving, preaching, singing, dancing, and loving everybody like it was her job and hers alone" (137). The autonomy and self-sufficiency of this family diminish the community by comparison and infuse it with the hope but also the fear of the lightning bolts.

Inevitably, the lightning bolt of slave law finds Baby's yard, driving Sethe to seek "safety in a handsaw," in defense of her commitment to "know what is" and to protect her children from what she "know[s] is terrible." Sethe is never repentant; though she is grieved by the loss of her daughter, she never doubts that she was correct in her effort to murder her children to protect them. Yet this shocking resourcefulness intensifies the community's fear and resentment of Sethe, so they ostracize her, a development which, in terms of the Pan-African worldview embedded in "bad" lore, is not mysterious, but quite practical. When white law fails to punish her, the woman whose uncompromising autonomy has made her the focal point of white violence returns to the heart of the black community. Therefore, both socially and spiritually, her residence becomes an impure periphery that the sacrifice has failed to purify, an area infected with violence and tragedy as if by a communicable disease. Her return is also a moral imposition since her presence has become a constant reminder of a standard of love they never risked living up to.

Upon Sethe's return, Beloved, the only child Sethe succeeds in murdering, begins haunting 124, first as an invisible disruptive force, then embodied as a woman the exact age that Beloved would have been had she lived. Evinced by Beloved's monopolization of all of Sethe's resources of love, food, and energy, Beloved's sole motivation is to feed on Sethe's remorse and guilt. Beloved's appetite is so great that she grows fat while Sethe and Denver, Sethe's other daughter, starve; Beloved drives Paul D away and isolates Sethe from Denver. Yet Beloved is not the only ghost haunting 124. Stamp Paid hears many voices haunting the house and recognizes them as "the people of broken necks, of fire-cooked blood and black girls who had lost their ribbons" (181). These are the ghosts of the entire history of black love ties that slavery had broken, bloodied, and cheapened. One viewing Sethe as a sacrificial victim, ritualistically expelled to the periphery of a desperately vulnerable community, has a basis for understanding why, on the novel's metaphysical dimension, Sethe becomes a woman haunted by ghosts. Such a congregation of ghosts suggests that, by condemning her "big, bad" love as "pride," then isolating her, the black community spiritually absolves itself of shamefully loving "small." But in so doing they have burdened Sethe with their own nagging guilt and remorse accompanying their own histories of lost love. She will remain burdened with the debilitating ghosts of this collective history until the black community abrogates its moral ascendency and embraces Sethe's burden as their burden.

In Morrison's revision of this sacrificial tradition, the redemption of sins comes full circle. When the community begins to fear the ghost devouring her more than they fear and resent Sethe, the women assemble in front of 124 to enact a ritual through which they again take up their rightful share of this grievous history. "Trembl[ing] like the baptized" (261), Sethe has the accumulated burden of African American history lifted from her shoulders by the community's collective grace. The ghosts of history are not exorcised out of existence, but the burden of them is redistributed. Although Sethe clearly retains some psychic damage as revealed by her attack upon Mr. Bodwin, her reintegration into the community signals the redistribution of a collective burden she has borne alone, freeing her to give her "big, bad" love to, and to accept love from, the living. "Me? Me?" is her gratefully astonished response to Paul D's living embrace, now that the dead no longer clamor for her kisses.

Notes

1. A videotaped interview with Toni Morrison. Produced and directed by Alan Benson. An RM Arts Production, 1987.

Works Cited

Baker, Houston A. 1984. *Blues, Ideology, and Afro-American Literature: A Vernacular Theory.* Chicago: The University of Chicago Press.

Drew, Benjamin. 1968 [1856]. *A Northside View of Slavery. The Refugee: Of the Narratives of Fugitive Slaves in Canada. Related by Themselves with an Account of History and Conditions of the Colored Population of Upper Canada.* New York: Negro Universities Press.

Dundes, Alan, ed. 1973. *Mother Wit from the Laughing Barrel.* Englewood Cliffs, NJ: Prentice-Hall.

Equiano, Olaudah. 1987. *The Interesting Narrative of the Life of Olaudah Equiano.* In *The Classic Slave Narratives,* edited by Henry Louis Gates, Jr., 1–83. New York: New American Library.

Gates, Henry Louis, Jr.. 1988. *The Signifying Monkey.* New York: Oxford University Press.

Genovese, Eugene. 1976. *Roll, Jordan, Roll.* New York: Vintage Books.

Lawal, Baba Tunde. 1970. "Yoruba Sango Sculpture in Historical Retrospect." Ph.D. diss., Indiana University.

Levine, Lawrence W. 1977. *Black Culture and Black Consciousness: Afro-American Folk Thought from Slavery to Freedom.* New York: Oxford University Press.

Morrison, Toni. 1987. *Beloved.* New York: New American Library.

Roberts, John W. 1989. *From Trickster to Badman: The Black Folk Hero in Slavery and Freedom.* Philadelphia: University of Pennsylvania Press.

Toomer, Jean. 1969. *Cane.* New York: Harper & Row.

Westcott, Joan, and Peter Morton-Williams. 1962. "The Symbolism and Ritual Context of the Yoruba *Laba Shango.*" *The Journal of the Royal Anthropological Institute of Great Britain and Ireland* 92: part 1 (January to June).

13 Baldwin, Bebop, and "Sonny's Blues"

Pancho Savery
University of Massachusetts–Boston

Well before James Baldwin died in 1987, the literary critical establishment had made up its mind about him. Thus, there was hardly any surprise when Lee A. Daniels's front page *New York Times* obituary lauded, "James Baldwin, Eloquent Essayist In Behalf of Civil Rights, Is Dead." Equally unsurprising was Mark Feeney's *Boston Globe* "Appreciation" entitled "A Forceful Voice on the Issue of Race." What James Baldwin had become was, to a large extent, black America's interpreter of black America to and for white America. As such, Baldwin was essentially mummified into the "Voice of the Civil Rights Movement," a historical relic of the 1950s through the 1970s. But even in this position, Baldwin was not always on solid ground. In 1963, the same year Baldwin published *The Fire Next Time*, considered by many his quintessential work, Amiri Baraka called Baldwin, in "Brief Reflections on Two Hot Shots," the "Joan of Arc of the cocktail party" and characterized his work as "the *cry*, the spavined whine and plea" (later published in 1966, 117). Three years later, Larry Neal would declare that "Baldwin has missed the point by a wide margin," because his "uncertainty over identity and his failure to utilize, to its fullest extent, traditional aspects of Afro-American culture has tended to dull the intensity of his work" (later published in 1989a, 61). And although Baraka would change by the time of Baldwin's death, calling him in "Jimmy!" "this glorious, elegant griot of our oppressed African-American nation" (1989, 127) who "made us feel . . . that we could defend ourselves and define ourselves" (129), it still seems that Baldwin will go down in literary history primarily as the witness to and conscience of America's years of racial confrontation. But is this accurate? What of the eight books of fiction Baldwin published? Not only do I want to suggest that we need to reevaluate the fiction, but I want to do so

For Gerald Byron Johnson.

by looking at Baldwin's most celebrated short story and suggest that, even here, there is more to be seen than has been previously, and that "Sonny's Blues" demonstrates a full use of "traditional aspects of Afro-American culture."

In his 1937 Emersonial manifesto "Blueprint for Negro Writing," Richard Wright asserted the existence of "a culture of the Negro" whose main sources were "(1) the Negro church; and (2) the folklore of the Negro people" (39). For Wright, this folklore expressed itself in "Blues, spirituals, and folk tales recounted from mouth to mouth." Wright criticized writers for not making more use of the folk tradition in their work, because in folklore "the Negro achieved his most indigenous and complete expression" (1978, 40). Two years later, Saunders Redding published the first in-depth, full-length work of African American literary criticism, *To Make a Poet Black* (1987 [1939]). There, Redding, following up on Wright, read African American literature from the beginning to the end of the Harlem Renaissance, and found that only two writers had escaped the two traps he found continually lurking. These were the traps of writing from a "very practical desire to adjust himself to the American environment" (1987, 3), and the trap of having to simultaneously write for two audiences in order to succeed. The two writers Redding found to be most successful, Sterling Brown and Zora Neale Hurston, were successful because of their works' immersion in "folk material" (122).

The most successful African American writers have continued to mine this vein, but the critics have often been behind. I would like to suggest that Baldwin is a case in point. Although there have been interesting analyses of "Sonny's Blues," none of them has gotten to the specificities of the music and the wider cultural implications.[1] Music is not simply the bridge the narrator crosses to get closer to Sonny, nor is it sufficient to point out that the music in the climactic scene is labeled as blues. What kind and form of these particular blues make all the difference.

An interesting way to begin thinking about "Sonny's Blues" is to think about when the story is supposed to be taking place. We know from the acknowledgments that it was first published in the summer of 1957, but can we be more precise? Part of the story takes place during "the war," but which one is it, Korea or World War II, and does it matter?

Baldwin tells us that Sonny's father "died suddenly, during a drunken weekend in the middle of the war, when Sonny was fifteen" (1966, 97). "[J]ust after Daddy died" (97), Sonny's brother, whom we know is seven years older (93), is "home on leave from the army"

(97) and has his final conversation with his mother. In the passage, which begins with that wonderful evocation of the coming of the darkness on Sunday afternoon with the old and young together in the living room, "Mama" admonishes her older son to watch out for Sonny "and don't let him fall, no matter what it looks like is happening to him and no matter how evil you gets with him" (101). But the narrator tells us that he did not listen, got married, and went back to war. The next time he comes home is "on a special furlough" for his mother's funeral. The war is still going on. The narrator reminds Sonny that Sonny must "finish school," "And you only got another year" (106). The school that Sonny must finish is obviously high school. Thus, no more than a year or so has passed since the death of the father, who died "in the middle of the war." The United States was in World War II from December of 1941 until August of 1945. "The middle of the war" would have been approximately 1943, or 1942 if you start from the beginning of the war in Europe. Thus, the crucial conversation between Sonny and his brother, in which Sonny first says he wants to be a jazz musician, takes place about 1944. If, on the other hand, the war being fought is the Korean War (June 1950 to July 1953), the conversation takes place about 1952.

When Sonny reveals to his brother that first he wants to be a musician, and then a jazz musician, and then not a jazz musician like Louis Armstrong but one like Charlie Parker, the brother, after asking "Who's this Parker character," says, "I'll go out and buy all the cat's records right away, all right?" (104). From 1942 to 1944, there was a ban on recordings, at least in part due to a scarcity of materials because of the war. In 1944, Sonny's brother would not have been able to go out and buy new material by Bird (Parker) because there wasn't any. Bird's seminal recordings were made between 1945 and 1948.[2] It is, thus, reasonable to conclude that the war is the Korean.

By 1952, Bird had already revolutionized music. And so when Sonny's brother asks Sonny to name a musician he admires and Sonny says "Bird" and his brother says "Who?," Sonny is justified with his, "Bird! Charlie Parker! Don't they teach you nothing in the goddamn army?" (103).[3] Sonny's brother, at age twenty-four in 1952, can certainly be expected to have heard of Bird. After all, he has heard of Louis Armstrong.

But it is in Sonny's response to Armstrong that one of the keys to the story lies. Sonny's brother admits that, to him, the term "jazz musician" is synonymous with "hanging around nightclubs, clowning around on bandstands," and is, thus, "beneath him, somehow" (103). When, from this perspective, jazz musicians are "in a class with . . . 'good-time people'," his mentioning of Louis Armstrong needs to be looked at.

From one perspective, Louis Armstrong is one of the true titans of jazz.[4] On the other hand, to many of the Bebop era, Armstrong was considered part of the old guard who needed to be swept out with the new musical revolution, and Armstrong himself was not positively disposed towards Bop. One turning point came in February of 1949 when Armstrong was chosen King of the Zulus for the Mardi Gras parade in New Orleans. To many, he seemed to be donning the minstrel mask of acceptability to the larger white world, and this seemed confirmed when, the same week, he appeared on the cover of *Time* (February 21, 1949).[5] It would be "natural" that Sonny's brother, the future algebra teacher, would have heard of Armstrong, here the symbol of the old conservative, but not of Parker, not only the new and the revolutionary, but the "had been a revolutionary" for seven years. Sonny's response to Armstrong makes this clear:

> I suggested, helpfully: "You mean—like Louis Armstrong?"
> His face closed as though I'd struck him. "No. I'm not talking
> about none of that old-time, down home crap." (103)

But the differences between Armstrong and Parker represent something much larger. Throughout history, African Americans have been engaged in intramural debate about the nature of identity. Du Bois, of course, put it best when he defined "double-consciousness" in *The Souls of Black Folk* and concluded:

> One ever feels his twoness,—an American, a Negro; two souls,
> two thoughts, two unreconciled strivings; two warring ideals in
> one dark body, whose dogged strength alone keeps it from being
> torn asunder. (1969, 45)

Du Bois's battles with Booker T. Washington and later with Marcus Garvey are one of the major moments in African American history when this debate was articulated. But there have also been many others; for example, Frederick Douglass and Martin Delany debating whether Africa or America was the place for blacks, and King and Malcolm on the issue of integration. But in order to look at African American culture fully, we cannot limit ourselves to the study of politics and history. As numerous commentators have pointed out, music is the key to much of the African American dispute over this issue of culture; and, therefore, knowledge of it is essential. For example:

> The complexities of the collective Black experience have always
> had their most valid and moving expression in Black music; music

is the chief artifact created out of that experience. (Williams 1972, 136)

To reiterate, the key to where the black people have to go is in the music. Our music has always been the most dominant manifestation of what we are and feel. . . . The best of it has always operated at the core of our lives, forcing itself upon us as in a ritual. It has always, somehow, represented the collective psyche. (Neal 1989b, 21–22)

I think it is not fantastic to say that only in music has there been any significant Negro contribution to a *formal* American culture. (Baraka 1963, 130–31)

The tenor is a rhythm instrument, and the best statements Negroes have made, of what their soul is, have been on tenor saxophone. (Ornette Coleman, quoted in Spellman 1970, 102)

There has never been an equivalent to Duke Ellington or Louis Armstrong in Negro writing, and even the best of contemporary literature written by Negroes cannot yet be compared to the fantastic beauty of the music of Charlie Parker. (Baraka, "Myth," 1966, 107)

Houston Baker has gone as far as suggesting that there is a "blues matrix" at the center of African American culture and that "a vernacular theory" of African American literature can be developed from this idea.

What I am arguing in general is that music is the cornerstone of African American culture; and that, further, Bebop was an absolute key moment. In African American culture, Bebop is as significant as the Harlem Renaissance, and Armstrong and Parker's roles somewhat resemble those of Washington and Du Bois, and Du Bois and Garvey. Armstrong, Washington, and Du Bois (to Garvey) represented the known, the old, and the traditional whose accomplishments were noted but who were considered somewhat passé by the younger, more radical Parker, Du Bois (to Washington), and Garvey.

Musically, Bebop was to a large extent a revolt against swing and the way African American music had been taken over, and diluted, by whites. Perhaps no more emblematic of this is that the aptly named Paul Whiteman and Benny Goodman were dubbed respectively "The King of Jazz" and "The King of Swing." As Gary Giddins succinctly puts it:

Jazz in the Swing Era was so frequently compromised by chuckle-headed bandleaders, most of them white, who diluted and undermined the triumphs of serious musicians that a new virtuosity was essential. The modernists brandished it like a weapon. They confronted social and musical complacency in a spirit of arrogant romanticism. (1987, 78)

Ortiz Walton describes the musical revolution as "a major challenge
to European standards of musical excellence and the beginning of a
conscious black aesthetic in music" (1972, 104) because of Bebop's
challenge to the European aesthetic emphasis on vibrato. This emphasis
produced music that was easily imitable, and thus open to commer-
cialization and co-optation. By revolting against this direction the music
had taken and reclaiming it, "Afro-American musicians gained a
measure of control over their product, a situation that had not existed
since the expansion of the music industry in the Twenties" (106).

Another aspect of this Bop reclamation was a renewed emphasis
on the blues. Although some people seem to think there is a dispute
over this issue, it is clear from listening to Parker's first session as a
leader that "Billie's Bounce" and "Now's the Time" are blues pieces.
In his autobiography, Dizzy Gillespie asserts:

> Beboppers couldn't destroy the blues without seriously injuring
> themselves. The modern jazz musicians always remained very
> close to the blues musician. That was a characteristic of the bopper.
> (1979, 294)

To this we could add the following from Baraka:

> Bebop also re-established blues as the most important Afro-
> American form in Negro music by its astonishingly comtemporary
> restatement of the basic blues impulse. The boppers returned to
> this basic form, reacting against the all but stifling advance artificial
> melody had made into jazz during the swing era. (1963, 194)

We could also look at Bebop in terms of the movement from the
diatonic to the chromatic, from a more closed to an open form, a
movement in the direction of a greater concern with structure, the
beginning of jazz postmodernism that would reach its zenith in the
work of Ornette Coleman. In "The Poetics of Jazz," Ajay Heble
concludes, "Whereas diatonic jazz attempts to posit musical language
as a way of thinking about things in the real world, chromaticism
begins to foreground *form* rather than *substance*" (1988, 62).

What becomes clear in most of the above is that Bebop must be
viewed from two perspectives, the sociopolitical as well as the musical.
In Gary Giddins's words, "The Second World War severely altered the
texture and tempo of American life, and jazz reflected those changes
with greater acuteness by far than the other arts" (1987, 77). When
Bebop began in the 1940s, America was in a similar position to what
it had been in the 1920s. A war had been fought to free the world
(again) for democracy; and once again, African Americans had participated and had assumed that this "loyal" participation would result

in new rights and new levels of respect. When, once again, this did not appear to be happening, a new militancy developed in the African American community. Bebop was part of this new attitude. The militancy in the African American community that manifested itself in the 1941 strike of black Ford workers and the 1943 Harlem riot also manifested itself in Bebop. As Eric Lott notes:

> Brilliantly outside, bebop was intimately if indirectly related to the militancy of its moment. Militancy and music were undergirded by the same social facts; the music attempted to resolve at the level of style what the militancy combatted in the streets. (1988, 599)

Of course, this made Bebop dangerous and threatening to some, who saw it as (or potentially as) "too militant," and perhaps even un-American. And in response to this, Dizzy Gillespie retorts:

> Damn right! We refused to accept racism, poverty, or economic exploitation, nor would we live out uncreative humdrum lives merely for the sake of survival. But there was nothing unpatriotic about it. If America wouldn't honor its Constitution and respect us as men, we couldn't give a shit about the American way. And they made it damn near un-American to appreciate our music. (1979, 287)

The threat represented by Bebop was not only felt by the white world, but by the assimilationist black middle class as well. Baraka offers these perspectives:

> When the moderns, the beboppers, showed up to restore jazz, in some sense, to its original separateness, to drag it outside the mainstream of American culture again, most middle-class Negroes (as most Americans) were stuck; they had passed, for the most part, completely into the Platonic citizenship. The willfully harsh, *anti-assimilationist* sound of bebop fell on deaf or horrified ears, just as it did in white America. (1963, 181–82)
>
> Bebop rebelled against the absorption into garbage, monopoly music; it also signified a rebellion by the people who played the music, because it was not just the music that rebelled, as if the music had fallen out of the sky! But even more, dig it, it signified a rebellion rising out of the masses themselves, since that is the source of social movement—the people themselves! (1979, 236)
>
> What made bop strong is that no matter its pretensions, it was hooked up solidly and directly to the Afro-American blues tra-dition, and therefore was largely based in the experience and struggle of the black sector of the working class. (1979, 241)

In light of this historical context, Sonny's brother's never having heard of Bird is not just a rejection of the music of Bebop; it is also a rejection of the new political direction Bebop was representative of in the African American community.

When the story picks up several years later, some things have changed. Sonny has dropped out of high school, illegally enlisted in the navy and been shipped to Greece, returned to America, and moved to Greenwich Village. Other things have not changed: his brother has become an algebra teacher and a respected member of the black bourgeoisie. After Sonny has been released from prison, he invites his brother to watch him sit in "in a joint in the Village" (1966, 113).

What is usually discussed concerning this final scene is that the brother enters Sonny's world, recognizes that he is only a visitor to that world tolerated because of Sonny, that here Sonny is respected and taken care of, and that here is Sonny's true family:

> I was introduced to all of them and they were all very polite to me. Yet, it was clear that, for them, I was only Sonny's brother. Here, I was in Sonny's world. Or, rather: his kingdom. Here, it was not even a question that his veins bore royal blood. (118)

When the music Sonny plays is discussed, it is usually done either abstractly, music as the bridge that allows Sonny and his brother to become reunited and Sonny to find his identity, or simply in terms of the blues. It is, of course, totally legitimate to discuss the music in either of these ways. After all, music does function as a bridge between Sonny and his brother; and twice we are reminded in the same page that "what they were playing was the blues," and "Now these are Sonny's blues" (121).

At the climactic moment of the story, when Sonny finally feels so comfortable that his "fingers filled the air with life" (122), he is playing "Am I Blue." It is the first song of the second set, after a tentative performance by Sonny in the first set. Baldwin presents the moment of transition between sets by simply noting, "Then they finished, there was scattered applause, and then, without an instant's warning, Creole started into something else, it was almost sardonic, it was *Am I Blue*" (121). The word "sardonic," it seems to me, is key here. One of the characteristics of Bebop is taking an old standard and making it new. As Leonard Feather explains:

> In recent years it has been an increasingly common practice to take some definite chord sequence of a well-known song (usually a standard old favorite) and build a new melody around it. Since there is no copyright on a chord sequence, the musician is entitled to use this method to create an original composition and copyright it in his own name, regardless of who wrote the first composition that used the same chord pattern. (1977, 55–56)

This practice results in a song with a completely different title. Thus, "Back Home Again in Indiana" becomes Parker's "Donna Lee"; "Honeysuckle Rose" becomes "Scrapple from the Apple"; "I Got Rhythm" becomes "Dexterity," "Confirmation," and "Thriving on a Riff"; "How High the Moon" becomes "Bird Lore"; "Lover Come Back to Me" becomes "Bird Gets the Worm"; and "Cherokee" becomes "Warming Up a Riff" and "Ko-Ko." But it is also characteristic of Bebop to take the entire song, not simply a chord sequence, and play it in an entirely different way. Thus, for example, Bird's catalogue is filled with versions of tunes like "White Christmas," "Slow Boat to China," "East of the Sun and West of the Moon," "April in Paris," and "Embraceable You."[6] As Baraka notes:

> Bebop was a much more open rebellion in the sense that the musicians openly talked of the square, hopeless, corny rubbish put forth by the bourgeoisie. They made fun of it, refused to play it except in a mocking fashion. (1979, 237)

Baldwin's use of the word "sardonic," therefore, is clearly intended to tell us that something more is going on than simply playing a standard tune or playing the blues. "Am I Blue" is exactly the type of song that by itself wouldn't do much for anyone, but which could become rich and meaningful after being heated in the crucible of Bebop.

The point of all this is that, through his playing, Sonny becomes "part of the family again" (121), his family with the other musicians; likewise, Sonny's brother also becomes part of the family again, his family with Sonny. But in both cases, Baldwin wants us to view the idea of family through the musical and social revolution of Bebop. Note the brother's language as Sonny plays:

> Then he began to make it his. It was very beautiful because it wasn't hurried and it was no longer a lament. I seemed to hear with what burning we had yet to make it ours, how we could cease lamenting. Freedom lurked around us and I understood, at last, that he could help us to be free if we would listen, that he would never be free until we did. (122)

In the mid to late 1950s, the word "freedom" is obviously a highly charged one. Not only does it speak to the politics of the Civil Rights Movement, but it also points forward to the "Free Jazz" movement of the late 1950s and 1960s, the music of Ornette Coleman, Cecil Taylor, Albert Ayler, and Eric Dolphy. Baldwin's concept of family is, therefore, a highly political one, and one that has cultural implications.

In *Black Talk*, Ben Sidran concludes about Bebop:

The importance of the bop musician was that he had achieved this confrontation—in terms of aesthetics and value structures as well as social action—well before organized legal or political action. Further, unlike the arguments of the NAACP, his music and his hip ethic were not subject to the kind of rationalization and verbal qualification that had all too often compromised out of existence all middle-class Negro gains. (1971, 115)

In "Sonny's Blues," Baldwin makes clear that, contrary to many opinions, he is in fact a major fiction writer; and that, Larry Neal notwithstanding, he *has* used to its fullest extent "traditional aspects of Afro-American culture." The implications are clear. Not only does Baldwin's fiction need to be looked at again, but when we are looking at it, writing about it, and teaching it, we need to be conversant with the specific cultural context he is writing in and from. And when we are, new things are there to be seen and heard.

Notes

1. The two best treatments of "Sonny's Blues" are by Sherley Anne Williams and John Reilly. While Williams discusses music, she sees the musician in Baldwin as "an archetypal figure" (1972, 145). Reilly's 1974 " 'Sonny's Blues': James Baldwin's Image of the Black Community," the single best essay on the story, actually does mention Bebop, but only in one paragraph, and then concentrates more on the importance of the blues.

2. For a description of Parker's first session as a leader, recorded on November 26, 1945, see Giddins 1987, 87–90.

3. Interestingly, Baraka notes that "Trane first heard Bird and Diz in the Navy, as the first records were beginning to get released" (1979, 234).

4. On the connection between Armstrong and Parker, see Williams, 1971, 108–9.

5. On Armstrong and the Mardi Gras see Murray, 1976, 190–91; and Albertson, 1978, 24 and 29.

6. It seems to me that this characteristic activity of Bebop is similar to Henry Louis Gates's theory of signifying, although Gates limits the concept to African American writers signifying on each other. On this issue, see both Gates (1988) and Cain (1990).

Works Cited

Albertson, Chris. 1978. *Louis Armstrong*. Alexandria: Time-Life Records.

Baker, Houston A., Jr. 1984. *Blues, Ideology, and Afro-American Literature: A Vernacular Theory*. Chicago: University of Chicago Press.

Baldwin, James. 1966. *The Fire Next Time*. New York: Dial.

―――――. 1965. "Sonny's Blues." In *Going to Meet the Man*, 86–122. New York: Dial Press.

Baraka, Amiri. 1963. *Blues People: Negro Music in White America*. New York: Morrow.

―――――. 1966. "Brief Reflections on Two Hot Shots." In *Home: Social Essays*, 116–20. New York: Morrow.

―――――. 1966. "The Myth of a 'Negro Literature.'" In *Home: Social Essays*, 105–15.

―――――. 1979. "War/Philly Blues/Deeper Bop." In *Selected Plays and Prose of Amiri Baraka/LeRoi Jones*, 228–41. New York: Morrow.

―――――. 1989. "Jimmy!" In *James Baldwin: The Legacy*, edited by Quincy Troupe, 127–34. New York: Simon and Schuster/Touchstone.

Cain, William E. 1990. "New Directions in Afro-American Literary Criticism." *American Quarterly* 42: 657–63.

Daniels, Lee A. 1987, December 2. "James Baldwin, Eloquent Essayist in Behalf of Civil Rights, Is Dead." *New York Times*, A1.

Du Bois, W. E. B. 1969 [1903]. *The Souls of Black Folk*. New York: Signet-NAL.

Feather, Leonard. 1977 [1949]. *Inside Jazz (Inside Be-bop)*. New York: Da Capo.

Feeney, Mark. 1987, December 2. "James Baldwin Dies: A Forceful Voice on Issue of Race." *The Boston Globe*, 1.

Gates, Henry Louis, Jr. 1988. *The Signifying Monkey: A Theory of Afro-American Literary Criticism*. New York: Oxford University Press.

Giddins, Gary. 1987. *Celebrating Bird: The Triumph of Charlie Parker*. New York: Beech Tree Books/Morrow.

Gillespie, Dizzy, with Al Fraser. 1979. *To Be Or Not . . . To BOP: Memoirs*. Garden City: Doubleday.

Heble, Ajay. 1988. "The Poetics of Jazz: From Symbolic to Semiotic." *Textual Practice* 2: 51–68.

Lott, Eric. 1988. "Double V, Double-Time: Bebop's Politics of Style." *Callaloo* 11: 597–605.

Murray, Albert. 1976. *Stomping the Blues*. New York: McGraw-Hill.

Neal, Larry. 1989a. "The Black Writer's Role, III: James Baldwin." In *Visions of a Liberated Future: Black Arts Movement Writings*, edited by Michael Schwartz, 57–61. New York: Thunder's Mouth.

―――――. 1989b. "And Shine Swam On." In *Visions of a Liberated Future: Black Arts Movement Writings*, edited by Michael Schwartz, 7–23. New York: Thunder's Mouth Press.

Parker, Charlie. 1976. *Bird/The Savoy Recordings (Master Takes)*. Savoy, SJL 2201.

Redding, J. Saunders. 1987 [1939]. *To Make a Poet Black*. Ithaca, NY: Cornell University Press.

Reilly, John M. 1974. " 'Sonny's Blues': James Baldwin's Image of Black Community." In *James Baldwin: A Collection of Critical Essays*, edited by Keneth Kinnamon, 139–46. Englewood Cliffs, NJ: Prentice-Hall.

Sidran, Ben. 1971. *Black Talk*. New York: Holt, Rinehart, and Winston.

Spellman, A. B. 1970. *Black Music: Four Lives (Four Lives in the Bebop Business)*. New York: Schocken.

Walton, Ortiz M. 1972. *Music: Black, White & Blue: A Sociological Survey of the Use and Misuse of Afro-American Music*. New York: Morrow.

Williams, Martin. 1971. *The Jazz Tradition*, New York: Mentor-NAL.

Williams, Sherley Anne. 1972. *Give Birth to Brightness: A Thematic Study in Neo-Black Literature*. New York: Dial.

Wright, Richard. 1978. "Blueprint for Negro Writing." In *Richard Wright Reader*, edited by Ellen Wright and Michel Fabre, 36–49. New York: Harper & Row.

14 Filiative and Affiliative Textualization in Chinese American Literature

David Leiwei Li
University of Southern California

Part I

Although Chinese American literature has gained significant recognition since its re-emergence in the late 1960s, critical output on this expansive body of texts has not yet matched its intensity and complexity. Oftentimes, there is a persistent gaze on the canonical token, Maxine Hong Kingston's *The Woman Warrior* (1976) in this case, which is upheld as the ultimate representative of Asian American creativity. This narrow focus on a single ethnic work tends to have an ahistorical effect—it encourages the cult of a minority genius, it isolates the value of the text, and it shows a disregard of the fundamental relatedness of ethnic literary production. While acknowledging the individuality of the imaginative act, here I try to locate contemporary Chinese American work in its own tradition formation. One aspect of this formation is its dual movement toward "filiation and affiliation." Edward Said argues that the failure of natural biological reproduction (filiation) in the modern era propels individuals to generate culturally compensatory orders (affiliation) that will reinstate the lost sense of an old system (1983, 16–20). While concurring with Said's basic formulation, I am not abandoning the role of filiation, as Said probably would. Rather, I am intent on etymologizing the word, to see "filiation," for instance, along with "filial piety." In the Chinese American literary context, "filiation" can be literally defined as a line of descent and practically used as a narrative device to trace paternity *and*, as the texts have so emphatically embodied, maternity as well. It figures a diachronic movement toward the possible beginnings of nascent Chinese American families. Affiliation, on the other hand, indicates a synchronic movement when the multifarious quests for the potential origins of individual families connect and parallel to form an album of an extended Chinese American family. Thus, filiation and affiliation are not oppositional terms but complementary ones; both are extensions of the same trope of "parent-child" that apparently espouses a natural relationship only to serve the cultural interest of community construction. Filiation and affiliation are the thematic and rhetorical strategies that lie in the heart of the Chinese American intertexts that I am about to review. Together, they serve to animate memory, rekindle a sense of communal history, and establish bonds of a shared identity.

I wish to begin this section with a poem fittingly called "The End of a Beginning." "The beginning is always difficult," Marilyn Chin writes, "The immigrant worked his knuckles to the bone / only to die under the wheels of the railroad . . . And I, / the beginning of an end, the end of a beginning, / sit here, drink unfermented green tea, / scrawl these paltry lines for you [Grandfather]" (1987, 3). The description captures the apparent contrast between the hand that worked its knuckles to the bone to construct the transcontinental railroad and the hand that scrawled these paltry lines to commemorate the event. The heroic gesture of the grandfather and the humble reverence of his granddaughter seem, however, to merge hand in hand. The grandfather buried under the rail of oblivion springs to life on his "one-hundredth birthday," resurrected under the pen of the granddaughter (3). The beginning and the end lose their demarcating functions; in their place is a revivified continuity that matters. Consciously pursuing the line of descent, the poem re-marks the presence of the rail, restores a historic foundation, and repairs the broken links between the past and present. It provides, as Chin genuinely believes, "The Parent Node" for the group of her poems and, I believe, for the sheaf of other Chinese American verse as well.

The parent node is a filial image aimed at creating a sense of cohesive kinship. Sometimes, it is invoked to counter the crevice caused by language, as in Mei-mei Berssenbrugge's "Chronicle":

> Grandfather talked to me, taught me.
> At two months, my mother tells me,
> I could sniff for flowers,
> stab my small hand upwards to moon.
> Even today I get proud
> when I remember
> this all took place in Chinese. (1982, 41)

Other times, the parent node conjures up the desire of identification, as in Nellie Wong's "Dreams in Harrison Railroad Park":

> I turn and touch my mother's eyes.
> They are wet
> and I dream

and I dream
of embroidering
new skin. (1977, 18)

Still other times the parent node expresses intimacy, enhanced by the
knowledge of its imminent loss, as "The Youngest Daughter" of Cathy
Song recalls:

It seems it has always
been like this: the two of us
in this sunless room,
the splashing of the bathwater.
. . . .
She knows I am not to be trusted,
even now planning my escape.
As I toast to her health
with the tea she has poured,
a thousand cranes curtain the window,
fly up in a sudden breeze. (1983, 6)

Or, later in her life when the daughter artist comes to rest at her
mother's feet, to hear "the ticking of the china clock, another heartbeat,"

It has taken me all these years
to realize that this is what I must do
to recognize my life.
When I stretch a canvas
to paint the clouds,
it is your spine that declares itself:
arching,
your arms stemming out like tender shoots
to hang sheets in the sky. (48)

Whether it is at play, at rest, bathing, or reminiscing, the imagistic
field of the poems we read is invariably particularized: "When I think
of Hawaii, / I do not fancy myself lolling under palm trees, / a
backdrop of verdant cliffs, caressed by a balmy breeze"; Wing Tek
Lum opens our eyes, "instead I give thanks for classmates and our
family graves, / this unique universe that we have called home."
Admittedly inspired by Frank Chin, Lum aptly names the poem "Local
Sensibilities," suggesting a unique universe of homespun rhymes in
which living friends and dead spirits co-inhabit the poetic self (1987,
67). Here, the parent node signifies a most local Chinese American
space where the intersubjective relationships between generations are
manifested. For Lum, looking at "A Picture of My Mother's Family"
becomes a moment of intense self scrutiny (24–25); grave sweeping is
"Something Our Family Has Always Done" (35–36); and above all,
"The Poet Imagines His Grandfather's Thoughts on the Day He Died,"

reaching into the recesses of an ancestral memory, made integral and intact through poetic ideation, "still one in my mind" (37).

The parent node is a rhetorical mode of search for a vision of one's own. The overriding concern, as Marilyn Chin has it, is, "How can we remake ourselves in his [great grandfather's] image?" (1987, 29). Elsewhere, she has attempted an answer: "I laugh at the sun; I take in air; / I whistle in sleep, let cicadas within / murmur their filial rapture / my father's dream is my dream" (68). Projecting fatherhood and carrying on parental aspiration are filial acts of respect and rejoicing, a moment of reciprocal togetherness as rendered in Alan Lau's "a father's wishes—the birthday letter" (1980):

> father
> it's hard for me
> to talk to you
> listen to the sound of my voice
> pay no attention
> to the words
> they are only wagons in the wind
> instead hear the creek
> of the wheels pleading for oil
> it is my young pain
> with your old pain
> moaning the boatman's blues
> together

Togetherness is hyperbolized in Lau's two-part poem "the sun eaten, the son born" when we are first told that the father "exposed jaws / in a yawn wide enough / to eat the sun / turned yellow / as if he had swallowed / fields of light," then, "his head" turned into "a bulb / illuminating characters / I cannot read . . . they dance luminous rhythms / in my unshaped head / not knowing their meaning." The second part recorded a happening years later when "father's head is with me still":

> walking thru the gate
> I sport a similar shape
> with my wool hat on
> winter reflection
> the shadow on the temple wall
> shows only a black circle of light
> against the moon
> a monk's head
> with no ears
> to get in the way

In a radiant display of symbolic reincarnation, Lau's formerly "unshaped head" takes "a similar shape" as his father's, luminous, cosmic, and determinate, emitting "a black circle of light / against the moon" like the birth of a star—"the sun eaten, the son born." The poem adroitly shapes a quotidian reproductive metaphor into a fresh generative impulse, couching familial descent in metaphysical succession, thus catapulting the reader into a new consciousness.

If the figure of filiation is deployed in Chinese American poetry in its most local geography and its most terse form, it is far more elaborated in its affiliated genre, the prose works, which, given the advantage of narrative duration, are often able to extend the journey back to the future. Laurence Yep's novel *Dragonwings* (1975) is such an example. Intrigued by a newspaper account of Fung Joe Guey, a Chinese American who flew a biplane over Oakland for about twenty minutes before a mishap on September 22, 1909, Yep decided to trace the story. A heap of questions ensued. "Did he ever build that new biplane?" Yep contemplated to himself, "I do not know. Nor do I know why he built that first biplane. I do not even know where he came from or whether he had a wife and a family" (247). However, Yep is deterred by neither the scarcity of information nor the obscurity of origin:

> Of the hundreds of thousands of Chinese who flocked to these shores we know next to nothing. They remain a dull, faceless mass: statistic fodder to be fed to the sociologists, or lifeless abstraction to be manipulated by historians. And yet these Chinese were human beings—with fears and hopes, joys and sorrows like the rest of us. *In the adventures of the various members of the Company of the Peach Orchard Vow, I have tried to make some of these dry historical facts become living experiences.* (247; my emphasis)

The attempt to humanize the faceless mass is strikingly carried out in the name of the Peach Orchard Vow, an allusion instantly revealing Yep's conscious alliance with an extant Chinese American tradition. A famous episode from the fifteenth century Chinese folk epic, *Romance of the Three Kingdoms*, the Peach Garden Oath relates the sworn brotherhood of three Shu Han heroes who vowed to a faithful comradeship that ends only with death. Such a brotherhood was later emulated, particularly by the secret societies of Canton that mushroomed in the nineteenth century against the Manchu Empire (Liu 1966, 202). Guan Gong, or Kwan Kung, one of the three sworn brothers, was ennobled and deified in Cantonese folklore to have become, in Frank Chin's words, "the god of war to soldiers . . . the god of literature to fighters who soldier with words, and the god patron protector of actors" (Chin 1981, xxvi).

Yep's move is meaningful because of his deliberate affiliation with a historical-literary model of alliance rooted in Chinese American practice, which is, interestingly enough, an attempt of *making* kinship, an act of affiliation that naturalizes social bonds for a common cause. More meaningful than this declared intention is the manner in which Yep executes it. *Dragonwings* becomes for him at once an occasion to understand the space between selves and an occasion to make Fung Joe Guey, the pilot, and Laurence Yep, the writer, take off together. To achieve this, Yep has chosen to become the narrator, Moon Shadow, *the son of his adopted father*, Fung Joe Guey, who has now become the fictive Windrider. Yep's narrative positioning combines both the tropes of filiation and affiliation. In the creative portrayal of a father-son bond, Yep has acted out the symbolic potentials of a communal identity. The father's fairy tale account of Dragon King's naming of him as Windrider, the "softskin" human embodiment of a former dragon physician whose dream it is to be "reborn again as a dragon," fires Moon Shadow's imagination to such an extent that he sees himself practically as a part of his father's journey back to heaven (34–47). "All about me," Moon Shadow tells us, "I had Father's dream taking visible form—first in the pictures . . . then in the models . . . and finally in the skeleton of the flying machine itself" (210). All the while, the reader sees a filial relationship taking shape: Windrider and Moon Shadow have together "learned about being a father and a son" (55). The lesson of *Dragonwings* transcends flight; as Father said toward the end, "Dragons have immense families too. It would be nice to live long enough to see my great-grandchildren. And it may be that my final test is to raise a brood of superior women and men" (242). Windrider's regenerative wish has certainly come true in the fictive field of dreams—in imagining an ancestor Yep has imagined a form of life, transferring the legitimacy of filiation to affiliation while bringing about a superior brood of men and women whose imaginative reading of the book will make them the proud progeny of the dragon.

Though apparently pursuing the theme of filiation, Yep's affiliative textualization suggests a reverse order of progenitoring. The true originator of the line of descent is not the father/grandfather, or mother/grandmother, but rather the author himself/herself. The use of a titular ancestor becomes a strategy of authenticating the ethnic self in significant traditions. Shawn Wong's 1979 novel, *Homebase*, stands out as yet another example of this family romance. The book catches its audience from its opening epigraph that reads: "AILAN-THUS altissima (*A. glandulosa*). Tree-of-Heaven. Deciduous tree. All Zones. Native of China. Planted a century ago in California's gold

country." The metaphoric implication of the tree's origin and trans-
plantation appears irresistible when the description continues, "Often
condemned as a weed tree because it suckers profusely, but it must
be praised for its ability to create beauty and shade under adverse
conditions—drought, hot winds, and every type of difficult soil."
Botanic classification transfers to biological filiation and sociological
affiliation. Shawn Wong has recovered the tenacity of the Chinese
American spirit in his imaged tree, surviving the American grain.

The tree is the novel's central organic trope, its most essential form,
and its most basic narrative intelligence. In its endowed human spirit,
the tree embodies an ancestral dream, as the protagonist Rainsford
Chan makes explicit:

> I will remember how my father showed me the stump of a once
> giant redwood tree, showed me its rings of growth. Like a blind
> man, he made me run my fingers over each year grain to feel the
> year of my great-grandfather's birth, my grandfather's birth, his
> own birth, and my birth. Out of all this I will see dreams, see
> myself fixed in place on the land. (23)

Indeed, the tree becomes the "homebase" that spawns Rainsford's life
stories:

> And it was here that I told all the stories of *four generations of my
> own life.* Out of this pure day where I rose up at sunrise to meet
> my grandfather's life here, where I felt the presence of his heart
> against the walls, heard it as noise in the night. . . . And out of
> so much *responsibility to create the whole vision of my life in
> America, of our lives in America,* their death gave me my own
> clear voice, gave me the heart speaking, but it was not my own
> heart to use. (57–58; my emphasis)

Vibrating with the tone of *Aiiieeeee!* that laments the racist suppression
of "seven generations of Asian-American voices" (xvi), Shawn Wong,
a coeditor of the anthology, realizes the "responsibility" of his mission,
for it is the writer who will recuperate historic personages and create
an intergenerational voice of Chinese America—the lives of the rail-
roader in the Sierra Nevada Mountains and of the detained immigrant
on Angel Island now breathe through the pages. "Wong's voice is the
orphan's wishing himself into family," novelist Diana Chang sharply
observes, "the orphan's loving the gone in order to hold onto their
presence, remembering his heritage to stave off his own dying through
their passing away" (1981, 137).

An orphan's devotion naturally turns into forms of emphathetic
perception. At times the son becomes the mother, who has "shaped
the style of my [Rainsford's] manhood in accordance with her own

competitive and ambitious self" (Wong 1979, 47, 38). Other times he is his own father or grandfather: hiking with "my patronizing blond-haired, whining, pouting bride of fifteen, known to me as 'The Body',"" Rainsford feels that he is "making up for those restless years, the lonely years of my grandfathers" (78, 76). Here, Wong's manner of speech is akin to his fellow writer Frank Chin's. One thinks of such a story as "The Eat and Run Midnight People" in *The Chinaman Pacific & Frisco R. R. Co.* (1988), which also bends on the same invocation of the grandfather. Like Rainsford who juxtaposes historical memory with day-to-day reverie, the narrative "I" of Chin chants, "Ride with me, Grandfather" when atop a horny white nun (23). While the theme of racial and sexual revenge has its uneasy nuances, such fictional acts of filial empathy serve not only as the grandson's compensation for the grandfather's lack, but also as poignant reminders of a history of Chinese exclusion and antimiscegenation laws whose impact are yet to be reckoned with. "The Body," as Rainsford remarks, "is America. She tells me things about me that I am not" (78). Nevertheless, in his resolute production of his progenitor, Rainsford has produced the self who is, let me make a similar affiliative shift, the child who is the father of man.

Part II

If Yep and Wong are keen on the narrative recalling of a family, an extended family that may embrace a Chinese American humanity, they are certainly not alone in their endeavor. Maxine Hong Kingston's 1980 book could be regarded as a sibling product, a sister's voice and a daughter's song commingling in the filial rapture of the time. *China Men* affiliates itself with the almost consensual quest for a cohesive Chinese American kinship by both establishing empowering origins and subverting hegemonic discursive formations. Though sharing the desire with Yep, Wong, and the tribe of poets discussed earlier to reconstitute an indigenous history, Kingston seems more interested in textual mediation, revision, and transformation. For her, *China Men* is "claiming America" in her Chinese American way. Following the example of William Carlos Williams's precursor text, *In the American Grain* (1956), which challenged, in Myra Jehlen's words, "the American teleology . . . that continues to animate the discovery story" by asserting the Icelandic legends (1986, 25), Kingston has seized upon the same dominant mythology of entelechy as a point of her departure by unfolding in her family saga more than a century of Chinese American experience.

Kingston's affiliation with China Men signifies a linguistic difference in naming. One recalls that Frank Chin's self-referential term has been consistently "Chinaman" from the 1970s "Chickencoop" to the 1980s "Pacific." Chin has traced the term to a time before it was even tarnished by racial slurs, and in his parodic essay "Chinaman's Chance" (1982) we hear him claim the name with pride:

> [W]e all feel "Chinaman" comes more naturally into the rhythm of the talk we're talking, especially if we are sucking and booming a railroad pace, reminiscent of an ancient back-breaking track-laying race, and our words want to wheel belly, shine and shine with a high iron.
>
> Let others be embarrassed by the little "Chinaman's" they have to abort and swallow down dead unspoken before they're heard. I'm talking *in tribute* to the Chinamans who took off their hats one Utah noon and looked west back over the six miles of track they'd laid since sunrise, and sighed, while further west, the Sierra they'd crossed, thundering applause they heard in their nerves.
>
> "Chinaman" is what we called ourselves, John. And "China-man" is what we answered to when called, John. "John" is what a Chinaman called a white. "Hey, John!" we said, the first to speak off the boat, as if we'd come home, and we had. *We came with a vision and put it into words*, first step on the American continent, home to Gum San, California Gold Mountain, to get rich in the mines. "Me longtime Californ'," we said. (167–69; my emphasis)

Chin has embraced the name with a celebration of its honorific intonations, cleansing its image from historical pollution. For him, "The Chinamans" are his forefathers who "carved the Sierras into their Plymouth Rock" and a name engraved in the mind of their filial descendants (170).

Tacitly responding to Chin and others' restorational champion of "Chinaman," Kingston writes in *American Heritage:*

> In the early days of Chinese American history, men called them-selves "Chinamen"... the term distinguished them from the "Chinese" who remained citizens of China, and showed they were not recognized as Americans. Later, of course, it became an insult. Young Chinese Americans today are reclaiming the word because of its political and historical precision, and are demanding that it be said with dignity and not for name-calling. (1978, 37)

However, if Chin has chosen to reimburse the currency of "Chinaman," Kingston takes a different shot at the term. She is more inclined to refute the authoritative oppression with which "Chinaman" seems to have been connoted. As Williams's *In the American Grain* opens with a proclamation, "It has been my wish to draw from every source one thing, the strange phosphorus of the life, nameless under an old misappellation" (1956, v), so Kingston begins her program of discovering America with a rectification of the name. *China Men* is Kingston's choice register, not Chinamen whose pejorative meaning predominates its usage, but China Men—a literal English translation of Chinese characters, meaning Chinese—who are also makers of American history.

Similar to Shawn Wong, who establishes his homebase by fondling the each year grain of the family tree, Kingston structures her work by kinship titles so that all characters are relatives, all stories are related, and all China Men are in the family. Unlike *The Woman Warrior,* whose naming strategy delineates the differences in an intergenerational matrilineal order, *China Men* uses generic designations like great grandfather, grandfather, father, uncle, and brother to punctuate continuation in patrilineal descent. "I thought that all of us see them as ancestors . . . mythic characters of a past golden age," Kingston explains, "it was all right to call them 'great grandfather' because they become the great grandfather of us all. Also they become the great grandfathers of our country in the sense of claiming America" (Islas 1983, 15). Thus, "The Great Grandfather of the Sandalwood Mountains" treks to Hawaii, hacking its jungles and harvesting sugarcane (Kingston 1980, 81–116); "The Grandfather of the Sierra Nevada Mountains" hammers against the granite, leaving a network of steel trails as the evidence of his presence (121–49); "The Father from China" (5–71) in his turn is "The American Father" (235–55), resolute in "The Making of More Americans" (163–221); and finally, "The Brother in Vietnam" brings us back to the present, refreshing our sense of a continual self (261–305). In this way, kinship titles provide *China Men* with the organizing code of the Chinese American epic experience. Kingston's use of the generational rhetoric of descent constitutes an alternative American historiography in a Chinese American point of view. Frank Chin's revulsion against the presumption that "yellow writers would tell their yellow literary time by a white clock" (1977, 42) and his fictional exercise of a different temporality in a story like "Railroad Standard Time" now find themselves together with Kingston's work in a congeneric enterprise of recovering their celebratory past.[1] The footprints of China Men across the North American continent also offer an alternative sociogeography in which Chinese Americans are to be re-viewed. Kingston's China Men are not confined in Chinatowns; they are both transoceanic and transcontinental, shuttling across spaces like the Monkey somersaulting in clouds. Kingston's mapping of their physical traces is in company with Shawn Wong, whose narrator Rainsford "see legends" while murmuring "the names of stations and towns like prayers, as if they belonged to me" (1979, 112).

Part III

The concluding vignette of *China Men*, "On Listening," shows Kingston's authorial postulations of her agency in the recovery of the familial storyline. In a manner strikingly similar to Kenneth Burke's fable of history as conversation in the parlor, Kingston orchestrates a party of disparate voices in which the motif of the myth of discovery recurs (Burke 1973, 110–11). A Filipino scholar states that the Chinese looked for the Gold Mountain in the Philippines while a young Chinese American interrupts him to say that a Chinese monk did indeed go to Mexico with Cortez. He is then disputed by someone else who claims that "some cowboys saw mandarins floating over California in a hot-air balloon, which came all the way from China." Kingston, the narrator, does not clearly "hear everything" said, and upon her request, the Filipino scholar promises "to write it down" for her. At this point, Kingston punctures her narrative by addressing both the audience at the party and at large: "Good. Now I could watch the young men who listen" (308–9).

To me, the anecdote not only unravels the nature of history as competitive stories, but more importantly it highlights the "twisted design," to use a phrase from *The Woman Warrior*, of Kingston's narrative plot. If Walt Whitman says to his audience that "you shall listen to all sides and filter them for yourself," he is asking them to actively participate in the song of democracy (26). If Ralph Ellison poses his rhetorical question in the last line of *Invisible Man*, "Who knows but on the lower frequencies, I speak for you?" he is appealing to his readers' imaginative identification (1972, 439). When Kingston says that "I could watch the young men who listen," she is investing her hope of revisioning a historical past and envisioning a prospective future in the new generations of her story community. A story is simply not a good one, the narrator turned onlooker seems to say, if it is unable to spawn its followers and regenerate its own follow-ups. Like Brave Orchid, the champion talker who talks Kingston into existence, the daughter storyteller is now wishing her genealogy to emerge.

David Henry Hwang hears the invitation to chorus, and he comes along with his own answering music. In a note to *FOB and Other*

Plays, his virgin play, first staged in 1979 at Stanford University, where he was a student, and then awarded an Obie in 1980 after Joseph Papp's Off Broadway production, the young playwright attributes his source of inspiration to the two "parental figures," as they were, of contemporary Chinese American literature:

> The roots of *FOB* are thoroughly American. The play began when a sketch I was writing about a limousine trip through Westwood, California, was invaded by two figures from American literature, Fa Mu Lan, the girl who takes her father's place in battle, from Maxine Hong Kingston's *The Woman Warrior*, and Gwan Gung, the god of fighters and writers, from Frank Chin's *Gee, Pop!* (3)

With this note, Hwang both declares the professed origin of his play and joins the inner literary circle of "us" in a family of ethnic solidarity. Such a gesture is also evident in his choice of a collective pronoun, the characteristic and charismatic "we" in the introduction to his anthology *Broken Promises* (1983), which he dedicates to the "Asian American theater people across this nation . . . as an offering" (xiii). It is small wonder that such an offering is graciously acknowledged by Maxine Hong Kingston in her foreword to that volume, later reproduced for Hwang's recent edition of *FOB and Other Plays*. Watching the young men who not only listen to but also renew her story, Kingston is exuberant that "our private Chinese lives and secret language can be communally understood. . . . Here is a community. We are proud to the bones" (Hwang 1990, vii).

FOB is a filial assertion of family membership, but more importantly it consciously affiliates itself with a recovered Chinese American tradition. Structurally, the play continues in the direction of Kingston's mixing of reality and fantasy in *The Woman Warrior* and Chin's dramatic shifts through limbo and ghetto in *The Chickencoop Chinaman*. Thematically, it confirms its predecessors' value in tapping the Chinese American mythic past as a potential avenue of freedom from the state of loss and alienation. Generically, it works in the vein of American immigrant literature, but subverts it by a refusal to embrace the assimilationist affirmation of the melting pot.

The prologue of the play directs the audience instantly to the center of Hwang's dramatic conflict: FOB vs. ABC. Dale, the native American-born Chinese (ABC) has this unflattering picture of his "sworn enem[y]," "F-O-B. Fresh Off the Boat. . . . Clumsy, ugly, greasy FOB. Loud, stupid, four-eyed FOB" (1990, 6). Grace, Dale's cousin and a naturalized Chinese American, seems far more tolerant of Steve, the son of a rich Hong Kong businessman and the FOB of the play. When the play evolves, the characters' sense of America and their sense of self in relation to it come into focus. Grace recalls her troubled adolescence when she bleached her hair and hung out at the beach in order to appear colorless and get along, and she is happy that she has outgrown that phase (30–31). Steve, however, is still unsure of his footing and tries to cover up his awkwardness with his chauffeur and limousine (22–23). Dale, the self-made-ethnic-turned-normal, is basking in his own success and eager to initiate Steve into his own mode of being:

> [Dale's parents are] yellow ghosts and they've tried to cage me up with Chinese-ness when all the time we were in America. *(Pause)* So, I've had to work real hard—real hard—to be myself. To not be a Chinese, a yellow, a slant, a gook. To be just a human being, like everyone else, *(Pause)* I've paid my dues. And that's why I am much better now. I'm making it, you know? I'm making it in America. (32)

> Coming to America, you're gonna jump the boat. You're gonna decide you like us ... you can't hold out—you're no different. You won't even know it's coming before it has you. Before you're trying real hard to be just like the rest of us—go dinner, go movie, go motel, bang-bang. And when your father writes you that do-it-yourself acupuncture sales are down, you'll throw that letter in the basket and burn it in your brain. And you'll write that you're gonna live in Monterey Park a few years before going back home—and you'll get your green card—and you'll build up a nice little stockbroker's business and have a few American kids before your dad realizes what's happened and dies, his hopes reduced to a few chattering teeth and a pack of pornographic playing cards. (26)

The scene of professing the uninitiated, like the one above between Dale and Steve, is not new in Chinese American literature. Fred's lecture of China MaMa in *The Year of the Dragon* is one, and Kingston's graphic representation of the girl who tortures her silent classmate in order to make her talk is another. What appears common among these scenes is not so much lending of a helping hand from the insider of a host society, but a rejected wanna-be's display of cultural know-how to the newcomer, or the less assimilated. The ostentation and condescension, most of the time inseparable from one another, are manifestations of the American-born Chinese's painstakingly acquired sameness with the dominant race and culture. The bildungsroman of Dale, at least from the way he presents and preaches to Steve, seems to be a theatrical shorthand for playwright Hwang to demonstrate the syndrome, in his own words, of "self-loathing." He continues, "Dale loathes the 'Fresh-Off-the-Boat' Steve precisely because the latter represents all the identifications Dale has spent a lifetime attempting to avoid" (xi). Knowing Hwang's affiliation with the Asian American theater movement in the 1970s and his proclaimed connection with Chin, one will have no trouble seeing *FOB* as a dramatic extension of one of the overriding thematic concerns of *Aiiieeeee!* (1983), which, we recall, associates almost all aspects of Asian American literary and cultural history with the cancer, in a slightly different wording, of "self-contempt."

Part of Hwang's theatrical prescription to this phenomenal malady seems to be setting Steve up as a possible model for his doppelgänger Dale so that the latter would become whole again by integrating with the former, his abnegated other. This works in the scene when Grace suggests that the three of them "play Group Story," or more aptly group therapy (42). Dale starts off as the bear of the story but soon quits his part. Steve and Grace square off as Gwan Gung and Fa Mu Lan in a series of exchanges in which Mu Lan wants to avenge herself on Gwan Gung's mindless slaughter of her family for sport. The anachronistic meeting of the mythic heroes conversing in a form close to Christian liturgy would become all too baffling for this reader if it were not for Steve's occasional monologue to link Gwan Gung with successive generations of Chinese immigrants, fighting their way into the United States. I am not so troubled by Hwang's antiheroic treatment of Gwan Gung in the exposition of his foolhardiness as I am by his haphazard use of folklore. Kingston notes in her foreword that Hwang "draws from Chinese mythology and asks what good those myths do us in America" (viii). Steve's revisionist impersonation of Gwan Gung coupled with his own romantic naïveté somehow makes me wonder about his connection with his folk god either in terms of the classic text or in the immigrant folk tradition. He appears less determined and less warriorlike than the historic personage that he is supposedly emulating. Therefore, when Steven and Grace finally join hands, suggesting perhaps that the former has awakened the latter's repressed memory of her cultural heritage, such a symbolic union in the name of the warriors seems to lack the sense of purpose one has encountered in Kingston's and Chin's re-creations of myths. Because of Hwang's ambivalence at the surrealistic level, the ultimate persuasiveness of *FOB* at the level of reality appears diminished.

Even if encouraged by the power of myth in the destiny of Steve and Grace, the audience will not fail to see that Dale is thrown off the boat, so to speak. The myth of Gwan Gung has done little good for Dale, who remains almost unchanged and untouched by the end of the play, "alone in the back room," once more cursing, "Clumsy, ugly, greasy FOB" (50). FOB and ABC seem to go their separate ways, with an unusual twist, though, that the immigrant is not only granted entrance into America, but is also positioned as the hero. Hwang thus reverses the role of theater as an instrument of Americanizing the newcomer into denouncing their affiliation with the place of their origin, and proposes a necessary maintenance of a home culture in a host society. *FOB* thus compounds the theme of assimilation as opposed to acculturation, chronicling its new meaning for the present generations.

Hwang's second work, *The Dance and the Railroad* (in *FOB* 1981), features two nineteenth century railroaders at the site of the construction camp. Against the backdrop of the workers' strike for better wages and working hours is a celebration of their creative urge, the determination to flex their muscles for operatic performance rather than being forced into service by "the white man" (64). The play also bears family resemblances to Kingston's and Chin's works. The railroad workers' demand, "Eight hours a day good for white man, all the same good for Chinaman" (65), is literally lifted out of the pages of "The Grandfather of the Sierra Nevada Mountains" chapter of Kingston's *China Men* (1980, 139). Hwang clearly joins Kingston's efforts to dismiss the myth of Chinese labor as inherently cheap and compliant. Meanwhile, he also takes up the line of the Lone Ranger in Chin's *Chickencoop Chinaman*, charging the "Chinamans with no songs, no jokes, no toasts, and no thanks" (1981, 37), by presenting the ritual and rhythm of Cantonese opera in the limelight.

In an even pithier form than *FOB*, *The Dance and the Railroad* quickly draws the audience into a similar master-pupil relation between Lone, the railroad old-timer/seasoned opera player, and Ma, the recent immigrant laborer/anxious student of opera. Though the structural pattern takes after the first play, the communication between the characters in the present work is more genuine and more nurturing. In their performing sessions, Lone and Ma help each other to shape a vision and revive a tradition so that the invocation of Gwan Gung is not an end in itself but a jumping board, as Ma sees it, to "immortalize my story" and to honor the victory of the strikers (78). Under the watching eyes of Gwan Gung, Lone and Ma measure their steps and shift their poses: water-crossing dance, labor dance, and battle dance succeed one another with dazzling intensity. With gangs banging, arias flowing, sticks twirling, Lone and Ma at once express an idiosyncratic cultural form and enact the spirit of Gwan Gung in the immigrants' undaunted passage to America and their subsequent forcing of the mountains and forcing of "the white devil to act civilized" (82).

With *Family Devotions* (in *FOB* 1981, 87–146), Hwang completes his Chinese American trilogy with a vibrant code. Returning from his excursion to the collective consciousness about the transcontinental railroad, Hwang probes into the more personal mythologies of his own family. The play rings an autobiographical note when he reconstructs his multigenerational saga from China to the Philippines and then to America. But "the lanai/sunroom and the tennis court of a home in Bel Air, California" definitely indicate an affluent contemporary setting (91). When the play opens, Ama and Popo, the eldest generation of the family, are waiting for their long-separated brother Di-gou to join them from China. Popo's daughter Hannah and son-in-law Robert are off to the airport while Ama's daughter Joanne and her husband Wilbur are home barbecuing chicken. Their seventeen-year-old Jenny is with her cousin Chester, a violinist who has just taken a job in the Boston Symphony and attempts to skip the family gathering. Ama and Popo are engaged in a heated chit-chat, first comparing their nisei (second generation Japanese American) son-in-law Wilbur to the Japanese in the World War II documentary who "always kill and laugh, kill and laugh" (97), and then drifting to Di-gou, who is made to work in the rice fields of China, where "all the people wear wires in their heads [which] force them to work all day and sing Communist song" (95). Finally, a revelation comes that Ama and Popo are to kick the communist demon out of their backslid brother by soliciting his testimony of their aunt See-goh-poh, the evangelist who is the "first in the family to become Christian [and made] this family chosen by God" half a century ago in China (102–3).

After Di-gou's arrival, Ama lights up her "neon cross" and commands, "We begin! Family Devotions!" (125). Popo begins her "Special Testimony" by reminiscing about the stormy boat trip from China to the Philippines and confirming it as God's plan (129). Everyone applauds. Jenny expresses her love for the family and everyone applauds (130). Wilbur reports his being voted "Mr. Congeniality" in his social club, but is pushed off the podium by Robert, who looks like a middle-aged version of Dale in *FOB* (131). Deciding to show his relative "American ways" (118), Robert relishes his celebrity status resulting from a kidnap incident by calling it his "American Dream. From rags to kidnap victim" (136). Soon the testimonies fall into shambles, everyone is disputing everyone else except Di-gou, who has by now become his sisters' most convenient diversion away from "this small family disagreement" (137). Failing to extract Di-gou's testimony of God's mercy, Ama and Popo decide to punish his body and save his soul. With the help of their daughters, they tie him to the table and begin scourging him with an electric cord, when Di-gou "suddenly breaks out of his bonds" and "grabs Chester," who just rushes in to his rescue. Miraculously, Di-gou "begins speaking in tongues!" and Chester "begins interpreting [his] babbling" (138–41). The story of See-goh-poh is, however, not about a missionary who marries God and converts hundreds of villagers, as Ama and Popo so believed, but about a woman who goes on an evangelical tour to give birth to her illegitimate child in order to avoid her family's condemnation. Faith and facts collide when the sisters and their brother start comparing notes on the biographical details of their aunt, See-goh-poh, until the weight of truth seems too much for Ama and Popo to bear. Both of them collapse dead, turning into "two inert forms" (141–45).

Hwang's black comedy of errors eventually jars the initially tranquil surface of the play not just to unsettle his audience's perspective, but to reorganize it through a glass darkly. The family is so enmeshed in its mythologies that not even a Christian vision is able to unify it. "Brainwash," a recurrent word in different contexts of the play, gives us perhaps an insight into the blindness of the characters' imprisonment in the various ideologies of religious fundamentalism, Communism, and the American dream. Can there be a family devotion that does not lead to fragmentation but integration? Beneath his exposé of the absurd in the main plot lies Hwang's pondering of such a question. Chester, whose circumstances of life are similar to Dale's in *FOB*, has originally no interest in meeting his granduncle Di-gou. When they do meet, however, they become the only people in the play who are really communicating:

> DI-GOU: There are faces back further than you can see. Faces long before the white missionaries arrived in China. Here. (*He holds CHESTER's violin so that its back is facing CHESTER, and uses it like a mirror*) Look here. At your face. Study your face and you will see—the shape of your face is the shape of faces back many generations—across an ocean, in another soil. You must become one with your family before you can hope to live away from it. (123)

Di-gou's rhetoric of filiation barely appeals to Chester, because for him "See-goh-poh's face is the only one that has any meaning here. . . . There's nothing for me" (123). Besides, holding the violin back to mirror Di-gou, Chester foresees change, "Before you know it, you'll be praying and speaking in tongues" (124). Yet, when the play reaches its climax, neither does Di-gou kneel before the neon cross nor does Chester reject the faces. Transformations indeed occur, however. The deaths of his sisters completely alters Di-gou's plan to bring them back to China; instead, he realizes that "no one leaves America" and wishes to "drive an American car down an American freeway" (145). After Di-gou exits the stage and before the curtain falls, *"(a single spotlight* [falls] *on CHESTER's face, standing where DI-GOU stood at the beginning of the play) (The shape of CHESTER's face begins to change)"* (146).

It is difficult to imagine Chester's face by reading the script alone, but Chester's taking of Di-gou's place seems to warrant a reading that the grandnephew may resemble his granduncle. Thus, in his theatrical signification, Hwang is using biological affinity as a vehicle to convey a newly found cultural affiliation, for indeed Di-gou and Chester are rebels of different generations but of the same kind against their family religion. The antinomians appear to have united, casting a ray of hope for continuity in an otherwise totally disintegrated family. Hwang obviously wants more than the repudiation of failing familial mythologies and wishes to salvage something meaningful for an alternative family tradition. In *Family Devotions* as in *FOB* and *The Dance and the Railroad,* Hwang has made the possibilities of connecting an immigrant culture his special province. The kind of renewed kinsman contact we have seen in his theater, between Di-gou and Chester or between Steven and Grace, is always invigorating. Although the quest for the common experiential denominator cannot eradicate discord, Hwang seems convinced in his trilogy that the self-conscious affiliation of native-born and immigrant Chinese Americans can enable the birth of a meaningful community.

Part IV

Hwang's thematic treatment of the family, however, bears some resemblance to Frank Chin's in that both playwrights express doubts about the effectiveness of the Chinese American family as a sustainable social form. *The Year of the Dragon* ends with the actual death of the patriarch, Pa, the hinted departure of Ma and the rest from Chinatown, and the stranded Fred, the main character who alone will or will not survive the shambles left by his next of kin. *Family Devotions* has a similar conclusion: the violent deaths of Ama and Popo, the feeling of utter loss and disorientation of Robert and Wilbur, and the flight of Chester from the mess add up to suggest sterility of the family. Hwang is, however, more optimistic than Chin because he injects hope into his work by suggesting kinsman contact outside the immediate family as a promising alternative. One wonders if the existing Chinese American familial order ails beyond treatment. Kingston's *The Woman Warrior* suggests otherwise. It expounds disruption of the family which embeds it within a Chinese box narrative that signifies its regenerative impulse. A more rosy outlook of this familial renewal can be found in Amy Tan's bestselling novel, *The Joy Luck Club*, which centers on a similar mother-daughter plot.

It is "[t]o my mother / and the memory of her mother" that Tan dedicates *The Joy Luck Club*, "You asked me once / what I would remember. / This, and much more." The dedication seems to have recapitulated one of the major themes of the book, the fictional act of re-membering by both recalling the past and by recreating a sense of membership in a forever tenuous formation of human community. Tan writes in her opening vignette:

> Now the woman was old. And she had a daughter who grew up speaking only English and swallowing more Coca-Cola than sorrow. For a long time now the woman had wanted to give her daughter the single swan feather and tell her, "This feather may look worthless, but it comes from afar and carries with it all my good intentions." And she waited, year after year, for the day she could tell her daughter this in perfect American English. (1989, 17)

The mother-daughter bonding hinges not so much on emotive links as it does on linguistic ones. On the one hand, the passage points to the difficulty of communication in an immigrant household where parental Chinese is not the mother tongue of the children and where the familial past of the elder generation is not automatically handed down to their American-born children. "In me," acknowledges the daughter narrator, "they see their own daughters, just as ignorant, just as unmindful of the truths and hopes they have brought to America. . . . They see daughters who will bear grandchildren born without any connecting hope passed from generation to generation" (41). On the other hand, the quotation from the opening vignette exemplifies the daughter's mindful attempt to continue the family aspiration. Her "perfect American English" is not an exclusionary language that separates her from her mother, but an inclusive language that brings them together. A bilingual reader may particularly appreciate the Pacific double-cross of Tan's English. The punning of "Coca-Cola" (which when translated in standard Chinese means "Tasty and Happy") with "sorrow" and the rendition of a Chinese idiom as "This feather may look worthless, but it comes from afar and carries with it all my good intentions" exhibits the enriching capacity of bilingual exchange.[2] *The Joy Luck Club* itself can be read as such an exchange both at the private, familial level of mother and daughter and at the level of the public sphere where ethnic characters of the book willingly converse with readers of the mainstream culture.

The Joy Luck Club is organized into four "sections" (my word instead of "chapters" because of the latter's suggestion of sequence) and each section contains four stories. All sixteen stories are told by a narrative "I" who is differentiated each time by her name and the title preceding the story. With the exception of the first and last stories—where Jing-Mei Woo substitutes her mother Suyuan Woo's narrative voice as she does in replacing her mother's place at the mah jong table—the first section of the book reads like the autobiographical narratives of the four mothers, the next two depict the journeys of the four daughters, and the last one returns to the mothers. For me, the temptation to find out whose daughter it is that I am reading begins with section two, an irresistible temptation that nudges me until the last section, when I realize to my surprise I have to discover whose mother it is that I am reading just for a change. The readers of the book, including the aforementioned reviewers, may experience the same, and I am told by many that they helplessly resort to the table of The Joy Luck Club, as I did myself. Maxine Hong Kingston, for example, was impressed by the book but troubled by the compulsion to go back to the table while other less assiduous readers may simply stop making distinctions among characters.[3]

Although The Joy Luck Club originated as a group of stories and still retains traces of short fiction, to dismiss the book on grounds of its insufficient command of novelistic form or its lack of mastery of the individual voices actually prevents the possibility of reading it as something novel. To read The Joy Luck Club as a novel, one has to understand the rhetorical device that has driven readers. To me, the structure of the book at once deconstructs the notion of novel as a personal heroic enterprise motivated by economic individualism and reconstructs it as a communal enterprise.

Crucial to this interpretation are the table of contents, which I will call table one, and the table of The Joy Luck Club, which I will refer to as table two. Table one has a familiar look: when sections of the novel are introduced and interspliced with vignettes, The Joy Luck Club at least in its visual format takes after Kingston's China Men. However, Tan's work is different from Kingston's in two significant ways. While China Men delineates a patrilineal order, The Joy Luck Club follows a matrilineal one. While China Men pursues the line of descent, The Joy Luck Club does not. How can a novel with a mother-daughter plot eschew descent? My answer to this question is that it apparently does not, but in effect redefines descent as such. The assertion needs some further clarification. Table one is arranged in the fashion that follows: the stories by Jing-Mei Woo, An-Mei Hsu, Lindo Jong, and Ying-Ying St. Clair form the first section; the stories by their daughters Waverly Jong, Lena St. Clair, Rose Hsu Jordan, Jing-Mei Woo, and Lena St. Clair, Waverly Jong, Rose Hsu Jordan, and Jing-Mei Woo form the next two sections; and the stories by An-Mei Hsu, Ying-Ying St. Clair, Lindo Jong, and Jing-Mei Woo conclude the last section. Despite the ostensible mother-daughter division, there is no conceivable order that facilitates the reader's quest of family lineage.

Table two does something that seemingly contradicts my foregoing argument:

The Mothers	The Daughters
Suyuan Woo	Jing-Mei "June" Woo
An-Mei Hsu	Rose Hsu Jordan
Lindo Jong	Waverly Jong
Ying-Ying St. Clair	Lena St. Clair

This table certainly has a semblance to the kind of family tree format of the nineteenth century realistic tradition, but the analogy stops there. Instead of a hierarchical genealogy, Tan's is a horizontal one. Instead of tracing the progenitor of a family, Tan groups four families unrelated by blood under the seal of the club, signifying a formal sharing of communal identity. If the readers are unsatisfied with table one because it fails to deliver their query of who is who, they will remain discontent with table two for the same reason—Amy Tan, in my view, has played a tricky narrative game of hide-and-seek only to question our (the readers') taken-for-granted sense of individuality and community. The mothers "who spent a lifetime comparing their children" and the daughters who rivaled one another like siblings indicate not so much a desire for difference as a range of closeness among the members of the club (37). *The Joy Luck Club* is a sworn sisterhood—not quite unlike the sworn brotherhood in *The Three Kingdoms*—through which the mothers of "unspeakable tragedies they had left behind in China and hopes they couldn't begin to express in their fragile English [in 'Bible study class' and 'choir practice']" consciously pledge their alliance for mutual well-being (20). The daughters' relation to each other seems to have been a reproduction of their mothers'. "All of us are like stairs, one step after another, going up and down, but all going the same way," An-Mei Hsu remarks (215). Though sounding a bit fatalistic, this could be Tan's self-referential comment on her novel: the destinies of mother-daughter are filiated as the course of life among mothers and daughters are affiliated. When the money from the mah jong table is not for an individual's gain but for the interest of the club, and when the aunties saved money for June Woo to fulfill her mother's wish to find her lost daughters in China, one begins to understand the transgenerational and transfamilial tenacity of a community (39).

The tables with which Tan begins her novel are therefore ploys that may give illusory satisfaction to those of us who are prone to identify the individual heroines of the book, while they serve others as a moral about enabling communions. In a decade of greed when American individualism takes the shape of predatory egoism, the narrative structure of Amy Tan's novel may be suggesting an alternative of a fructifying collectivity—so ancient and so Oriental by nature that it probably never fails to appeal—where shared purpose and endeavor constitute the kernel of human experience. The blurring of voices and indistinguishable qualities of the characters therefore help to create a narrative sense of personal and social dependency not as symptoms of immaturity as male-centered Western psychology will diagnose it, but as signs of healthy human relationships. In this way, *The Joy Luck Club* has materialized in fictional form a way of Chinese American life not precisely filial or familial, but certainly related to it.

The abundant poetic, dramatic, and novelistic gestures of family devotion, be it biological or cultural, demonstrate some consensual movement toward the end of Chinese American literary reconstruction. The filiative tribute to ancestors and the affiliative effort at community building interact to claim both historical anchorage and present legitimacy for the ethnic entity. What appear at first glance as separate textual maneuvers have, in fact, constituted a nourishing dialogue, ensuring the continuity and contemporaneity of Chinese American expression.

Notes

1. "Railroad Standard Time" is collected in *The Chinaman Pacific & Frisco R.R. Co.* (1–7).

2. A more literal translation of Tan's quoted idiom would be, "Sending a goose feather from a thousand *li* [measure of length about half a kilometer] afar: the gift is light but the affection is heavy."

3. Conversation with Kingston, March 28, 1989, at the University of Texas, Austin.

Works Cited

Berssenbrugge, Mei-Mei. 1982. *Summits Move with the Tide.* Greenfield Center, NY: Greenfield Review.

Burke, Kenneth. 1973. *The Philosophy of Literary Form: Studies in Symbolic Action.* Berkeley: University of California Press.

Chang, Diana. 1981. "Homebase" (review). *Amerasia Journal* 8(1): 136–39.

Chin, Frank, Jeffery Paul Chan, Lawson Fusao Inada, and Shawn Wong, eds. 1983. *Aiiieeeee! An Anthology of Asian-American Writers.* Washington: Howard University Press.

Chin, Frank. 1982. "Chinaman's Chance." *WCH Way* 4: 167–81.

———. 1977. "Letter to Y'Bird." *Y'Bird Magazine* 1(1): 42–45.

———. 1981. *The Chickencoop Chinaman; and, The Year of the Dragon: Two Plays.* Seattle: University of Washington Press.

———. 1988. *The Chinaman Pacific & Frisco R.R. Co.* Minneapolis: Coffee House.

Chin, Marilyn. 1987. *Dwarf Bamboo.* Greenfield Center, NY: Greenfield Review.

Ellison, Ralph. 1972. *Invisible Man.* New York: Vintage.

Hwang, David Henry. 1983. *Broken Promises: Four Plays.* New York: Avon.

———. 1990. *FOB and Other Plays: With a Foreword by Maxine Hong Kingston.* New York: New American Library.

Islas, Arturo. 1983. "Maxine Hong Kingston." In *Women Writers of the West Coast: Speaking of Their Lives and Careers,* edited by Marilyn Yalom, 11–19. Santa Barbara: Capra.

Jehlen, Myra. 1986. *American Incarnation: The Individual, the Nation, and the Continent.* Cambridge: Harvard University Press.

Kingston, Maxine Hong. 1980. *China Men.* New York: Ballantine.

———. 1982. "Cultural Mis-readings by American Reviewers." In *Asian and American Writers in Dialogue: New Cultural Identities,* edited by Guy Amirthanayagam, 55–65. London: Macmillan.

———. 1978. "San Francisco's Chinatown: A View of the Other Side of Arnold Genthe's Camera." *American Heritage* Dec.: 35–47.

———. 1976. *The Woman Warrior: Memoirs of a Girlhood among Ghosts.* New York: Vintage Books.

Lau, Alan Chong. 1980. *Songs for Jadina.* Greenfield Center, NY: Greenfield Review.

Liu, Wu-Chi. 1966. *An Introduction to Chinese Literature.* Bloomington: Indiana University Press.

Lum, Wing Tek. 1987. *Expounding the Doubtful Points.* Honolulu: Bamboo Ridge.

Said, Edward W. 1983. *The World, the Text, and the Critic.* Cambridge, MA: Harvard University Press.

Song, Cathy. 1983. *Picture Bride.* New Haven, CT: Yale University Press.

Tan, Amy. 1989. *The Joy Luck Club.* New York: Putnam's.

Whitman, Walt. 1959. *Complete Poetry and Selected Prose,* edited by James E. Miller. Boston: Houghton Mifflin.

Williams, William Carlos. 1956. *In the American Grain*. New York: New Directions.

Wong, Nellie. 1977. *Dreams in Harrison Railroad Park*. Berkeley: Kelsey Street.

Wong, Shawn. 1979. *Homebase*. New York: I. Reed Books.

Yep, Laurence. 1975. *Dragonwings*. New York: Harper and Row.

15 The Unheard: Vietnamese Voices in the Literature Curriculum

Renny Christopher
University of California, Santa Cruz

> I could never understand Americans. First they came to Viet Nam,
> they killed my family, injured my neck with a grenade. . . . After
> what they did, they tried desperately to save my life, all the way
> from Viet Nam to San Francisco. Today I'm an American, too.
> Does that make me crazy?
> —Than Pham

> Learning . . . is, to no small extent, whether in elementary school
> or the university, learning to be stupid.
> —Jules Henry

Of the seven thousand or so books published in the United States
dealing with the Vietnam war, fewer than a dozen are by Vietnamese
American authors. Of those Vietnamese American books that have
been published, very few are read in college classes dealing with the
war (or with Asian American studies, or with anything else), because
they are not readily available, because they are not "literature," because
they do not "fit in." We can, in fact, watch the canon-formation process
at work in the area of Vietnam war literature. If we look at what is
being taught in college classes, at what is being written about in
literature journals, we can see that the emerging canon is almost
exclusively male, almost exclusively Euro-American, and, with the
exception of Ron Kovic's *Born on the Fourth of July*, exclusively middle-
class. There are works by women, by people of color, by working-
class writers out there, but they are being ignored. Prominent among
those being ignored are the works of Vietnamese Americans.

Vietnamese American literature is an emerging literature that is both
similar to and different from other immigrant literatures, and vitally
important in the ongoing efforts of the United States to understand
its role in the war, and the impact of the war on American culture.
Furthermore, Vietnamese American students from the population of
almost one million refugees now in this country are present in our
classrooms.

What can be gained by reading Tran Van Dinh's novel *Blue Dragon, White Tiger* (1982, published by a small press, and largely unread although it was reviewed by *The New York Times* when it came out), by reading Truong Nhu Tang's *A Vietcong Memoir* (1985), by reading Le Ly Hayslip's *When Heaven and Earth Changed Places* (1989)? What is the point of multicultural education, anyway?

What can be gained are insights into the nature of both Vietnam and the United States. What can be gained is an understanding of the full parameters of the war, the full costs, as well as insight into the newest U.S. immigrant group—a group that has already begun to make a major impact in American life. Vu-Duc Vuong ran for the Board of Supervisors in San Francisco in 1990, the first Vietnamese American candidate for a U.S. public office; Vietnamese fishermen are challenging discriminatory and selectively enforced U.S. fishing laws; and the Vietnamese American community is waging its own political conflicts, especially over the issue of normalization of relations with the Socialist Republic of Vietnam, over which several Vietnamese Americans, including writer Doan Van Toai and columnist Triet Le, have been killed or wounded.

Myra Jehlen has proposed a solution to cultural studies' problem of universality versus radical otherness. Her proposal suggests that neither universality nor radical otherness explains contemporary reality. As she says, "If difference ever existed, it is long lost." In other words, shared particular, historical experience is what overcomes otherness. Jehlen's term for this is "communality" (1990, lecture, University of California, Santa Cruz). Because colonizers and colonized (her example is the Spanish conquest of the Aztecs) are both present in the colonizing experience, they share that reality. Even if the two peoples come at the experience from different, unshared, realities, the shared historical experience is a place to begin talking.

This communality is precisely what the Vietnamese American works assert. Their goal is to explain that shared history to a U.S. audience from the side of the Vietnamese. So far, the U.S. audience has not really been listening. Even Hayslip, whose book is selling well, seems to be misread. The U.S. audience seems to be rejecting the possibility of communality. Or, rather, the U.S. audience, for the most part, doesn't even seem to recognize the possibility of communality, a possibility spread out richly in all the Vietnamese American works about the war.

Hayslip, in a prologue to her narrative, addresses both U.S. veterans of the war and civilians who did not go to the war, with a message not just of reconciliation but, more importantly, of the need to *mutually* learn from the experience of the war and to move forward together:

> The least you [veterans] did—the least any of us did—was our duty. For that we must be proud. The most that any of us did—or saw—was another face of destiny or luck or god. Children and soldiers have always known it to be terrible. If you have not yet found peace at the end of your war, I hope you will find it here. We have important new roles to play. . . .
>
> If you are a person who knows the Vietnam war, or any war, only by stories and pictures, this book is written for you too. . . . The special gift of that suffering, I have learned, is how to be strong while we are weak, how to be brave when we are afraid, how to be wise in the midst of confusion, and how to let go of that which we can no longer hold. In this way, anger can teach forgiveness, hate can teach us love, and war can teach us peace. (1989, xv)

The "here" that Hayslip refers to is her book. Her book is not intended to be just "literature"; it, like the organization she founded, the East Meets West Foundation, is intended as activism. She seeks, through the foundation and the book, to change U.S. thinking about the war.

Hayslip's final sentence, with its reconciliation of opposites, might be dismissed as just so much "Oriental mysticism" by readers seeking to reject her message of communality. However, the whole of her narrative goes on to support the assertions she makes in that sentence, that there are positive values to be learned from the horrifying experiences of war.

Tran Van Dinh, in his novel *Blue Dragon, White Tiger,* goes even further than Hayslip in his demand for recognition of communality. He asserts that the destinies of the United States and Vietnam are interlinked, and his novel is designed to foster recognition of that linked destiny in U.S. readers.

Dinh stresses not only the interlinked present and future of the two nations and two peoples, but of their interlinked past as well, a past not recognized by a Western-centered world view. The main character of the novel, Minh, a professor who returns to Vietnam in 1967 after teaching in the United States for several years, plans to lecture to his students at the University of Hue on

> such concepts as "life, liberty and the pursuit of happiness"; the influences of Confucianism on French philosophers like Voltaire, Montesquieu, and Diderot, who in turn had influence on American revolutionaries like Thomas Jefferson; and the role of Thomas Paine in the 1776 revolution. (1983, 124)

Dinh is thus asserting that the communality between the two nations stretches far back into both their pasts—that East and West have long influenced each other, and that the direction of influence has not flowed one way. Dinh, by tracing a line of thought from Confucianism through the French philosophers to Jefferson, author of the American Declaration of Independence, is also pointing to the next step in the linkage. In 1945 Ho Chi Minh modeled the Vietnamese declaration of independence on the American Declaration, and on the writings of the French Revolution:

> "All men are created equal. They are endowed by their Creator with certain inalienable Rights; among these are Life, Liberty and the pursuit of Happiness."
>
> This immortal statement appeared in the Declaration of Independence of the United States of America in 1776. In a broader sense, it means: All the peoples on the earth are equal from birth, all the peoples have a right to live and to be happy and free.
>
> The Declaration of the Rights of Man and the Citizen, made at the time of the French Revolution, in 1791, also states: "All men are born free and with equal rights, and must always remain free and have equal rights."
>
> These are undeniable truths. (1973, 53)

Students in my American studies class on the Vietnam war in American popular culture are always astonished to discover that this is the Vietnamese declaration of independence, but it is an excellent point at which to begin talking about communality and shared ground.

Truong Nhu Tang, in *A Vietcong Memoir,* makes the same demand of his U.S. readers that the other two authors do. (Tang is not Vietnamese American; he lives in Paris. His book, however, was written in English and aimed at a U.S. audience, so I am considering him along with Hayslip and Dinh, both Vietnamese Americans.) Tang writes in his foreword:

> [I]t is only through understanding the Vietnamese who fought on the other side that Americans will have anything like a complete portrait of a war upon which they have been reflecting so deeply—the only war they have ever lost. (1985, xiv)

Despite the growing number of works available by or about the Vietnamese, the U.S. public and teachers of literature have not taken note of the message so eloquently stated by these authors.

How *can* we teach these works that lie so far outside the discourse that we are familiar with? Actually, none of them is difficult, because the books do the work themselves. Designed by their authors to communicate with American audiences, they go far more than halfway in building the bridges. As Reed Way Dasenbrock writes in chapter 3 of this volume, "You can trust them . . . to give you the assistance you need."

Blue Dragon, White Tiger is the story of Minh, a Vietnamese professor of politics who has been living and teaching in the United States for several years when the story opens. He returns to Vietnam in 1967, joins the National Liberation Front (NLF), becomes part of the negotiating team in Paris, serves under the new regime after liberation, then ultimately defects back to the United States. One review said of the novel,

> Unlike many of the popular war novels, wherein the action is fast and the world is black and white, Tran Van Dinh's work leaves much room for reflection while telling his story against the background of the war, and, what is more important, within the texture of Vietnamese culture. It is a story that challenges the intellect and the imagination. (Crown 1985, 160)

More, the novel actually blends American and Vietnamese storytelling conventions. While it uses plot, character, dialogue, and the other traditional elements of American fiction, it also uses elements of fate and symbolism from the Vietnamese tradition. Monocultural American readers might mistake the workings of fate in the novel for contrived coincidence; to do so is to miss part of the point. Events in the novel (especially the appearances of three women: the American Jennifer and the Vietnamese Xuan and Thai) occur because Minh's fate requires that they appear to teach him particular lessons.

Minh's quest throughout the novel is to fit Marxist doctrine into Vietnamese culture. His friend, Loc, explains to Minh:

> Marxism, a humanist philosophy basically, is made up essentially of two interrelated foundations that we Vietnamese have discovered and lived with for thousands of years. These are *Tinh*, feeling, and *Ly*, reason. At the present time, our *Tinh* is grounded in our culture and our *Ly* is rooted in our just struggle for independence, freedom, and socialism. *Ly* helps us clarify our *Tinh* and devise appropriate strategies and tactics for the revolution. *Tinh*, in turn, humanizes our *Ly* and transforms our strategies into understandable, popular, workable programs of action. *Tinh* and *Ly* form the unbroken circle in which our national communication operates. (96)

Ultimately, though, Minh is unable to reconcile the postliberation Vietnamese state with his ideal of Vietnamese culture, and he returns to the United States, where he will hold "the spirit of the historic Vietnam" in his heart (334). It is Minh's ironic destiny that he will be able to be "truly Vietnamese" only if he lives in exile in the West. Minh thus embodies the experience of biculturality.

The entire novel is driven by Minh's political quest. The actions of the characters in the novel are motivated by their political understand-

ings. This is a foreign concept to most American readers, who, for the
most part, do not see humans as being motivated by politics. I would
argue that, indeed, we are motivated by politics (and not just in such
obvious examples as the civil rights movement, the antiwar movement,
or the protest of the closing of the Green Giant cannery in Watsonville,
California). Our understandings of the world—the goals we strive for,
our belief in "upward mobility," in individualism, in "fairness," in the
quest for economic power—all arise from our politics. But we are
taught to see these phenomena as "natural," rather than as a political
ideology. Therefore, *Blue Dragon, White Tiger,* even while it works to
underline many basic similarities between Vietnamese and Americans,
may seem very foreign to some American readers. But it can also begin
a thinking process which might lead students to throw off some of
their parochialism.

Tang's memoir describes the effects of colonialism on bright, young,
upper-class Vietnamese like himself. He also shows us the intricacies
of politics in postcolonial Vietnam. His story is of interest to American
audiences because it reveals how differently he went about negotiating
the course of his life from the way so many young American men
went about making their decisions about what their participation in
the war would be. For example, the stories that Tim O'Brien, in *If I
Die in a Combat Zone,* and William Broyles, in *Brothers in Arms,* tell
about how they decided what to do about their military service differ
enormously from Tang's presentation of his developing politics. Broyles,
already in the marines, decides to desert on the eve of being shipped
to Vietnam:

> And so an idea began to build in my mind. I would do what
> [Siegfried] Sassoon had done. I would refuse to go. A Marine
> lieutenant refusing to board the plane to Vietnam because he was
> against the war—it would be a great gesture. Unlike my going to
> Vietnam, which was a moral gesture that would most likely go
> unnoticed and which could leave me dead, this gesture would
> definitely be noticed—and I would live. (1986, 74)

Talked out of it by a friend, Broyles changes his mind:

> Jan was right about one thing. I did compose that statement to
> conceal a simple fact: I was afraid. Worse, I had tried to conceal
> my fear behind morality and principle. If I were going to take a
> stand against the war, I should have done it long before. (76)

O'Brien was drafted after graduating from college. After considering
the alternatives of evading or being inducted, he decides to submit to
the draft. He writes:

> It was an intellectual and physical stand-off, and I did not have the energy to see it to an end. I did not want to be a soldier, not even an observer to war. But neither did I want to upset a peculiar balance between the order I knew, the people I knew, and my own private world. It was not just that I valued that order. I also feared its opposite—inevitable chaos, censure, embarrassment, the end of everything that had happened in my life, the end of it all. (1973, 31)

The point to note about O'Brien and Broyles is that their explanations are focused on the self. Their experiences are described in terms that place the personal at the center of the discussion—both of their own inner discussions in deciding what to do and in their recounting of those discussions to us, their readers.

Tang's decision processes are very different—focused more on his place within his family and society, on political and historical movements. He talks of his "initiation into the mysteries of colonialism" (1985, 5) and of how his "heart had embraced the patriotic fire, and my soul was winging its way toward the empyrean of national liberation" (22). I am not suggesting that either cultural style is better than the other—what I am suggesting is that American readers are much more used to the kind of personalism represented by Broyles and O'Brien than the style represented by Tang.

Truong Nhu Tang, the son of a wealthy Saigon family, became politically active while he was a university student in Paris. He returned to Vietnam and helped found the NLF. He worked undercover in Saigon for several years, was arrested and tortured, then released in a secret exchange of prisoners. He joined the Provisional Revolutionary Government (PRG) as Minister of Justice and lived at PRG headquarters in the jungle near the Cambodian border, enduring American B-52 bombing attacks, for several more years before being transferred to Hanoi as a liaison. After the liberation he became disillusioned over the northern, Communist domination of the new unified government (despite his activities with the NLF and PRG, he was not a Party member). He became a boat person and ultimately settled in Paris.

The project of Tang's *A Vietcong Memoir* (1985) is to educate its readers. It presents itself as a historical work, equipped with maps, index, glossary of names, and an appendix containing several documents of the NLF. The book also contains many pictures which seem to act as authentication. Many of the pictures show Tang with other prominent revolutionary figures.

This is not a *personal* narrative in the usual Western sense. Although it does narrate Tang's life story, the focus is not primarily on Tang's personal life, but on his participation in revolutionary politics. Political maneuvering and historic events always take center stage. For example, during the years that Tang lives at PRG headquarters in the jungle, he is separated from his family. There is no mention of any attempts to communicate with them, no mention of missing them. When he returns to Saigon after the liberation, he discovers that his wife has divorced him and left the country, and that one of his children is living in France, the other in the United States. But even this personal information is offered more as an illustration of the disruption that returning cadres found in Saigon than as part of a detailed personal account. Tang has five brothers, all of whom were on the other side— two as ARVN (Army of the Republic of Vietnam) officers, one as a government official, two in business. Despite this rift in his family, he mentions them only once, in the context of reunion after the liberation.

Tang is a transnational cosmopolite at the same time that he is a Vietnamese nationalist. This is shown clearly in his description of his meeting with Ho Chi Minh in Paris in 1945. Ho's appeal is familial: "Almost immediately I found myself thinking of my grandfather" (12), but at the same time world-historical: "I sat next to him, already infusing this remarkable person . . . with the schoolboy reverence I had felt toward the personal heroes adopted from my reading of history: Gandhi, Sun Yat-sen, and especially Abraham Lincoln" (12).

Hearing Ho Chi Minh compared to Abraham Lincoln might be a shocking thing for many American readers. Yet it seems perfectly natural to Tang, who, as a young student, has not yet discovered the hypocrisy of the West, and who will always be able to contain paradoxes because of the transnational cultural influences of his upbringing.[1] Because he has not yet discovered the hypocrisy of the colonial West, he is able to say that "already in love with French culture, I was now utterly fascinated by the spirit and vitality of French political life. . . . Meanwhile, I decided to join the movement for Vietnamese independence that was beginning to percolate in the Paris streets and debating halls" (19) and see no contradiction there. Rather, he makes an international synthesis, writing that "I began to envision a radical westernization of Vietnam along the lines of Japan's miraculous industrialization of the late nineteenth and early twentieth centuries. . . . [Vietnam could] adopt the best from the world's political and economic cultures: the American approach to economics, the German scientific spirit, the French fervor for democracy" (20).

Like Tran Van Dinh, Tang is interested in the ways in which Vietnamese culture can absorb and transform Marxism (another Western invention). He describes the early formation of the NLF and its division of its membership into "cells": "This cell structure is sometimes thought of as a communist innovation, but for the Vietnamese, with their long history of secret societies, it is practically second nature" (70). But, like Tran Van Dinh, he ultimately believes he has been betrayed by the Marxist revolution.

There are many similarities between Tang and Tran Van Dinh. They are from a similar class background, although Tang is much wealthier. They both joined the NLF and left in disillusionment after 1975. They both continue to respect and admire the person of Ho Chi Minh and to believe that his writings are true and correct, while his followers have led Vietnam into a government that betrays the revolution that Ho led. Both take a cosmopolitan, internationalist view of both culture and politics. Tang and Dinh are a type of exile intellectual like many others produced by the second half of the twentieth century. The First World would do well to learn the lessons that those like Tang and Dinh are trying to teach.

Even when the U.S. reading public does adopt a Vietnamese American work as its own, as seems to be the case with Le Ly Hayslip's *When Heaven and Earth Changed Places* (1989)—which has been widely reviewed in the press, distributed by the Quality Paperback Book Club, and taught in college courses—there are attempts to shape that work into a denatured, apolitical human-interest story with no implications for present or future public policy.

David Shipler's front-page review in *The New York Times Book Review* (1989), titled "A Child's Tour of Duty," praises Hayslip's book for managing "so gracefully to transcend politics, keeping her humaneness as the focus." He goes on to quote a passage from the book in which Hayslip describes playing war games as a child:

> When I played a Republican [a South Vietnamese soldier] I always imagined that the laughing face at the end of my stick-rifle was my brother Bon Nghe, who had gone to Hanoi and who might one day come back to fight around Ky La. . . . When I played a Viet Cong, I could think only of my sister Ba in Danang, who, being married to a policeman, locked her door every night out of fear of "those terrorists." (1)

Shipler is emptying this passage of any political content by declaring that the book "transcends politics" and by focusing on her "humaneness." But it is precisely Hayslip's inability to negotiate the political mine field created by the civil war in her nation that creates the problems she must overcome. Further, Shipler emphasizes the part of the book that covers Hayslip's childhood, barely mentioning the later parts of the book.

> But the most touching and illuminating sections of the book are those set in her lovingly described home village, for there is nothing more anguishing to read than portrayals of a war through a child's eyes.

Of course Shipler is correct about the anguish of war through a child's eyes, but by focusing on Hayslip's childhood, he displays the usual attitude of paternalism that Americans take toward Third World peoples. It seems that still, despite all the discussions of the last twenty years, Euro-Americans, unlike their Vietnamese American compatriots, are unable to stand toe to toe with adult others and deal with them as equals who share a complicated history.

There are two other major works that are worth consideration in any project involving the teaching of Vietnamese literature. Both are oral histories: David Chanoff and Doan Van Toai's *Portrait of the Enemy,* and James Freeman's *Hearts of Sorrow.*

Chanoff and Toai's *Portrait of the Enemy* presents the stories of several former members of the NLF. This book is a problematic oral history because, rather than presenting each person's story in its entirety, it breaks the stories into several pieces and slots them into thematically organized sections. By breaking up the personal stories so that the voices support the themes, it thwarts the move toward communality and disguises the personal and particular.

The book must also be read in the context of a political awareness that recognizes that these speakers all began as North Vietnamese Communists or South Vietnamese National Liberation Front members. They then defected after the war was won, for a variety of reasons, including the mistreatment of NLF leaders after the victory because of longstanding Vietnamese sectional rivalries. But in a country where, even during the war, few Americans knew the difference between the North Vietnamese Army and the VC (Vietcong), let alone anything of Vietnamese internal politics, history, and customs, such an understanding will probably be rare.

However, teaching these books can sometimes result in transformative experiences for teacher and students alike. In a core first-year humanities course called Social Change in the Third World, I have seen students' attitudes almost completely transformed by reading Hayslip's autobiography. In class discussions after reading the book (and after a lecture given by Hayslip herself), students expressed new attitudes. Several students who had remained entrenched in ignorance about the Third World and Third World cultures and peoples for much of the quarter came to class after reading *When Heaven and Earth Changed Places* with a feeling of having had the scales lifted from their eyes. Many students indicated that their picture of the war in Vietnam was now very different from the one they had entered the class with—largely formed by movies, TV, and high school history texts.

In an upper division course about the representation of the war in American popular culture, a similar transformation took place in some students' attitudes. Despite extended discussions about the racism against Vietnamese that informs most of the other works students read and viewed in this class, several students failed to "see" where the Euro-American texts were racist. These students remained locked in the framework of the dominant American discourse. After reading Hayslip's narrative toward the end of the course, most of the students who previously failed to "see" could then "see" quite clearly. Again, reading the Vietnamese refugee point of view became a transformative experience for these students in the context of discussions of the war.

I believe that these texts possess enormous power to educate—not only about an important period in U.S. history, but also about another culture, their perceptions of the war, and their perceptions about their adopted country. I hope this literature will gain a wider audience.

In the words of Le Ly Hayslip:

> I can only say what I myself have learned: that life's purpose is to grow. We have time in abundance—an eternity, in fact—to repeat our mistakes. We only need to correct them once, however—to learn our lesson and hear the song of enlightenment—to break the chain of vengeance forever. (366)

Notes

1. The comparison of Ho and Lincoln is actually not an uncommon one among Vietnamese. Thu Huong, one of the women who broadcast as "Hanoi Hannah," said recently in an interview with Don North in *Indochina Newsletter* (1990), "I have always compared our traditions of liberty, like those of Abraham Lincoln and Ho Chi Minh."

Works Cited

Broyles, William. 1986. *Brothers in Arms*. New York: Avon.

Crown, Bonnie R. 1985. "Review of *Blue Dragon, White Tiger* by Tran Van Dinh." *World Literature Today* 59(1): 160.

Hayslip, Le Ly with Jay Wurts. 1989. *When Heaven and Earth Changed Places: A Vietnamese Woman's Journey from War to Peace*. New York: Penguin.

Ho Chi Minh. 1973. *Selected Writings*. Hanoi: Foreign Languages Publishing House.

Jehlen, Myra. 1990. "Why Did the European Cross the Ocean? Or, Montaigne's Dilemma." Invited public lecture at the University of California, Santa Cruz, October 16.

Kovic, Ron. 1976. *Born on the Fourth of July*. New York: McGraw-Hill.

North, Don. 1990. "The Voice from the Past: The Search for Hanoi Hannah." *Indochina Newsletter* 63, 1–8.

O'Brien, Tim. 1973. *If I Die in a Combat Zone*. New York: Dell.

Shipler, David K. 1989, June 25. "A Child's Tour of Duty." Review of *When Heaven and Earth Changed Places*, by Le Ly Hayslip. *New York Times Book Review*, 1.

Tran Van Dinh. 1983. *Blue Dragon, White Tiger: A Tet Story*. Philadelphia: TriAm Press.

Truong, Nhu Tang, with David Chanoff and Doan Van Toai. 1985. *A Vietcong Memoir*. New York: Vintage.

16 Narrative Theory in Naguib Mahfouz's *The Children of Gebelawi*

Suzanne Evertsen Lundquist
Brigham Young University

> Each culture has a special pan-
> human contribution for all our
> thinking, remembering species.
> —Victor Turner

Amidst the profusion of varied critical approaches to literature existing in the West, using the words "narrative theory" in the title of an essay about a novel from the Middle East is fraught with possible expectations. In current academic settings, it might seem appropriate to filter Naguib Mahfouz's novel through the narrative theories of Mikhail Bakhtin, Roland Barthes, Claude Bremond, Jacques Derrida, Algirdas Julien Greimas, Wolfgang Iser, and Shlomith Rimmon-Kenan. And yet, Mahfouz has a narrative theory of his own upon which *The Children of Gebelawi* is predicated. *Theory,* from the Greek *theamai,* means "I behold." Mahfouz, much in the fashion of a cultural anthropologist, has observed how stories function within cultural contexts; and he dramatizes, through telling a story, how storytelling is the way humans communicate the complexity of human existence.

Perhaps central to cross-cultural concerns is the assertion that the receiving culture allows the giving one to define or explain how stories appear to work within their own cultural contexts. If, for example, we go looking for proof of our own theories, we will surely find evidence that they work in foreign settings and can thus assume that our categories are universal. And yet, beginning with or imposing some kind of similarity often obscures difference and therefore diminishes cross-cultural contributions. It is not that Western notions of story do not apply: it is the pattern or method of application that makes the difference.

To transcend the boundaries of our own view of literary criticism, we can use a simple process. First, we can explore the assertions being made by the author from the Other culture. Next, we can explore fundamental similarities and differences between Western constructs and those of the Other. In this regard, it is safe to say that Mahfouz's approach to narrative is different from most contemporary Western approaches and more like Native American approaches or those of novelists like Reynolds Price. For example, Kenneth Lincoln, in discussing the Native American conception of storytelling, maintains that "the Indian storyteller weaves a narrative less as a point of view, detached on the crosshairs of art, more as a human presence, attended by an audience taking part in the story. It is not a question of the 'rhetoric of fiction,' in Western terms for the novel, but of historical witness to human events" (1983, 223). It is within such parameters that Mahfouz works. And finally, we can consider what the Other (Mahfouz) has to offer the West.

In *The Children of Gebelawi*, Mahfouz asserts that audience reactions to the sacred narratives-core culture stories—of Jews, Christians, and Muslims—advance the greatest hope for overcoming existing social unrest while paradoxically creating the very boundaries that are at the heart of cross-cultural strife. The usefulness of Mahfouz's novel in teaching cross-cultural awareness might be found in this very assertion: that sacred stories construct social realities, create cultural boundaries, and can—through revision, re-creation, and reenactment—offer hope for more healing human experiences.

In *The Children of Gebelawi*, Mahfouz allegorically discusses the history of humankind from Adam to the present. The general appeal of this and other of Mahfouz's works is so great that twenty foreign language editions have been published, with another twenty being negotiated for publication (Luxner 1989, 16).[1] Originally published serially in *Al-Ahram*, a Cairo newspaper, during 1959, *The Children of Gebelawi* was not published in novel form until 1967 and even then in an abridged version. In fact, the book was banned in most Arab nations until after Mahfouz won the Nobel Prize in 1988. Although publishers in Lebanon finally did publish an Arabic version of the text, the first complete edition of *The Children of Gebelawi* appeared in English in 1981. In this novel, Mahfouz is critical of political and religious leadership. He is also very liberal with his interpretation of traditional sacred narratives. In fact, while showing how cultures remember, retell, or reenact these stories, he revises and reinterprets them.

In *The Children of Gebelawi*, Mahfouz traces the Jewish, Christian, and Islamic traditions back to the story of Gebelawi and his sons and grandsons—Adham (Adam), Gebel (Moses), Rifaa (Christ), Kassem (Mohammed), and Arafa (a name, according to Roger Allen, that comes from the verb meaning "knowledge" and, by implication, "scientia" [1990, 255]). Following the "Prologue," the major chapters of the novel are "Adham," "Gebel," "Rifaa," "Kassem," and "Arafa." Translated, *Gebelawi* means "Mountain Dweller." With all the biblical allusions surrounding mountains, Gebelawi can be understood as the father of the covenant; he is the covenant maker, the father of the book, the beginner of stories. And his message is: When true holiness is set free in the world and shared through sacred narrative, it is possible that peace might exist and that cruelty and humiliation might cease. However, during the novel, the "ten conditions" of the covenant remain vague and ambiguous except through the interpretations given them by Gebel, Rifaa, and Kassem. Gebelawi keeps a copy of the "ten conditions" in a secret book locked in a vault in his bedroom. For most of the descendants of Gebelawi, the "ten conditions" are the provisions of a will that simply outline the correct division of property. Arafa, however, believes that the book contains the secrets to Gebelawi's power or magic; indeed, Arafa is willing to risk his life to know "the ten conditions of the endowment" (312).

The setting of the entire novel is Gebelawi Alley, a district in Cairo. The general condition in the alley is one of poverty, bigotry, and oppression. For literary critic Jareer Abu-Haidar, this novel is "essentially a parable of authority and power, not only in Egypt (its author's country), but everywhere in the Arab world, or rather in the Middle East" (1985, 119). Abu-Haidar further claims that this novel is the story of an "endless struggle for power, a perpetual Armageddon, in which nothing seems to avail except Machiavellian machinations in their most sinister and primeval aspects" (119). Indeed, once Gebelawi casts Adham and Omayma out of the estate, most of their posterity live in hovels. The streets of the alley are described as being "crowded and noisy, with barefoot children, almost naked, playing in every corner, filling the air with their squeals and covering the ground with their filth. The doorways [are] surrounded by women, chopping jute leaves, peeling onions, lighting charcoal, gossiping and joking, cursing and swearing" (Mahfouz 1981, 73). Fights break out often amid the meowing of cats, the growling of dogs, and the running of rats and mice about the yards. Men spend their idle time in cafés smoking hashish, listening to storytellers, or discussing the injustice of the trustees of the estate, who claim to represent Gebelawi and his wishes, but only bully the people into submission while extorting funds from the estate.

However, two activities break the constancy of this human condition: the sharing of stories in the cafés and the rise of prophets who act upon the stories in an attempt to bring salvation to those living in a rubbish heap. While history might indeed be a chronicle of intimidation, humiliation, greed, and murder among peoples and nations, historians of Greek, Hebrew, and Christian history suggest another dimension. Historian Arnaldo Momigliano concludes that "history is to the Greeks and consequently to the Romans an operation against Time the all-destroying in order to save the memory of events worth being remembered" (1966, 15). For Jews, and later for Christians, says Momigliano, history is the story of "a privileged line of events represented and signified [by the] continuous intervention of God in the world he [has] created" (19). The added dimension included by Christians to the concept of time and history is the notion of continual rebirth and renewal (21). Certainly Muslim historians share similar ideas about events surrounding the revelations given to Mohammed. And, significantly, it is also the duty of Jews, Christians, and Muslims to remember the past. *The Children of Gebelawi* shows a people who rely on their prophets to periodize their history. Essentially, all other events constitute chaos or nonhistory.

In light of Momigliano's discussion of the type of story we term *history,* Mahfouz's "Prologue" to *The Children of Gebelawi* provides a fuller context:

> This is the story of our alley, or these are its stories. I myself have lived only through the most recent events, but I have written down everything as it is told by our many professional storytellers who learnt them in the cafés or from their fathers.
>
> The tales are told on a thousand and one occasions. Whenever people are wronged or injured they point to the Big House at the top of the alley, where it meets the desert, and say sadly: "There is our ancestor's house. We are all his children and we all have a right to his estate; why should we be hungry and wretched?" Then they tell the stories of the great heroes of our alley: Adham and Gebel, Rifaa and Kassem. (1981, 1)

The themes in this novel are numerous and powerful in their implications and treatment. However, it is in the very assertion that storytelling can have a positive role in the creation, maintenance, and re-creation of cultural and individual identity that Mahfouz offers an alternative to the hungry and wretched condition of common, collective, or communal beings.

American novelist Reynolds Price also attempted a retelling of sacred narratives in his work *A Palpable God.* Price's introductory essay to *A Palpable God* contains his discovery about the impact of sacred stories on human history. Price's ideas (or theories) about narrative are similar to Mahfouz's treatment of storytelling and, therefore, provide a clear access to Mahfouz's more fictive account. Price claims that "a need to tell and hear stories is essential to the species Homo Sapiens—second in necessity apparently after nourishment and before love and shelter. Millions survive without love or home, almost none in silence" (1985, 3). And indeed, when the children of Gebelawi lose faith in the stories, the novel ends. The last character, Arafa, reflects, "When would the alley stop retelling stories?" (Mahfouz 1981, 295). And in the same passage, Arafa also asks, "What had the alley gained from these stories?" (295). The entire novel is an answer to both questions.

But it is a particular kind of story through which the children of Gebelawi are nourished. Says Price, "We crave nothing less than perfect story; and while we chatter or listen all our lives in a din of craving—jokes, anecdotes, novels, dreams, films, plays, songs, half the words of our days—we are satisfied only by the one short tale we feel to be true: History is the will of a just god who knows us" (14). Gebelawi is the God-figure in Mahfouz's novel—the just grandfather who knows his children. He rejects racism, selfishness, and disobedience; he also reveals his will to his children in times of need. In the "Adham" section of the novel, for example, Gebelawi tells his sons, "It will be best for someone else to manage the estate instead of me." Instead of choosing the birthright son, Idris, Gebelawi chooses Adham to manage the estate under his supervision. The other brothers are shocked and enraged. Screams Idris, "I and my brothers are sons of a fine lady, an aristocrat, but this fellow is the son of a black maid." Idris continues to roar, "He's the youngest of us, too; give me one reason why you should prefer him to me. Is this the age of servants and slaves?" (6). Gebelawi answers with calm and reason, "Adham knows the tenants and most of their names. He also knows how to write and do sums" (7).

This answer is not acceptable to Idris. His further raging causes him to be the first man to be cast out of the estate never to return. Idris, outside the estate, behaves horribly. He becomes a drunk and a womanizer, brash and unseemly. However, on one of Adham's trips into the alley he is approached by a seemingly repentant Idris, who begs Adham to have mercy on him. He wants Adham to find out if he has been cut out of his father's will. Says Idris, "He will certainly have written it into the book which contains everything about the estate." This book, however, "is in a secret chamber in father's bedroom" (23). This book contains "the ten conditions"—conditions that Idris wants Adham to secure by stealing into his father's chambers and sneaking a look at the contents of the book. With encouragement from his wife Omayma, Adham tries to obtain the secrets of the book through stealth. He is caught by his father and also exiled from the gardens and estate. Both Idris and Adham are thrust into the desert to find their way in life. However, Adham's only dream is to return to the estate through obtaining the forgiveness of Gebelawi. After a long and harsh life, Adham finally receives Gebelawi's forgiveness; this is the revelatory moment in the Adham section. "Have you forgiven me?" Adham asks the huge person whose image seems to fill the doorway of his hut. The answer, "after a pause: 'Yes'" (71). This metaphor of the human condition—exile and return—fills sacred narratives. In fact, from the story of the Fall to narratives about Jesus Christ, the history and theology of Jews, Muslims, and Christians pivot around this idea.

As Mahfouz's narrative continues, Omayma and Adham have "gone hardly any distance from the house when a drunken laugh [rings] out. They [look] in that direction, and there they [see] Idris, in front of the hut he had built of tins and sticks" (31). This is the real Idris, the incarnation of evil (31). Indeed, in Arabic, the Devil's name is "iblis." And, as Mattityahu Peled tells us, in the Koran, Satan steals into Heaven to look at the secrets of the book (1983, 188).

In focusing on Mahfouz's narrative theory, it seems important to note that only two written texts are mentioned in *The Children of Gebelawi*. The implied narrator mentions the first text when he reports that he has "written down everything as it is told by our many professional storytellers who learnt them in the cafés or from their fathers" (1). The second book, and the one upon which all other stories depend, is Gebelawi's "fat book," the one that includes "everything about us" (23). No Old Testament, New Testament, or Koran are generated out of the lives of Gebel, Rifaa, and Kassem. Mahfouz suggests that there is really only one book: Gebelawi's.

Mahfouz, however, does not create a dichotomy between oral and print traditions. Philosophically, Mahfouz's novel is not grounded upon a bipolar scheme. And, therefore, Gretchen Ronnow's theory about the literacy-illiteracy or print-orality dichotomy in this novel is not defensible. Certainly, as Ronnow so capably points out, Western writers like John Oxenham and Walter Ong have invented oppositional or polar existences for those living in literate societies as opposed to oral cultures. From Western intellectual sources, Ronnow concludes that "an oral culture tends to be over-communal, non-individualistic, and authoritarian" as well as violent, while a literate culture "isolates the individual from the group, mutes and minimizes interpersonal communication, and encourages individual thinking as the preferred route to truth" (1984, 95). As the words used to describe oral cultures accumulate, however, it is easy to see the privileged status given to print societies. Oral cultures are described as being "authoritarian," "communal," "dependent," "performance oriented" (relying on formulaic modes of expression), "unoriginal," and "reductive." Heroes, for example, are reduced to types (92–97).

The oral versus written interpretation of Mahfouz's novel simply does not work. Gebelawi's book of secrets—with implied fixed meaning and human destiny—remains out of reach; the contents of the book are never certain. However, belief in revealed words that transcend the sayings of professional storytellers as well as the written parameters of books suggest or speak of a mythic notion of orality. Rather than being static, formulaic, and reductive, orality in Mahfouz's novel is dynamic, active, and revolutionary. That is, the new stories—the stories of a just father who knows and cares about his children—offer the possibility of renewal.

There are also many layers of textual interplay in this novel. The most essential level of interplay, however, comes from reliance on the readers' knowing traditional sacred narratives. The storytelling, the revelations, written texts, and the reader's knowledge of the texts from which Mahfouz creates his fictions work together. This work simply plays off of the traditional stories, challenging, interpreting, and rendering them powerful for audiences from the Jewish, Christian, and Islamic traditions. And because Mahfouz renders these tales in a fiction, with assertions and implications not literally from the Torah, Old Testament, Koran, or Gospels, he implies things about the content of these texts that make readers ask: What about race? What about a black Adham being rejected by his fair brother Idris? If there is one father, how did the idea of a privileged lineage evolve? How many sacred texts suggest a premortal reality? What are the ramifications of the temptation to know the secrets of God and his ten conditions? How do individuals and cultural leaders use sacred narratives—to relieve or cause human suffering and humiliation? Is there revealed truth? Are some texts, some narratives, more significant to cultural identity than others? In a postmodern era, such as ours, that either rejects or criticizes metaphysical discourse on social and political grounds, is Mahfouz suggesting a rereading of sacred texts that will give us a more healing context from which to examine world affairs? And what about this desire to return to the estate? The number of deaths caused by contention over who should inherit the land of Israel, for example, is overwhelming. And don't these "holy" wars pivot around interpretations of sacred narratives?

While such questions have generally been examined by philosophers, historians, or theologians, contemporary thinkers suggest that modern novelists best explore the contingent nature of the issues such questions pose. Walter R. Fisher, for example, suggests that Western intellectual systems have presumed argumentative discourse superior to other forms. No matter how strongly proponents of this view argue, however, their presumptions ignore the fact that all logic is situated—or based—in narrative. That is, all logic "will always be a story, an interpretation of some aspect of the world that is historically and culturally grounded and shaped by human personality" (1987, 49). Fisher's "logos/mythos" conception of human reason, his narrative rationality, has broad implications for literary critics, ethnographers, and philosophers. Fisher further contends that "human communication in all of its forms is imbued with mythos—ideas that cannot be verified or proved in any absolute way" (19).

Mahfouz's novel is also founded on these premises; the contingent nature of stories told about revelations given to Mahfouz's central characters is fundamental to the narrativity of Mahfouz. Each story, each episode, is full of ambiguity, an ambiguity that both challenges the metaphysical presumptions of Jews, Muslims, and Christians as well as suggests the mythic nature of logical and theological propositions. In the Gebel section, for example, Gebel (Moses) goes to the desert to work through the tensions existing between the two people he is—one of them loyal to his mother who raised him (the wealthy leaders of the estate), the other one concerned with the trials of his people (the poor commoners). Before he is fully conscious about what is happening, he almost bumps into "a huge person." Says Gebel, "At first I thought it was one of the chiefs, but he seemed unlike anyone from our alley, or any human being at all, tall and broad like a mountain. I was filled with terror and tried to retreat, but a strange voice said 'Stop Gebel'" (114). After the figure announces, "Don't be afraid; I am your grandfather, Gebelawi," and Gebel responds that he "never dreamt of meeting [Gebelawi] in this life," Gebel strains to see the face of the figure speaking to him. "You will not be able to see my face while it is dark" (114–15). Gebelawi, then, remains hidden in ways that create narrative ambiguity. The same holds true with the experiences of Rifaa and Kassem with Gebelawi.

Mahfouz does not privilege the descriptions of reality offered by any single character. On the contrary, he demonstrates the unique contribution of each central character to the children of Gebelawi. He also exposes the ironic way that these same children have divided up their inheritance (by establishing quarters) to the detriment of all the children—followers of Gebel (Moses), Rifaa (Christ), and Kassem (Mohammed) alike. Gebelawi, rather than being a supreme judge who authorizes only one description of reality or a father who cares only for people in one quarter of the alley, is a figure who intervenes when his children need to reestablish true human community and dissolve arbitrary boundaries.

Mahfouz also does not privilege traditional interpretations of good and evil characters. In exposing the contingent nature of events of major consequence, Mahfouz generally does not create characters that are fully good or bad. For example, in the story paralleling the Abel and Cain episode, Mahfouz exposes the problems of favoritism and envy in family relationships. Hammam (Abel) is invited back to the estate, Kadri (Cain) is not. In a jealous moment, Kadri strikes a fatal blow to his brother's head. But Mahfouz does not portray Kadri as being evil—he is rash and envious. And it is envy, according to Ann and Barry Ulanov, that creates the greatest wounds of all—"Envy, that great distance maker, that connection destroyer" (Ulanov 1983, 10). It is envy that separates Cain from Abel, Esau from Jacob, and Joseph from his brothers. And the sibling rivalry between Ishmael and Isaac persists down to the present day. Mahfouz clearly sees the distance caused by this envy and is sympathetic to both the envied and the enviers. For example, he says of the Cain figure Kadri, after he killed his brother:

> He threw himself down exhausted, feeling all force had gone out of him. He wanted to cry, but the tears would not come. He thought: "Death has defeated me." He had not invited it, nor intended it, but it had come as it pleased. If he could have turned into a goat he would gladly have disappeared amongst the flock. If he could have become a grain of sand he would gladly have been buried in the ground. "I can't claim any strength, for I can't give back the life I have taken. That sight will never leave my memory. What I buried was neither living nor lifeless, but something else that my hand has made." (61)

This story is echoed throughout the book whenever a murder takes place: when Gebel (Moses) kills a fellow Gebelite, for example (84), and at the end of the novel when Arafa (323), while sneaking into Gebelawi's estate, inadvertently kills Gebelawi (symbolically equating the rise of science with the death of God). The story of brother killing brother is retold in different settings and circumstances, but it is the same story. The causes are always envy, inequality, cruelty, greed, or ignorance. And the question that this type of story always implies is, "Am I my brother's keeper?" To this question, the central characters always answer in the affirmative. In his Nobel Prize lecture, Mahfouz gives a "Yes" to this question:

> In this decisive moment in the history of civilization . . . the human mind now assumes the task of eliminating all causes of destruction and annihilation. And just as scientists exert themselves to cleanse the environment of industrial pollution, intellectuals ought to exert themselves to cleanse humanity of moral pollution. It is both our right and our duty to demand of the great leaders in the civilized countries, as well as of their economists, to effect a real leap that would place them in the focus of the age. . . . Today the greatness of a civilized leader ought to be measured by the universality of his vision and his sense of responsibility toward all humankind. The developed world and the third world are but one family; each human being bears responsibility toward it to the degree that he has obtained knowledge, wisdom and civilization. I would not be exceeding the limits of my duty if I told [the leaders] in the name of the Third World: Be not spectators to our miseries. . . . We have had enough of words. Now is the time for action. (1989, 16)

Mahfouz makes several other assertions about storytelling similar to those Price articulates in his introduction to *A Palpable God*. Says Price, story is "the chief means by which we became, and stay, human" (1985, 14). Price also claims

> there is a clear fact that narrative, like the other basic needs of the species, supports the literal survival of man by providing him with numerous forms of nurture—the simple companionship of the narrative transaction, the union of the teller and the told; the narrator's opportunity for exercise of personal skill in telling and its ensuing rewards; the audience's exercise of attention, imagination, powers of deduction; the spiritual support which both parties receive from stories affirming our importance and protection in a perilous world; the transmission to younger listeners of vital knowledge, worldly and unworldly; the narcotic effect of narrative on pain and boredom; and perhaps most importantly, the chance that in the very attempt at narrative transaction something new will surface or be revealed, some sudden floater from the dark unconscious, some message from a god which can only arrive or be told as a tale. (26)

And finally, there is the insurance that it is story that brings order into an otherwise chaotic world.

In the sections dealing with Gebel, Rifaa, and Kassem, all of the above assertions hold true. In Gebel's time, for example, the café is narrow but runs "back a long way to the storyteller's bench at the far

end, under a painting of Adham on his death bed looking at Gebelawi
who stood at the door of the hut. . . . All eyes [are] on the storyteller
and the men [nod] their heads at the beauty of the telling or the
goodness of the moral" (Mahfouz 1981, 75). When Gebel is exiled
from the home of his adoptive parents, he gives "a parting look at
the garden and the garden house and [remembers] the tragedy of
Adham which was recited to the music of the fiddle every evening"
(95). He remembers the "ten conditions" and is drawn to his people,
wants their happiness and their ability to share equally in the inheritance from the estate because of his understanding of the truthfulness
contained in the stories he has heard throughout his life.

Price's assertion that "in the very attempt at narrative transaction
[we hope that] something new will surface or be revealed . . . some
message from a god which can only arrive or be told as a tale" holds
particularly true in *The Children of Gebelawi*. Gebel, Rifaa, and Kassem
each hear and relate the story of their own meeting with Gebelawi.
No other humans in the book meet him. Indeed, life is so miserable
that many characters feel that Gebelawi has forgotten them. But at
moments of particular chaos, Gebelawi comes or sends a messenger
to each of these men. And something new can then be told, retold,
and through the retelling, the alley is renewed and once again receives
"the spiritual support" from the stories which affirm the people's
"importance and protection in a perilous world" (Price 1985, 26). For
example, in the desert, Gebelawi comes to Gebel during the night and
says, "Don't be afraid; I am your grandfather, Gebelawi" (Mahfouz
1981, 114). And when Gebel is retelling the event to his friends, he
explains to them that Gebelawi told him: "You, Gebel, are a man who
is much relied on, yet you have left your comfortable life out of
indignation at the way your people are oppressed. But your people
are my people, and they have rights in my estate which they must
take. Their honor must be defended, and their life must be
good. . . . Success will go with you" (115). From this visit, Gebel and
his followers gain the strength to overcome the chiefs in the alley and
gain equality for their fellows. This peace and equality exist until the
people in the alley are "plagued with forgetfulness" (136).

And Rifaa, the Christ-figure in the novel, is told by a blind storyteller
(as he feels Rifaa's face with his hands) that his features are much
like Gebelawi's (141). Rifaa walks like a bridegroom and is found to
be constantly nurtured by the storytellers in the alley. The text explains
that "the storyteller carried on the story to an attentive audience. Rifaa
followed him eagerly; this was a true reciter and these were the real
stories" (145). These "real stories" transform Rifaa, give him the desire

to create happiness in the hearts of the people in the alley by encouraging them not to make their happiness dependent on the estate but rather on purifying their hearts. During Rifaa's encounter with Gebelawi, he is told: "How wrong it is for a young man to ask his old grandfather to act; the beloved son is the one who acts." Rifaa then asks, "What device can I who am weak use against those chiefs?" Gebelawi replies, "The true weakling is the fool who does not know his inner strength, and I do not like fools" (160). From this hour on, Rifaa knows what is wanted of him. As a result, he begins to share his story and thereby to retell, to re-create, the story of the alley. This narrative re-creation both reinterprets former stories as well as suggests narrative probabilities.

The idea of "narrative probability," as Fisher uses the phrase, means "what constitutes a coherent story" as well as "narrative fidelity, whether or not the stories [that a people from a particular culture experience] ring true with the stories they know to be true in their lives" (1987, 5). Certainly Rifaa's story enjoys this kind of narrative probability. The people in the alley know that Gebelawi also revealed his will to Gebel in a similar desert setting to that reported by Rifaa. Certain patterns of behavior remain constant over time. Rifaa, for example, (1) heard the old stories, (2) from the old stories he feels called to do something about the poor conditions of his people, (3) Gebelawi reveals his will to Rifaa in a desert setting, and (4) he returns to the people and tries to make a difference in their lives. This pattern is followed by Gebel and later by Kassem. Because the pattern is constant, many from the culture believe the stories are probable.

However, I would add to Fisher's notion of "narrative probability" the dimension a physicist might imply while using the term "probability"—to suggest that, under certain circumstances, future events might break with old patterns. T. S. Eliot expressed a similar idea in "Little Gidding":

> History may be servitude,
> History may be freedom. See, now they vanish,
> The faces and places, with the self which, as it could, loved them,
> To become renewed, transfigured, in another pattern.
>
> (1952, 142)

Three statements made by Rifaa demonstrate these elements of Mahfouz's narrative theory. Full of confidence, Rifaa draws on the old stories to narrate his re-vision.

> Adham longed for a pure life of happiness. Gebel did so too, and he only wanted the estate as a way to that life; but he got the

idea that it wouldn't be possible for anyone unless the estate was shared out equally so that each man received his due and enjoyed the use of it, released from toil and free to live the happy life. But the estate is such a petty thing; it is possible to attain true life without it and anyone who wants to can. It's in our power to be rich from this very hour. (1981, 160)

The probability of narrating new stories, then, comes out of the narrative moment when something new is revealed.

The something new revealed through Rifaa is the fact that humans are "better and finer when [they] conquer vanity" (172). It is not where people live or what portion of the estate they are able to acquire and maintain that makes them the children of Gebelawi—it is an inward purity. Says Rifaa:

The Gebelites [Jews] are not the best people in our alley; the best are those who do most good. I used to make the same mistake as you, and paid attention only to the Gebelites. But the people who deserve happiness are those who seek it sincerely. Look at the way the poor accept me and are cured of evil spirits. (172)

Rifaa chooses four of his patients to be his friends and brothers. Through Rifaa's curing spirit, each disciple is transformed—one from being "a layabout and . . . an incurable opium eater"; another from being "a hardened bully and . . . pimp." They help him heal the poor and weak—to free them from "evil spirits and from hatred and greed and malice" (173). Old stories have been changed; people have new narrative possibilities through individual transformation.

Rifaa also explains, through a reinterpretation of the Gebel narrative, what portions of the old stories have become distorted:

Ever since the story has been told that Gebelawi asked Gebel to make the houses of his quarter magnificent like the Big House, people have had their eyes fixed on Gebelawi's magnificence. They have forgotten his other virtues. That's why Gebel was unable to change people by merely winning their rights in the estate, so when he died the strong took over and the weak became full of hatred and misery came back. But I'm opening the gates of happiness without any estate or power. (173)

However, it is because Rifaa attempts a reinterpretation of the stories that he is finally killed. There is danger in suggesting narrative probability. During Rifaa's trial, for example, he is accused of many crimes—of leaving his quarter to work among those in other quarters, of despising the people of power and importance, of claiming to know what Gebelawi wants for his people. In response to the accusation that people say Rifaa repeats only what he has "heard from Gebelawi himself," Rifaa answers, "That's how I understand his words to Adham and Gebel." His accuser shouts back: "His words to Gebel don't bear interpretation" (181). Still another angrier leader asserts, "No one can speak in the name of Gebelawi except the Trustee of his estate and his heir" (182). Another element of narrative probability, then, is the question of authority. Who are the keepers of the stories? Who are the official interpreters?—the theologian, the historian, the literary critic, the philosopher, or relatives?

Rifaa's reform movement gains more success after his death than during his life. Despite the fact that Rifaa's followers try to maintain the belief that Rifaa's mission was to "heal the sick and that he despised importance and power," the Rifaaites are, ironically, "recognized as a new quarter, with the same rights and privileges as Gebel's quarter" (197). The continual creation of boundaries hedging people in is also one of the plagues in Gebelawi Alley. And then, once again, the people in the alley divide themselves into Gebelites and Rifaaites and slip into forgetfulness.

The story of Kassem (Mohammed) is also powerful. It is through him that the people in the alley come to realize that Gebelawi is the ancestor of us all. It is through the stories told to Kassem that he discovers Gebelawi's will and learns how the people can live up to the "ten conditions" contained in Gebelawi's book. It is Kindil, Gebelawi's servant, who reveals the will of Gebelawi to Kassem (227). This time, Gebelawi—who knows "everything and is aware of every event, big or small"—informs Kassem "that all the people of the alley are equally his children, that the estate is equally their inheritance, that chiefs are an evil that must end and that the alley must become an extension of the Big House" (228). Kassem is also told that he must bring this condition about. As he goes about interpreting this message, however, the implications for Islam become revolutionary. For example, Kassem says, "If God grants me victory, I shan't stop women from sharing the income of the estate" (234). As might be expected, resistance to this idea is great. And yet Kassem explains, "Our ancestor told me through his servant that the estate belongs to everyone. Half the people are women; it is amazing that the alley doesn't respect them; but it shall respect them on the day that it knows the meaning of justice and mercy" (234). Kassem's revision of the old stories, his revision of the "ten conditions," is collective. His task was to "achieve the honor that Gebel gave to his people, and the love that Rifaa called for; more than that, the happiness that Adham dreamed of" (235). Through force and love, the alley once again comes to know peace. But, in the end, the people are once more plagued with forgetfulness.

"Arafa," the final chapter of the novel, begins:

> No one who contemplates us now will believe those tales. Who were Gebel and Rifaa and Kassem? Where are the achievements that are talked of in the cafés? The eye sees only an alley sunk in darkness and storytellers singing of dreams. How have things come to such a pass? (287)

This section focuses on a character whose life is compelled by curiosity, the desire to solve problems through magic (science), and by revenge. In his compulsion to prove Gebelawi's continued existence and to read, for himself, the actual contents of the book which contains the "ten conditions," Arafa sneaks into the estate and, by accident, causes the death of Gebelawi. The irony and ambiguity contained in the events surrounding the death of Gebelawi are powerful. On the one hand, Arafa wants to become a good enough magician that he will be "able to restore Gebelawi to life, Gebelawi whom it had been easier to kill than to see" (323). And on the other hand, Arafa also feels that "a word from our ancestor used to cause the best of his children to act for him until death. His death is more powerful than his words; it makes it necessary for the good son to do everything, to take his place, to be him" (323). The death of God, the rise of magic, and the power of the trustee's cudgels dominate this chapter. Men also fight over who can own the best products of the magic. Rumors fill the hashish dens and people live in a "terrible atmosphere of fear and hatred and intimidation" (355). But once again, whenever the people suffered injustice, they said, "Oppression must cease as night yields to day. We shall see the end of tyranny and the dawn of miracles" (355). This, the last sentence of the novel, can be read as full of satire. Humankind continues to be ruled by the trustees and to live in a state of forgetfulness.

Adham, Gebel, Rifaa, Kassem, and the characters that make their lives worth remembering and retelling are the cultural heroes of the Jews, Christians, and Muslims. And, says Mahfouz, their memory "remains, and is worth more than flocks and flocks of sheep and goats" (206). These men—Adham, Gebel, Rifaa, and Kassem (and the stories about them)—are the world's share of goodness. Their message? Equality, righteousness, and brotherhood, and our common love and dependence on Gebelawi, the father of the book. And their stories are what we have to move us to a full life shared with those who are not of our race, kindred, tongue, or people. It would seem that Mahfouz is suggesting, in this novel, that these stories must be read collectively. They represent the contributions of the Jews (who number 18,169,340 or 0.3 percent of the world's population), the Christians (who number 1,669,520,440 or 32.9 percent of the world's population), and Muslims (who number 880,552,210 or 17.4 percent of the world's population) (*The World Almanac* 1990, 611).

Literary critic Abu-Haidar claims that Mahfouz's *Children of Gebelawi* is not just another Arabic novel, but "an important event" whose message is for "the powers that be, not only in Egypt and other Arab countries, but everywhere in the world" (1985, 119). Perhaps "the powers that be" should be the group credited with being plagued with forgetfulness. Of this kind of forgetfulness, African writer Chinua Achebe tells us, "A fool alone will / contest the precedence of ancestors and gods; the wise wisely sing them grandiloquent lullabies / knowing they are children / those omnipotent deities" (1977, 46). To remember and know the old stories, then—the stories of the ancestors whose lives gave us moments of true peace and vision—and even to celebrate those narratives with "grandiloquent lullabies" is to understand that the old narratives create new narrative probabilities. The ancestors become the children in this regard. And, finally, this discussion of narrative theory affirms Mircea Eliade's contention that "the [modern] novel continue[s the] mythological narrative, though on a different plane and in pursuit of different ends" (1963, 190). Certainly the mythos of this novel transcends traditional mythological boundaries; it becomes a call to stop quartering the alley, the land of inheritance. It is also a call to worship true goodness and not power or science. If Mahfouz's critics are correct, if Mahfouz has accomplished what critics believe he has, then his narrative is well worth our consideration. After all, the English words "story" and "narrative" come to us through "Greek, Latin, and French from two Proto-Indo-European roots—*weid* and *gno, seeing* and *knowing,*" explains Price (1985, 14). Perhaps Mahfouz's implied narrative theory has just such purposes: that we might see, know, remember, and change.

Notes

1. Mahfouz has written thirty-eight novels and twelve volumes of short stories; twenty-six of his narratives have been made into films. His topics range from the Pharonic period of human history to more recent Islamic and global concerns.

Works Cited

Abu-Haidar, Jareer. 1985. "Awlad Haratina by Najib Mahfuz: An Event in the Arab World." *Journal of Arabic Literature* 16: 119–31.

Achebe, Chinua. 1977. *Beware Soul Brother.* London: Heinemann.

Allen, Roger. 1990. "Najib Mahfuz: 1988." In *Nobel Laureates in Literature,* edited by Rado Pribic, 251–57. New York: Garland.

Eliade, Mircea. 1963. *Myth and Reality.* New York: Harper.

Eliot, T. S. 1952. "Little Gidding." In *The Complete Poems and Plays: 1909–1950,* 142. New York: Harcourt.

Fisher, Walter R. 1987. *Human Communication as Narration: Toward a Philosophy of Reason, Value, and Action.* Columbia: University of South Carolina Press.

Lincoln, Kenneth. 1983. *Native American Renaissance.* Berkeley: University of California Press.

Luxner, Larry. 1989. "A Nobel for the Arab Nation." *Aramco World* 40(2): 14–16.

Mahfouz, Naguib. 1981. *The Children of Gebelawi,* translated by Philip Stewart. London: Heinemann.

—————. 1989. "Nobel Prize Lecture." *Aramco World* 40(2): 16.

Momigliano, Arnaldo. 1966. "Time in Ancient Historiography." In *History and the Concept of Time.* Beiheft 6 *History and Theory,* 1–23. Middletown, CT: Wesleyan University Press.

Peled, Mattityahu. 1983. *Religion, My Own: The Literary Works of Najib Mahfuz.* New Brunswick: Transaction Books.

Price, Reynolds. 1985. *A Palpable God.* San Francisco: North Point Press.

Ronnow, Gretchen. 1984. "The Oral vs. the Written: A Dialectic of Worldviews" in Najib Mahfouz's *The Children of Our Alley. Al-ʿArabiyya: Journal of the American Association of Teachers of Arabic* 17(1): 87–118.

Ulanov, Ann and Barry. 1983. *Cinderella and Her Sisters.* Philadelphia: Westminster Press.

The World Almanac and Book of Facts: 1990. 1990. "Estimated Religious Population of the World, 1988," 611. New York: Pharos Books.

17 The Mixed Blood Writer as Interpreter and Mythmaker

Patricia Riley
University of California, Berkeley

Don't offend
the fullbloods,
don't offend
the whites,
stand there in
the middle
of the god-
damned road
and get hit.

—Gogisgi/Carroll Arnett
"Song of the Breed"

As I sit staring at the face of one of technology's latest gods, my hands on a keyboard that functions as its messenger, I find myself "standin' in the middle of the road" with the rest of my brothers and sisters. Therefore, before leaping headlong into a discussion of the mixed blood writer and the peculiar problematics involved in this occupation that so many of us have found ourselves in, I feel compelled to talk about how mixed bloods came into existence and how they have been perceived by others and by themselves, since I believe this will shed considerable light on the subject at hand.

There was a time in so-called Early American History when inter-marriage between whites and Indians was advocated as a means of achieving a "bloodless" conquest, one that could be arrived at not by the spilling of blood, but by the mixing of it. Thomas Jefferson expressed these sentiments in 1803:

> In truth, the ultimate point of rest and happiness for them is to let our settlement and theirs meet and blend together, to intermix, and to become one people ... and it will be better to promote than retard it. (Bieder 1980, 19)

"Song of the Breed" is reprinted here by permission of Carroll Arnett.

Missionaries seeking to convert and civilize Indians also held a similar stance, believing the mixed blood was more malleable and would "espouse the interests of civilization and Christianity" (Bieder 1980, 19). A common observation of the time was that mixed bloods were "the first to take on 'white ways': to start farming and acquire an education," as well as serve the quite useful purpose of interpreting (19–20). In the 1830s, Alexis de Tocqueville held that "the half-blood forms the natural link between civilization and barbarism" (20). The idea of the mixed blood as a bridge between cultures may have had its roots in this period.

However, by the middle of the 1800s these beliefs began to deteriorate as reports came in that the mixed blood had failed to live up to white expectations. Mixed bloods quickly became marked as "faulty stock." Since they often chose tribal life over a white one, "Like the Indian, the mixed-blood was viewed as headed for extinction" (Bieder, 27). More than one hundred years later, we continue to disappoint the white man. We continue to live, to acquire education and link our lives to that of our tribes, and we continue to define ourselves in spite of a society that would do that defining for us.

There is no definition for *mixed blood* according to *Webster's Encyclopedic Version of the New Lexicon Dictionary;* however, the definition of the pejorative term *half-breed* reads as follows: "n. someone of mixed breeding, esp. of mixed white and American Indian parentage" (434). While this clinical definition may satisfy the question of the genetic "what," it gives no real insight of any substance.

In the Lakota language, the word used to describe a mixed blood is *iyeska;* however, its meaning does not end there. According to Orval Looking Horse, keeper of the sacred Pipe of the Lakota people, the term *iyeska* embodies the concept of one who not only interprets between the red and white worlds, but between the world of spirits and of human beings as well.[1] I believe the fullness of this definition places the mixed blood firmly within spiritual and mythic traditions and is the most descriptive of the way the mixed blood writer approaches the writing of literature. It is also a definition which enables one to begin to understand the predicament and complexity of the mixed blood writer as a producer of contemporary Native American literature.

In the introduction to *That's What She Said,* mixed blood Cherokee writer Rayna Green describes the contemporary Native American author as someone who walks "a new Trail of Tears," one that was blazed by the government policy of relocation:

> They go to the towns for jobs or to follow their husbands and
> families. They go to school someplace and they never go home
> again permanently, or the city becomes home. Sometimes they
> get to go back to the Rez. Maybe it's someplace they never were
> before, and that new experience becomes part of the searching.
> They can be looking for something Indians call "Indianness"—
> what sociologists call "identity." . . . Because most of them—with
> few exceptions—are "breeds," "mixed-bloods," not reserve-raised,
> they aren't "traditional," whatever that might mean now. Some
> might say that writing is just their role. That's what breeds do.
> They stand in the middle and interpret for everyone else, and
> maybe that's so. That's what they are. But "identity" is never
> simply a matter of genetic make-up or natural birthright. Perhaps
> once, long ago, it was both. But not now. For people out on the
> edge, out on the road, identity is a matter of will . . . a face to be
> shaped in a ceremonial act. (1984, 7)

While Green focuses on the idea of the mixed blood as interpreter,
she also brings up the notion of the quest for identity. Underlying this
quest is a sense of alienation which drives the seeker and permeates
much of Native American literature today. In *The Sacred Hoop: Recovering the Feminine in American Indian Traditions*, Paula Gunn Allen
discusses this preoccupation with alienation in Native American literature and offers insight into the experiences which often shape mixed
blood consciousness, while pointing out that acculturated fullbloods
can also qualify for a kind of mixed status:

> What is the experience that creates this sense of alienation? The
> breed (whether by parentage or acculturation to non-Indian so-
> ciety) is an Indian who is not an Indian. That is, breeds are a bit
> of both worlds, and the consciousness of this makes them seem
> alien to traditional Indians while making them feel alien among
> whites. Breeds commonly feel alien to themselves above all. (1986,
> 129)

Allen also mentions the fact that the writers of contemporary Native
American literature are predominantly mixed bloods of one description
or another and adds that "exactly what this means in terms of writers'
rendering of personal experience is necessarily a central concern of
American Indian literary criticism" (129). Unfortunately, the import of
Allen's observation, as it relates to the complexity and construction of
contemporary Native American literature, cannot be fully discussed
here. However, a more limited inquiry is possible by examining some
of the ways in which Leslie Silko's mixed blood status affected the
way her novel *Ceremony* was constructed.

If Silko has inherited the mixed blood's historical role of interpreter,
she has also inherited a mixed bag full of weighty problems and thorny

questions that must of necessity be wrestled with. After a work has been completed, the first problem generally encountered by any writer is getting it published. This can be particularly problematic for a writer of Native American literature.

The American public has not a few preconceived notions about Indians, and they would generally prefer not to have these images disrupted. If the disruption were too severe, would the American public read the books? Most likely not. America knows how it likes its Indians, preferably on film or on the pages of books looking savagely exotic, nobly hovering on the brink of extinction or extinct by the last page. The American public dotes on such dramatic endings as the one non-Indian novelist, Marilyn Harris, gave to her "Oh, so sympathetic novel" written in 1974, *Hatter Fox*.

Harris's novel is a variation of the "vanishing American" theme that has been repeated over and over in American literature and is a favorite with the reading public. Hatter Fox is a poor, alienated, Navajo Indian princess, abused by white and Indian alike. She winds up in an insane asylum and is eventually rescued from the horrors of this snake pit by a good white doctor who works for the Bureau of Indian Affairs and decides it is his sole mission in life to civilize and make a proper American out of her. Of course, he fails because Hatter is too much of a "childlike" Indian to ever learn to be a responsible citizen. She is subsequently killed off by not looking where she is going and stepping into the street in front of a tourist bus. The novel ends on these overly dramatic, tragic notes:

> I should have been content to let her be what she was. But there was no room in the world for what she was. And now there is less room for me.
> I hear from our bench the chiming of bells for matins coming furiously from the cathedral. The hour before dawn. The last hour of the condemned. How many more are waiting for death? . . .
> Now is my night upon me. I still wait for her. But she doesn't come. It is the silence that frightens me.
> I miss her . . . I miss her . . .
> I miss her . . . (273)

Harris's interpretation of Native American experience is the stuff American dreams are made of and, unfortunately, it is what many major publishing houses are generally in the market for. The reader can have a good time feeling bad over the fate of the American Indian, have a good cry, turn over, go to sleep, and forget it. After all, "there [is] no room in the world for what [we are]" (273).

In light of this Western penchant for the "vanishing American," what is the tribal writer to do? How does one present an accurate portrayal of Native American people, one that does not stink of noble savagery on the brink of doom, and still manage to get into print at the same time?

To begin to uncover some of the answers to the dilemma of publishing, we need to look at audience. Who will read these novels? Certainly publishers assume the audience will primarily be a non-Indian one and that assumption may well be true. However, within the last ten to fifteen years there has been an increase in Native American readers as Indian-written novels and anthologies find their way into classrooms at the secondary and college levels. In spite of this increase in tribal readership, the question of audience remains a valid one, since the number of tribal readers alone is not sufficient incentive for the novels to become published by major publishing houses. The answer to the difficult question of audience is that Silko has written and continues to write for both. However, it is important to note that the audience she writes most directly *to* is a tribal one, while the audience she writes for, in terms of numbers of book sales, is not. The operative word here is "to." The problem that Silko faces lies within this inherited role of interpreter, which requires that she translate tribal realities for a large audience whose culture is distinctly different from that of the tribal audience with whom the author is most concerned.

Situated between worlds, the mixed blood writer faces a difficult task. Clearly, Silko stands in the middle of that road which Arnett speaks so bluntly about in his poem (1983, 14). If the non-Indian audience is going to read the novel, it must somehow appeal to non-Indian tastes, and that taste has been established, but for the novel to hold up under the scrutiny of Native American readers, it must maintain cultural integrity at the same time. What Silko has done in the face of this perplexity is to take the trickster's path. She wrote a novel which is partly Western and partly tribal and which, as Paula Gunn Allen says, may appear to almost give America what it wants:

> [A]s a result of following western literary imperatives, most writers of Indian novels create mixed blood or half-breed protagonists, treating the theme of cultural conflict by incorporating it into the psychological and social being of the characters. (1986, 81)

However, an important factor to keep in mind is that Silko has created a written work which has been fueled by oral traditions and, like the old stories, this new work is coded or written in layers. Such layered writing works to subvert aspects of the text which may appear at first glance to be stereotypical, while opening it up on another level to a deeper and different understanding by Native American readers. Hence, the appeal to a number of audiences on a number of different levels. This is certainly the case in *Ceremony*.

On the surface, *Ceremony* uses the popular Western themes of alienation and cultural strife, aspects that are, according to Allen, embedded in the consciousness of the breed (1986, 129), as well as the consciousness of the dominant culture. The idea of an alienated hero at odds with the world appeals to the American reading public because it is also such a completely American theme. American literature abounds with stories about alienation. However, the alienation found in *Ceremony* is alienation with a twist, and the twist is a distinctly tribal one which works at deflecting the text from Western stereotypes, while turning it towards a more tribal mode of perception.

Silko, as mixed blood trickster writer, created a hero who is in opposition to the usual Western protagonist. Euro-American cultural demands for individuality in the extreme dictate that the protagonist must leave home in order to experience full self-realization. Tayo, Silko's tribal protagonist, must do the opposite. Haunted by his experiences in World War II and alienated by his "half-breed" status in a tribal society that places a great deal of value on "pure" bloodlines, the road to healing lies in Tayo's ability to find his way back to his community and his traditions. Silko's literary resolution to Tayo's estrangement accurately reflects the consciousness of her Laguna people.

In *Recovering the Word*, William Bevis describes this need to return to community as "homing in":

> In marked contrast, most Native American novels are not "eccentric," centrifugal, diverging, expanding, but "incentric," centripetal, converging, contracting. The hero comes home. "Contracting" has negative overtones to us, "expanding" a positive ring. These are cultural choices we are considering. In Native American novels, coming home, staying put, contracting, even what we call "regressing" to a place, a past where one has been before, is not only the primary story, it is a primary mode of knowledge and a primary good. (1987, 582)

In contemporary Native American novels, the most common way for the protagonist to "come home" is through a return to spirituality and the ritual tradition. Certainly the use of the ritual tradition within *Ceremony* represents far more than some idea of accommodating Western publishing tastes for the exotic Indian. According to Allen, it functions as an important counterdevice that works against the novelist's acquiescence to the theme of alienation:

> But at least since the publication of Cogewea, the Half-Blood . . . in
> 1927, this acquiescence to western publishing tastes is offset by
> a counterdevice. The protagonists are also participants in a ritual
> tradition, symbolizing the essential unity of a human being's
> psyche in spite of conflict. This development implies integration
> in the midst of conflict, fragmentation, and destruction and pro-
> vides literary shapings of the process of natavistic renewal, a
> process that characterizes American Indian public life in the last
> quarter of the twentieth century. (1986, 82)

Allen also notes that the focus Native American novelists have
chosen is counter to that of the Western protest novel, which concerns
itself with the oppressor, rather than the oppressed (82).

Unlike *Hatter Fox*, which portrays a solitary Indian awash in an
urban sea of whiteness that ultimately spells her doom, *Ceremony* takes
place in a tribal world, peopled with tribal characters. Though the
white man's handiwork is seen and discussed, he is largely absent
from the novel. The white doctor from the veterans' hospital makes
only a brief appearance in *Ceremony*. As she focuses on the oppressed
rather than the oppressor, Silko defuses the Western notion of the
"vanishing American." Though there are dead Indians at the novel's
close, there are still a good number of Indians left alive and kicking.

By limiting the white characters' time in the novel, Silko articulates
the reality that Native American people have largely opted to direct
their attention to their own traditions and customs and, as Allen points
out, "ignore the white man as much as possible" (1986, 82).

Lakota historian Vine Deloria, Jr., bears this out in *We Talk, You
Listen*:

> In many areas whites are regarded as a temporary aspect of tribal
> life and there is unshakeable belief that the tribe will survive the
> domination of the white man and once again rule the continent.
> (1970, 13)

This belief is illustrated by Silko's creation of the "witchery" story
in *Ceremony*. When Tayo meets the old mixed blood medicine man,
Betonie, he is told that the white man is not the "demi-god" he thinks
he is, and neither does he possess the power the world has attributed
to him. According to Betonie, white people can be managed because
Indians created them:

> But white people are only tools that the witchery manipulates:
> and I tell you, we can deal with white people, with their machines
> and their beliefs. We can because we invented white people; it
> was Indian witchery that made white people in the first place.
> (1978, 139)

Is Silko's invention of the "witchery" and her use and interpretation of tribal beliefs accommodationist? Has her translation perhaps made the white folks feel more comfortable? I think not. Silko's idea that Indians created white people in no way absolves the white man from historical responsibility in the genocide of Native American people. Throughout the novel, Silko has attached responsibility for what evil has occurred through the white man to the white man, and she has attached what has occurred through the Native American to the Native American, but the blame has been firmly affixed to that force which is truly responsible for man's inhumanity to man. She has moved beyond blaming all white people for what some chose and continue to choose to do, and has opted instead to focus on the greater issue at hand, the resistance of the "witchery" which drives human beings to destroy one another. Silko makes this clear in an interview with Jane B. Katz in *This Song Remembers:*

> In the novel, I've tried to go beyond any specific kind of Laguna witchery or Navajo witchery, and to begin to see witchery as a metaphor for the destroyers, to the counterforce, that force which counters vitality and birth. The counterforce is destruction and death. I tried to get away from talking about good and evil, and to return to an old, old, old way of looking at the world that I think is valid—the idea of balance, that the world was created with these opposing forces.
>   I try to take it beyond any particular culture or continent, because that's such a bullshit thing—it's all Whitey's fault. That's too simplistic, mindless. In fact Tayo is warned that *they* try to encourage people to focus on certain people or groups to blame them for everything. Another name for the counterforce is "the manipulators," those who create nothing, merely take what is around. (1980, 193)

Silko uses the story of the "witchery" to point out that *how* this counterforce came into existence is not the most important thing. What must be acknowledged is the fact that it does exist and that it will manipulate anyone who allows it to do so. The real importance lies in accepting the fact that the "witchery" itself is inextricably a part of our human existence and that it cannot be destroyed. However, one *can* choose not to participate in it, as Tayo did. One can refuse to be manipulated by it and in doing this live a life that is balanced and complete, rather than suffer the fragmentation and chaos experienced by the characters of Harley, Leroy, Pinkie, and Emo.

Lost in the throes of desire for life as they have been told to want it, they exist in a shadowland. Each stumbles through his personal darkness, feeding on beer and twisted memories of wartime mutilations and liaisons with uniform-enamored blondes who do not want them anymore. Tayo, in contrast, recognizes the "witchery" for what it is and moves increasingly away from the material world and into the sacred.

However, could it be said that, even as Silko enabled the character of Tayo to overcome the "witchery," she became tangled in it herself? To more traditional Native Americans, the exposure of the ritual tradition constitutes a violation of the sacred. Silko's novel could possibly be considered the most problematic in this area, because she chose to incorporate a sacred Laguna clan story into the narrative itself, unlike James Welch, who disguises the sacred so thoroughly in his novels that only an "insider" can recognize what is going on mythologically.

In what way should we view Silko's actions? Has she mistaken her role as interpreter for that of ethnographic informer? Since the entire novel rests on and incorporates myth, old and new, I began to explore the possibility of some sort of mythological explanation for her actions. (For clarification, I would like to add that I do not equate explanation with justification in any way.) In order to do this, I turned to my own mythic traditions for insight.

I began to see not only Silko, but many mixed blood poets and writers as analogous or metaphorically related to the mythic Cherokee Wild Boy or Orphan, who insisted that he was also the son of First Man and First Woman, and brother to their original offspring, in spite of the fact that he had been produced through the mixing of blood and water and not in the ordinary way. This mythic mixed blood, if you will, spent his life in the pursuit of hidden knowledge and often disclosed secrets.[2]

According to Charles Hudson in *The Southeastern Indians*, the Wild Boy-Orphan is the result of mixing categories and is therefore

> anomalous in two ways: in his strange birth and in his peculiar relationship to his brother. One of the most important features . . . is that he came from the water, and water is associated with disorder, innovation, and fertility; thus Wild Boy was always breaking rules and doing new things. (1987, 148–49)

There are several aspects of the Orphan's story and Hudson's analysis that deserve exploration. The relationship between the Orphan and the contemporary fact of the existence of the mixed blood is extremely interesting. Like the Orphan, the "breed" is a product of mixed blood, blood that has been thinned or watered down, so to speak. It is also true that the outside blood that led to the creation of the mixed blood came through or across the water. The association of the mythic mixed blood and the "real world" mixed blood with water is strong. And it is certainly true that many times the mixed blood feels like an orphan and is often treated that way as well. All of the mixed blood characters in *Ceremony* are orphans of one sort or another or in some way associated with abandonment. Silko herself lived on the edges of Laguna society and felt this keenly. It is important to mention that she lived near the river and attached special significance to that fact:

> Look where all the Marmon houses are here by the river, down below the village. I always thought there was something symbolic about that—we're on the fringe of things. The river's just a short walk from here, and I was always attracted to it as a kid. I knew it was a small river, and I didn't make any great demands on it. It was a great place to go and play in the mud and splash around. There are willows and tamarack, and there are always stories. You just hear them. I guess from the beginning there was the idea that the river was kind of a special place where all sorts of things could go on. (Silko 1980, 189)

Perhaps by taking the clan story, Silko was guilty of bad judgment, but she has certainly followed the Wild Boy's lead. Like her mythic predecessor, she created some chaos, broke the rules by exposing what had once been hidden, and gave birth to something new and innovative. She sees herself directly connected to the stories told by the Lagunas about mixed bloods and the "wild, roguish things they did" (189). As a mixed blood, Silko believes she has more latitude, more possibilities for expression than a fullblood writer like Simon Ortiz, whom she sees as possibly constricted by his family's ties to community religious life (190).

Though Silko constructs the majority of the novel around the bones of Laguna mythology, one may conclude from her remarks that she did not draw on Laguna or Navajo mythology to illustrate the concept of the "witchery" in the novel. The invention of the story of the "witchery" and the casting of Tayo, who, according to Allen, is a traditional Keres mythological character (1990, 383), as a mixed blood in a mixed blood story is not so much an act of accommodation to the exotic tastes of a non-Indian audience, as it is an attempt to move towards the creation of a new, mixed blood mythology which demonstrates one way for mixed bloods to become whole within the conflict they are born into.

If one examines the novel carefully with an eye to the mythic dimension, one can see that Silko is doing something very important.

At the novel's center is the idea that what is needed is a new ceremony. By calling for this, she is functioning as what comparative mythologist Joseph Campbell called "the secondary hero" who breathes new life into ancient, sacred traditions so that they continue to function in modern times. Campbell describes this role in an interview with Bill Moyers in *The Power of Myth*:

> There is a kind of secondary hero to revitalize the tradition. This hero reinterprets the tradition and makes it valid as a living experience today instead of a lot of outdated clichés. This has to be done with all traditions. (1988, 141)

The idea of Silko as "secondary hero" fits well within the Lakota definition of the mixed blood as interpreter between the human world and the spirit world. By placing the mixed blood within the existing Laguna mythic tradition through the characterization of Tayo and thereby creating a new mixed blood mythology, she is showing contemporary Native Americans, mixed bloods and fullbloods, a way to live in modern society. Tayo and the other important mixed blood characters, Betonie and the Night Swan, represent the kind of adaptation that is necessary for survival in the face of contemporary reality. By creating a new ceremony, one that is inclusive rather than exclusive, she has also opened a road upon which the mixed blood can return home to ritual traditions which have fueled the endurance of tribal people for thousands of years and which now have room for him or her as well.

Though Silko cautions all of her readers against acquiescing spiritually to a mechanistic society which erects altars to technology at the expense of humanity, I believe her primary interest is in sending a signal to tribal people everywhere that a resistance path remains. Whether on the land or tied to urban areas for economic reasons, a sacred space must be created that allows one to remain Indian. Through *Ceremony*, Silko demonstrates that there is a way to live in the modern world without giving in to the "witchery." That way is through remembrance, adaptation, and recreation. At the onset of the novel Silko writes:

> I will tell you something about stories,
> [he said]
> They aren't just entertainment.
> Don't be fooled.
> They are all we have, you see,
> all we have to fight off
> illness and death.

> You don't have anything
> if you don't have the stories.
> (1978, 2)

For a long time mixed bloods did not have the stories. Now, thanks to Silko, we have new stories and we are part of them as well. Throughout the novel, Silko has successfully translated tribal realities to non-Indians and mixed blood realities to fullbloods. True to form as a mythological descendant of the ancient Orphan-Wild Boy, she has broken some rules along the way, but she has also purchased a contemporary mythic space for mixed bloods everywhere, and through it all she sends a strong message to the camp of the "manipulators." We are being healed. We will return. We have not vanished from this red earth.

Notes

1. This definition was conveyed by Mr. Looking Horse during a conversation with a student following his appearance as a guest lecturer at San Francisco State University.

2. Many tribes have Wild Boy or Blood Clot Boy myths. There is a Pueblo myth about the Water Jar Boy that is somewhat analogous to this one. The Water Jar Boy came about through the mixture of earth and water. Those interested should see Elsie Clews Parsons, "Tewa Tales," *Memoirs of the American Folklore Society* 19(1926): 193.

Works Cited

Allen, Paula Gunn. 1986. *The Sacred Hoop: Recovering the Feminine in American Indian Traditions*. Boston: Beacon.

————. 1990. "Special Problems in Teaching Leslie Marmon Silko's *Ceremony*." *American Indian Quarterly* 14: 379–86.

Arnett, Carroll. 1983. "Song of the Breed." In *Songs from This Earth on Turtle's Back*, edited by Joseph Bruchac, 14. New York: The Greenfield Review Press.

Bieder, Robert E. 1980. "Scientific Attitudes toward Indian Mixed-Bloods in Early Nineteenth Century America." *The Journal of Ethnic Studies* 8(2): 17–30.

Bevis, William. 1987. "Native American Novels: Homing In." In *Recovering the Word: Essays on Native American Literature*, edited by Briann Swann and Arnold Krupat, 580–620. Berkeley: University of California Press.

Campbell, Joseph. 1988. *The Power of Myth*. By Bill Moyers. Edited by Betty Sue Flowers. New York: Doubleday.

Deloria, Vine, Jr. 1970. *We Talk, You Listen*. New York: Macmillan.

Green, Rayna. 1984. "Introduction." In *That's What She Said: Contemporary Poetry and Fiction by Native American Women,* edited by Rayna Green, 1–12. Bloomington: Indiana University Press.

Harris, Marilyn. 1974. *Hatter Fox.* New York: Bantam.

Hudson, Charles. 1987. *The Southeastern Indians.* Knoxville: University of Tennessee Press.

Parsons, Elsie Clews. 1926. "Tewa Tales." *Memoirs of the American Folklore Society* 19: 192–95.

Silko, Leslie Marmon. 1978. *Ceremony.* New York: Signet.

———. 1980. "Interview." In *This Song Remembers: Self Portraits of Native Americans in the Arts,* edited by Jane B. Katz, 186–94. Boston: Houghton.

Webster's Dictionary of the English Language. 1988. "Half-breed."

Index

Editors

Joseph F. Trimmer is professor of English at Ball State University, where he currently teaches courses in writing nonfiction and cross-cultural literature. He has published numerous articles on United States life and literature, directed international scholars' workshops at the Smithsonian Institution, and consulted on *Middletown,* a six-part film series that aired on PBS. His textbooks include *Writing with a Purpose, The Riverside Reader,* and *Fictions.* He was program chair for the 1989 NCTE Summer Institute for Teachers of Literature, which was devoted to cultural criticism.

Tilly Warnock is director of composition at the University of Arizona. She has published articles on rhetoric, writing centers, and literature, as well as a textbook titled *Writing Is Critical Action.* In 1990, she was program chair for the NCTE Summer Institute for Teachers of Literature; the topic was Cross-Cultural Criticism and the Teaching of Literature.

Contributors

Norma Alarcón is professor of ethnic studies at the University of California, Berkeley, where she teaches courses in Chicana feminism and literature and social movements and serves as the editor and publisher of Third Woman Press. She has published articles in collections of essays and in journals such as *Cultural Critique, Cultural Studies,* and *Americas Review.* She has also written a book titled *The Discourse of Difference,* a study of the poetry of Rosario Castellanos.

Robert S. Burton is assistant professor of English at California State University, Chico, where his teaching interests include multicultural, postcolonial, and twentieth-century British literature. His articles have appeared in *Critique, Notes on Contemporary Literature,* and *The Reference Guide to English Literature.* He has presented papers on Salman Rushdie, Kazuo Ishiguro, and Cynthia Kadohata.

Renny Christopher is a doctoral student in the Literature Board at the University of California, Santa Cruz, where she teaches courses in twentieth-century American literature and American studies. She has published articles on Vietnamese literature and working-class literature in journals such as *Vietnam Generation* and has contributed a chapter to an anthology, *Reading the Literatures of Asian America.* She is currently completing a study on Vietnamese works and the representation of Vietnamese in Euro-American works.

Reed Way Dasenbrock is associate professor of English at New Mexico State University, where he teaches courses in modern and non-Western literature and literary theory. His books include *The Literary Vorticism of Ezra Pound and Wyndham Lewis* and a collection of essays, *After Davidson: Contemporary Analytic Philosophy and Literary Theory.* He has written extensively on multiculturalism in journals such as *PMLA, College English,* and *Dissent.*

Anuradha Dingwaney is assistant professor of English at Oberlin College, where she teaches courses on Anglophonic literatures of the Third World. She has published articles on Salman Rushdie and other Third World writers and on feminist pedagogy. She is currently completing a longer study on the discursive resistance in the work of writers from the African and Indian diasporas.

Judith Scot-Smith Girgus teaches middle-school English at the Horpath Hall School in Nashville, Tennessee, and formerly taught middle and secondary

English in Albuquerque, New Mexico, and Eugene, Oregon. She has published articles on various professional issues in journals such as *Educational Leadership* and is currently researching the behavioral patterns of female students in the all-female classroom.

Sandra Jamieson is assistant professor of writing at Colgate University, where she also teaches courses in African American literature and cultural studies. She is completing a study of the role of textbooks in the teaching of reading and writing. She recently team-taught a course called The Poetics of African American Women Writers with Houston Baker of the University of Pennsylvania.

David Leiwei Li is assistant professor of English at the University of Southern California, where he teaches courses in Asian American and contemporary American literature. He has published articles on Maxine Hong Kingston in periodicals such as *Criticism* and *American Literary History*. He is currently completing a book on the dialogical formation of contemporary Chinese culture.

Suzanne Evertsen Lundquist is associate professor of English at Brigham Young University, where she teaches courses in Native American sacred texts and modern novels. Her publications include *Trickster: A Transformation Archetype, College Composition: A Course in Ethnographic Thinking,* and an essay in *Approaches to Teaching Momaday's The Way to Rainy Mountain*. Her interest in Mahfouz grew out of a course in novels of the Third World, which she taught to senior English majors.

Carol Maier is professor of Spanish at Kent State University, where she is affiliated with the Institute for Applied Linguistics, and teaches courses in the theory and practice of translation. She has published *In the Feminine Mode: Essays on Hispanic Women Writers* and has translated works by Severo Sarduy, Octavio Armand, and Carlota Caufield. Two of her current projects are a translation of Rosa Chacel's *Memorias de Leticia Valle* and a collection of essays she is editing with Anuradha Dingwaney, *Between Languages and Cultures: Translation and Cross-Cultural Texts*.

Reginald Martin is professor of English at Memphis State University, where he teaches courses in African American literature. His articles have appeared in *College English, Black American Literature Forum,* and *The South Atlantic Review,* and his books include *Ishmael Reed and the New Black Aesthetic Critics*. He has recently completed a Ford Foundation leave, during which he researched the politics of literary criticism.

H. W. Matalene is associate professor of English at the University of South Carolina, where he teaches courses in eighteenth-century British literature. He has edited a collection of essays, *Romanticism and Culture: A Tribute to Morse Peckman and a Bibliography of His Work,* and has published articles in journals such as *College English*. He recently team-taught a course in Chinese and Chinese American literature with Professor Yang Deyou of Shanxi University.

Mary Poovey is professor of English at Johns Hopkins University, where she teaches courses in nineteenth-century British culture. Her books include *The Proper Lady and the Woman Writer: Ideology as Style in the Works of Mary Wollstonecraft, Mary Shelley, and Jane Austen* and *Uneven Developments: The Ideological Work of Gender in Mid-Victorian England.* Her chapter in this book was first presented as the keynote address at the 1989 NCTE Summer Institute for Teachers of Literature and was subsequently published in *College English.*

Chauncey A. Ridley is assistant professor of English at California State University, Sacramento, where he teaches courses in African American literature. He has written on the relationship between African American folklore and contemporary short fiction in journals such as *Obsidian.* His essay on Toni Morrison is part of a larger study he is completing on the theme of "badness" in African American literature since Jean Toomer.

Patricia Riley is a doctoral student in ethnic studies at the University of California, Berkeley, where her teaching interests include contemporary Native American literature and Native American mythologies. Her publications include "The Death of Jim Loney: Ritual of Recreation" in *Fictional International.* A mixed blood Cherokee, she is currently editing a volume of essays, *Growing Up Native American.*

Mary C. Savage, a teacher of writing and literature and director of interdisciplinary programs at the college level for twenty years, is now a storyteller and consultant in multicultural education. At present, she is writing *We Are the Ones We've Been Waiting For: Essays in Literature and Liberation for Multicultural Times.* She directs the Parent Storytelling Workshops: A Home-and-School Literacy Project in several elementary schools on the lower east side of New York City as an artist-in-residence of the Henry Street Settlement.

Pancho Savery is associate professor of English at the University of Massachusetts, Boston, where he teaches courses in African American literature and modern and contemporary drama. He has published articles on Ralph Ellison, Saunders Redding, and Roy DeCarava in journals such as *Black American Literature Forum* and *The Journal of Urban and Cultural Studies* and has edited a collection of essays, *Approaches to Teaching Ellison's Invisible Man.* He is currently working on a study of critical and pedagogical issues in the teaching of African American literature.

James Slevin is professor of English at Georgetown University, where he regularly teaches courses in the theory and teaching of writing. He is the coeditor of two books, *The Future of Doctoral Programs in English* and *The Right to Literacy,* and numerous articles on the politics of reading and writing and their teaching. His chapter in this book was first presented at the Wyoming Conference on English and will appear as a chapter in his new book, *Introducing English.*